MERRILL Science

AUTHORS

Dr. Jay K. Hackett
University of Northern Colorado

Dr. Richard H. Moyer
University of Michigan-Dearborn

Dr. Donald K. Adams
University of Northern Colorado

Reading Consultant
Barbara S. Pettegrew, Ph.D.
Director of the Reading/Study Center
Assistant Professor of Education
Otterbein College
Westerville, Ohio

Safety Consultant
Gary E. Downs, Ed.D.
Professor
Iowa State University
Ames, Iowa

Gifted and Mainstreaming Consultants
George Fichter
Educational Consultant
Programs for Gifted
Ohio Department of Education
Worthington, Ohio

Timothy E. Heron, Ph.D.
Professor
Department of Human Services, Education
The Ohio State University
Columbus, Ohio

Content Consultants
Robert T. Brown, M.D.
Associate Professor of Clinical Pediatrics
Director, Section for Adolescent Health
The Ohio State University/Children's Hospital
Columbus, Ohio

Henry D. Drew, Ph.D.
Chemist
U.S. FDA, Division of Drug Analysis
St. Louis, Missouri

Judith L. Doyle, Ph.D.
Physics Teacher
Newark High School
Newark, Ohio

Todd F. Holzman, M.D.
Child Psychiatrist
Harvard Community Health Plan
Wellesley, Massachusetts

Knut J. Norstog, Ph.D.
Research Associate
Fairchild Tropical Garden
Miami, Florida

James B. Phipps, Ph.D.
Professor, Geology/Oceanography
Grays Harbor College
Aberdeen, Washington

R. Robert Robbins, Ph.D.
Associate Professor of Astronomy
Astronomy Department, University of Texas
Austin, Texas

Sidney E. White, Ph.D.
Professor
Department of Geology & Mineralogy
The Ohio State University
Columbus, Ohio

ACKNOWLEDGEMENT

The authors are deeply indebted to the late Robert B. Sund for his inspiration and guidance in the early development of this series.

MERRILL PUBLISHING COMPANY
A Bell & Howell Information Company
Toronto • London • Sydney

Merrill Science Program Components

Student Editions, K-6
Teacher Editions, K-6
Teacher Resource Books, K-6
  (Reproducible Masters)
Big Books, K-2
SkillBuilders: A Process & Problem Solving
  Skillbook, Student Editions, K-6
SkillBuilders: A Process & Problem Solving
  Skillbook, Teacher Editions, K-6
Poster Packets: Science in Your World, K-6
Color Transparencies, K-6
Activity Materials Kits, K-6
Activity Materials Management System
Awards Stickers
Science Words Software, 1-6
In-service Videotapes
Mr. Wizard Videos, 3-7
Science Fair Package

Dr. Jay K. Hackett is Professor of Earth Science Education at the University of Northern Colorado. He holds a B.S. in General Science, an M.N.S. in Physical Science, and an Ed.D. in Science Education with support in Earth Science. A resource teacher for elementary schools, he conducts numerous workshops and professional seminars. With over 20 years of teaching experience, he has taught and consulted on science programs across all levels and remains active in local, state, and national science professional organizations.

Dr. Richard H. Moyer is Professor of Science Education at the University of Michigan, Dearborn. He holds a B.S. in Chemistry and Physics Education, an M.S. in Curriculum and Instruction, and an Ed.D. in Science Education. With more than 19 years of teaching experience at all levels, he is currently involved in teacher training. He was the recipient of two Distinguished Faculty Awards. He conducts numerous workshops and in-service training programs for science teachers. Dr. Moyer is also the author of Merrill's *General Science* textbook.

Dr. Donald K. Adams is Professor of Education and Director, Education Field Experiences at the University of Northern Colorado. He holds a B.S. in Liberal Arts Social Science, an M.S. in Biological Science, and an Ed.D. in Science Education with support in Earth Science. In over 20 years of teaching, he has been instrumental in implementing personalized science and outdoor education programs and has served as a consultant to teacher preparation and science programs throughout the United States, Australia, and New Zealand.

Reviewers: Teachers and Administrators **Annette Barzal,** Walter Kidder Elementary School, Brunswick, OH; **Ronald Converse,** Conroe Independent School District, Conroe, TX; **Suzanne Doof,** C.E.S. 132, Fort Lee, NJ; **Shirley Gomez,** Luling Elementary School, Luling, LA; **Janice Gritton,** Gavin H. Cochran Elementary School, Louisville, KY; **Glenn Hubert,** Miami Shores Elementary School, Miami, FL; **Shirley Larges,** Azalea Middle School, St. Petersburg, FL; **Janet McDonald,** Pine Middle School, Los Alamitos, CA; **Marsha McKinney,** Pope Elementary School, Arlington, TX; **Jeffrey Moniz,** St. Philomena Elementary School, Portsmouth, RI; **Sister Pauline Elizabeth Neelon,** St. Teresa Elementary School, Providence, RI; **Lynda Taylor,** Alta Vista Elementary School, Waco, TX; **Joy Tingle,** Terrebonne Parish School System, Houma, LA; **Jay Woodard,** Waukesha Public Schools, Waukesha, WI; **Eugene Wozniak,** Dearborn Schools Resource Center, Dearborn, MI

Cover Photo: Planets—Saturn and moons by Jet Propulsion Labs
Series Editors: Karen S. Allen, Janet L. Helenthal; **Project Designer:** Joan Shaull; **Series Artist:** Dennis L. Smith; **Project Artist:** Shirley J. Beltz; **Illustrators:** Nancy Heim, Intergraphics, Kirchoff/Wohlberg, Inc., Jeanine S. Means, Jim Shough; **Photo Editor:** David T. Dennison; **Series Production Editor:** Joy E. Dickerson; **Project Production Editor:** Carole R. Hill

ISBN 0-675-03514-7

Published by
Merrill Publishing Co.
A Bell & Howell Information Company
Columbus, Ohio 43216

Copyright © 1989 by Merrill Publishing Co.
All rights reserved. No part of this book may be reproduced in any form, electronic or mechanical, including photocopy, recording, or any information storage or retrieval system, without permission in writing from the publisher.
Printed in the United States of America

Table of Contents

UNIT 1

Plants Around Us 2

1 Plants as Producers 4

1:1 Green Plants 5
Activity 1-1 Green Plants Produce Starch 7
Activity 1-2 Plants Produce a Gas 10
Science and Technology 11

1:2 Using Plants for Raw Materials . . 12
People and Science 17

2 More About Plants 20

2:1 Flowers and Seeds 21
Activity 2-1 Flowers 27

2:2 Plants Produce New Plants 28
Activity 2-2 Growing Plants from Parts of Plants 31
Language Arts Skills 33

UNIT 2

Light, Color, and Sight 38

3 Light and Color 40

3:1 Light 41
Activity 3-1 Refracting Light 48
People and Science 49

3:2 Color 50
Activity 3-2 Seeing Colors 51
Science and Technology 55

4 The Sense of Sight 58

4:1 How We See 59
Activity 4-1 Observing the Iris . . . 60

4:2 Problems and Proper Care 64
Activity 4-2 Making a Water Drop Lens 68
Language Arts Skills 71

UNIT 3

Our Solar System 76

5 Our Star 78
- 5:1 Comparing Stars 79
- 5:2 Solar Eclipse 84
  - Activity 5-1 Making a Model of an Eclipse 85
  - People and Science 87

6 Members of Our Solar System 90
- 6:1 Planets and Orbits 91
  - Activity 6-1 Sun, Planets, and Gravity 94
  - Science and Technology 95
- 6:2 The Inner Planets 96
- 6:3 The Outer Planets 100
  - Activity 6-2 Comparing Planets. 104
- 6:4 Other Members 106
  - Language Arts Skills 111

UNIT 4

Minerals, Rocks, and Fossils 116

7 Earth's Composition 118
- 7:1 Identifying Minerals 119
  - Activity 7-1 Mineral Properties . . 123
- 7:2 Rocks: Mineral Mixtures 126
  - Activity 7-2 Identifying Rocks . . 133
- 7:3 Useful Rocks and Minerals 134
  - People and Science 137

8 Using Rock Records 140
- 8:1 Fossil Records 141
  - Activity 8-1 Making a Fossil 143
  - Science and Technology 145
- 8:2 Using Fossils 146
  - Activity 8-2 Making Footprints . . 149
  - Language Arts Skills 151

UNIT 5

Animal Adaptations and Behavior 156

9 Adaptations for Survival 158

- **9:1** Adaptation of Body Parts 159
  - Activity 9-1 Fish Scales 162
  - Science and Technology 169
- **9:2** Special Adaptations 170
  - Activity 9-2 How An Animal Adapts to Its Environment 174
  - People and Science 175

10 Animal Behavior 178

- **10:1** Reflex and Instinct 179
  - Activity 10-1 Reflex Behavior of a Sow Bug 182
- **10:2** Learned Behavior and Social Behavior 186
  - Activity 10-2 Learning a New Behavior 188
  - Language Arts Skills 193

UNIT 6

Sounds We Hear 198

11 Making and Using Sound 200

- **11:1** Properties of Sound 201
  - Activity 11-1 Observing Vibrations 204
  - Activity 11-2 Investigating Pitch 208
- **11:2** Behavior of Sound 210
  - Activity 11-3 Reflected and Absorbed Sound 213
  - People and Science 215

12 How We Hear Sound 218

- **12:1** All About Ears 219
  - Science and Technology 223
- **12:2** Hearing Sounds 224
  - Activity 12-1 Finding Direction Using Sound 224
  - Activity 12-2 Measuring Sounds 228
  - Language Arts Skills 231

v

UNIT 7

Oceans of Earth — 236

13 The Ocean Around Us — 238

- **13:1** Oceans and Seas............ 239
  Activity 13-1 Using a Globe... 241
- **13:2** Properties of Ocean Water.... 242
  Activities 13-2 A Property of Ocean Water.............. 245
- **13:3** Ocean Movements........... 250
  Activity 13-3 Ocean Currents . 254
  Science and Technology 257

14 Probing the Ocean — 260

- **14:1** Ocean Life.................. 261
- **14:2** Mapping the Ocean.......... 264
  People and Science.......... 269
- **14:3** Deep Ocean Features........ 270
  Activity 14-1 Mapping the Ocean Bottom.............. 273
- **14:4** Protecting the Ocean........ 274
  Language Arts Skills 276

UNIT 8

Electricity and Magnets — 282

15 Electricity — 284

- **15:1** Static Electricity.............. 285
  Activity 15-1 Static Electricity . 288
- **15:2** Current Electricity............ 292
  Activity 15-2 Making a Circuit . 293
  Activity 15-3 Finding the Conductors 295
  Science and Technology 299

16 Magnetism and Electricity — 302

- **16:1** Magnets 303
  People and Science.......... 307
- **16:2** Magnets and Electricity....... 308
  Activity 16-1 An Electromagnet.............. 309
  Language Arts Skills 313

UNIT 9

Growing Up Healthy   318

17 Taking Care of Yourself   320

17:1 Exercise and Sleep 321
     Activity 17-1 Planning for
         Exercise 325

17:2 Personal Cleanliness 328
     People and Science.......... 333

18 Healthful Eating   336

18:1 Nutrients.................... 337
     Activity 18-1 Testing for Fats.. 342
     Science and Technology 345

18:2 Food Groups and Nutrition 346
     Activity 18-2 Checking Your
         Diet 350
     Language Arts Skills 353

Glossary 358

Index........................... 366

Science in Your World

Science can be a hair-raising experience! At least you might think so when you look at the picture on the opposite page. Imagine you are the person in this picture. What would you want to know? What is happening? Why is this happening?

Asking *why*, wondering *how*, and testing the *what if's* are some steps scientists use to find out about our world. Observation is another very important step. When you use these steps to study our world, you are using the same methods scientists use in their search for knowledge. This search is really an adventure!

The wonderful thing about this adventure is that it is happening NOW—all around you! Would you like to be a part of it? All you need is a sense of adventure and the key to your own imagination. This key is called *curiosity*.

Set your imagination free. Begin one of the great adventures of your life—the study of the world around you. No need to look somewhere else because, when you study science, the excitement is everywhere!

UNIT 1
Plants Around Us

Jokichi Takamine was a Japanese scientist who spent most of his adult life studying and working in the United States. He made several important contributions to the world of science. He became very fond of the United States. Because of this fondness, he gave a living gift to the country that was his second home. He arranged with the mayor of Tokyo to have cherry trees planted in Washington, D.C. These trees have given their beauty to the city since 1912.

Jokichi Takamine—1920

Cherry trees in bloom

Chapter 1
Plants as Producers

Plants are important to people in many ways. Plants or plant parts probably made up a part of your diet today. Your science textbook was made, in part, from a plant product. You may use plants at home and school to make your surroundings more attractive. How have you used plants today?

Plants are part of daily living

Green Plants 1:1

LESSON GOALS
In this lesson you will learn
- plants produce food.
- how plants make food.
- how plants and animals get energy.
- how respiration releases energy from food.

When you think of living things, you may think first of people you know, your pets, or animals in the zoo. Plants are living things, too. All living things need food to survive. Plants are different from animals in one important way. Plants can make their own food. Animals cannot make their own food. Animals must eat plants for food or they must eat other animals that eat plants.

How are plants and animals different?

Figure 1-1. Animals eat plants for food or they eat other animals that eat plants.

Photosynthesis

The process by which plants make food is **photosynthesis** (foht oh SIHN thuh sus). The word means "put together with light." A green plant makes food using light energy. Green plants get light energy from the sun.

What is the process by which plants make food?

PHOTOSYNTHESIS

Carbon dioxide + Water —is changed into→ Food + Oxygen

(with Light energy and Chlorophyll)

Energy from the sun is trapped by chlorophyll. Then carbon dioxide and water are combined to make food for growth. Oxygen is released into the air.

Figure 1-2. Photosynthesis is the process by which plants make food.

What parts of a plant produce food?

Figure 1-3. Plants store extra food in the form of sugar or starch.

The green parts of a plant can produce food. In most plants the leaves are the special parts where the most food is made. Leaves contain a chemical called chlorophyll (KLOR uh fihl). **Chlorophyll** is the green matter in plants that traps light energy to produce food.

Plants also use water and carbon dioxide to make food. Water is taken from the soil by the roots and travels up the stems to the leaves. Carbon dioxide is taken from the air. Air enters the plant through small openings in the leaves.

During photosynthesis, plants use water and carbon dioxide to make food. Photosynthesis can only begin during the day when there is sunlight. Light energy is changed to food energy and oxygen is released during photosynthesis. The oxygen passes out of the plant and into the air through small openings in the leaves.

Plants make more food than they need. The extra food is stored in the plant. Some plants store food in the form of sugar. Many plants store sugar in their fruits. These fruits taste sweet. Other plants such as potatoes, carrots, cauliflower, and beans make sugar that is turned into starch and then stored. These plants do not taste sweet.

Activity 1-1   Green Plants Produce Starch

QUESTION   How can you show that photosynthesis produces starch?

Materials

scissors
geranium plant
black paper
paper clips
shallow dish

alcohol
water
dropper
tincture of iodine
pencil and paper

What to do

1. Clip a strip of black paper across the upper surface of a geranium leaf and place the plant in a sunny window for two or three days.
2. Cut the covered leaf from the plant and remove the paper.
3. Soak the leaf overnight in alcohol.
   CAUTION: *Do not taste the alcohol.*
4. Rinse off the alcohol. Drop iodine on both parts of the leaf: covered and uncovered.
   CAUTION: *Do not get iodine on your skin or clothing. Do not taste iodine.*

What did you learn?

1. What did the black paper do?
2. What happened when the leaf was soaked in alcohol?
3. What happened when you dropped iodine on both parts of the leaf?

Using what you learned

1. Which part of the leaf contained starch?
2. Where does the energy come from that plants use to make food?

Respiration

All living things need energy. You need energy to walk, talk, and play. Energy comes from food made by plants. Oxygen combines with food and energy is released. **Respiration** (res puh RAY shun) is the process that breaks down food and releases energy.

Plants get energy from food they make. Animals get energy from food they eat. During respiration, sugars or other foods combine with oxygen. Energy, carbon dioxide, and water are released. Plants and animals need energy for all of life's activities. Energy is needed for growth, repair of tissues, movement, warmth, and all other body functions.

From what do plants and animals get energy?

Why is energy needed by plants and animals?

Figure 1-4. Respiration is the process that breaks down food and releases energy.

RESPIRATION

Food + Oxygen —is changed into→ Carbon dioxide + Water

Food and oxygen are combined. Energy is released from the food for use by the plant. Water and carbon dioxide are released into the air.

Respiration in plants and animals goes on all day and night. In plants, respiration is faster during warm seasons. There is more growth of buds, leaves, and seeds at this time. Respiration slows down during cold seasons because growth is slow.

Respiration and photosynthesis are different. During photosynthesis, carbon dioxide and water *are used* to make food. During respiration, carbon dioxide and water *are produced*. During photosynthesis, energy *is stored* in the food that is made. During respiration, energy *is released* from food in both plants and animals.

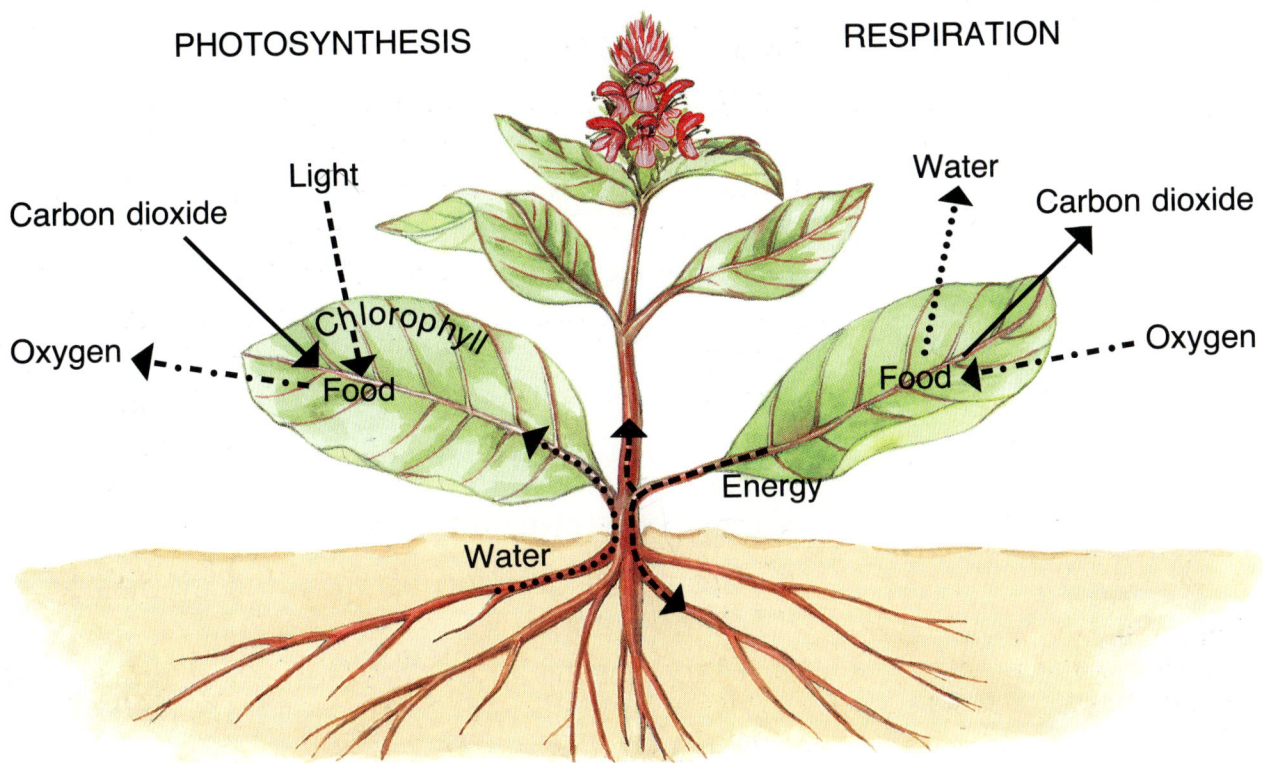

Figure 1-5. During photosynthesis, energy is stored; during respiration, energy is released.

Lesson Summary

- Green plants can make their own food.
- Photosynthesis is the process by which plants make food.
- Plants and animals get energy from food in a process called respiration.
- In respiration, food is combined with oxygen and energy is released for use by all living things.

Lesson Review

Review the lesson to answer these questions.
1. What is photosynthesis?
2. What are two products that are formed during photosynthesis?
3. What is respiration?
4. What are three products that are formed during respiration?

Activity 1-2 Plants Produce a Gas

QUESTION How can you observe plants producing a gas?

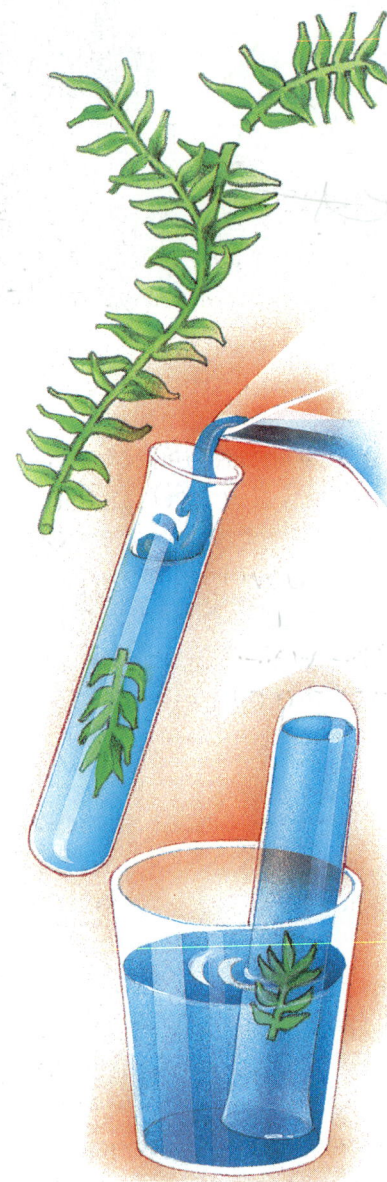

Materials

elodea plant
test tube
water
clear plastic cup
light source
hand lens
clock
pencil and paper

What to do

1. Break the growing tip from the elodea or other plant.
2. Place the tip in the test tube, top first. Fill the test tube with water. Fill the cup half full with water.
3. Cover the top of the test tube with your finger. Turn the test tube upside down into the cup. Be sure there are no air bubbles in the test tube.
4. Place the cup with the test tube in a bright light.
5. Use a hand lens to observe the elodea.
6. Record any changes after 15 minutes, 1 hour, 2 hours, 4 hours, 1 day, 2 days.

What did you learn?

1. What did you observe when the plant was first put in the light?
2. What did you observe after 15 minutes?
3. What did you observe after 2 days?

Using what you learned

1. How could you tell a gas was produced?
2. What gas do you think was produced?

Science and Technology

Plants in Space

Someday astronauts will be living in a space station somewhere between Earth and the moon. As they breathe, they will use up some of the oxygen in the air. When they exhale, they will add carbon dioxide to the air. Carbon dioxide is a poisonous gas. Some of the materials used to build the space station also release dangerous gases. These gases cause indoor air pollution. NASA scientists must find a way to keep indoor air pollution levels low so that the air will be safe for the astronauts.

One part of the answer to the problem is very simple. Houseplants can be used to lower indoor pollution and keep the air safe to breathe. Scientists have found that some houseplants remove dangerous gases from the air. Scientists think that the plants use these gases during photosynthesis. For example, the carbon dioxide exhaled by the astronauts is used by the plants. During photosynthesis, the carbon dioxide is broken down into oxygen and water. Astronauts can breathe the oxygen. The water given off by the plants keeps the air in the space station moist.

The NASA scientists plan to build a plant room in the space station. The room will be filled with plants. The plants will filter the air in the space station.

Anyone can use this space age technology. Plants can be used to lower indoor air pollution in homes, schools, and offices. Two houseplants that work well are the spider plant and philodendron. Indoor air pollution is a problem we must deal with on Earth also. Using houseplants wisely is a beautiful and easy way to help keep our air pure.

1:2 Using Plants for Raw Materials

LESSON GOALS

In this lesson you will learn
- plants and plant parts can be eaten.
- plants and parts of plants are used as raw materials.
- plants prevent erosion.
- plants can be used to beautify the environment.

Figure 1-6. Many different kinds of plants are sources of food.

People and other animals eat plants for food. More than 3,000 different kinds of plants supply people with food. Many different parts of plants are used as food by people. You eat the roots of beets, carrots, and turnips. You eat the stems of asparagus, potatoes, and kohlrabi. You eat the leaves of cabbage, lettuce, and spinach. You eat the seeds of wheat, corn, and peanuts. You eat the flower buds of cauliflower and broccoli. You eat the fruits of many plants. What plants have you eaten today?

Raw Materials from Plants

Plants provide you with many things other than food. Thousands of useful products are made from materials taken from plants. A **raw material** is any matter that can be made into useful products. Plants and parts of plants are used to make everyday products such as furniture, clothing, and medicine. The plants and parts of plants are called raw materials. Trees are raw materials for over 5,000 different products.

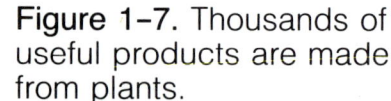

Figure 1-7. Thousands of useful products are made from plants.

Figure 1–8. Wood pulp is made from trees.

Wood pulp is a plant raw material that is a soft, spongy material made by cooking wood chips in strong chemicals with steam. Paper and paper products such as napkins, paper bags, food wrappers, and milk cartons are made from wood pulp. The chemical industry uses wood pulp to make some kinds of plastic housewares, toys, rubbing alcohol, and photographic film. What paper products have you used today?

Thousands of trees produce tannin. Tannin is taken from the bark and used to produce a chemical called **tannic acid**. Tannic acid is used by the leather industry. Leather is made from the hides of animals. Tannic acid is used to change the animal hides into soft and flexible leather. Then the soft leather can be cut and shaped into many patterns.

What is wood pulp?

What are some products made from wood pulp?

What is one use for tannic acid?

13

What are some plants used to make dyes?

What are two plants used to make medicine?

Figure 1-9. Latex (a) and cotton fiber (b) are raw materials obtained from plants.

a

b

Many dyes are made from plants. A **dye** is a substance that is used for coloring. Some people make dyes from onion skins, pokeberries, and the bark of the North American black oak tree.

Many bottles and containers use cork stoppers. **Cork** is the tough spongy bark of the European cork oak tree. A cork oak must grow for fifteen years before the bark can be used. Cork is also used for decorative wall coverings and for bulletin boards. Where do you see cork being used in your classroom?

Gums and resins are saps that ooze from the bark of tree trunks. **Resin** (REZ un) is a raw material from pine trees used to make turpentine, household cleaners, and other products. **Latex** (LAY teks) is a milky substance that comes from rubber trees. Latex can be made into a tough, long lasting product called rubber. Rubber gloves, elastic bands, and some tires are made from rubber.

The stems of many plants contain threadlike cells called **fiber**. Fibers can be spun into thread and woven into cloth. They can also be made into rope or string. Cotton cloth is made from fibers that come from the seeds of the cotton plant.

Plants were once the source of most remedies for disease. Foxglove leaves contain a drug used for certain types of heart disease. Quinine is a drug used to treat malaria. Quinine comes from the bark of a South American tree. Today, most medicines from plants are manufactured in special factories.

Plants Prevent Erosion

Compare the field in Figure 1-10a with the field in Figure 1-10b. One field is covered with plants. The plants hold the soil in place. The soil in the other field is bare. Without plants to help hold the soil, much of the topsoil has been blown or washed away. The removal of soil by wind and water is called **erosion** (ih ROH zhun).

What is erosion?

a

b

Figure 1-10. Plants hold soil in place (a); wind and water erode soil (b).

In the first field, the roots of plants hold the soil so that it cannot easily be blown or washed away. The roots of plants prevent erosion. The second field has been badly damaged by erosion. Plants cannot grow if the topsoil has been eroded away. Even if seeds germinate, they will probably die. If plants do not grow, erosion of the soil will continue and a desert will be produced. With proper care, it may be possible to improve the soil by getting plants to grow again.

Plants Add Beauty

Many plants are used to decorate our homes, schools, businesses, and parks. Plants have a natural beauty that is pleasing to most people. Some plants provide protection from wind, rain, and snow. They are also planted to provide shade. Plants improve our environment by providing pleasing shapes and colors.

Figure 1-11. Plants beautify our environment.

Lesson Summary

- Plant parts that can be eaten include roots, stems, leaves, flowers, fruits, and seeds.
- Plants and parts of plants are used as raw materials for many valuable products.
- Plants prevent erosion and help to beautify our environment.

Lesson Review

Review the lesson to answer these questions.
1. What is a raw material?
2. What are five products that are made from wood pulp?
3. What are three other products that are provided by plants?
4. How do plants prevent erosion?

People and Science

Gina's Garden Center

Have you ever seen a plant with yellow, orange, red, and green leaves? There is such a plant. It is called a croton (KROH tahn). There is even a plant with striped leaves called a zebra plant. Plants like the two just described can be found at Gina's Garden Center. Gina enjoys growing unusual plants.

Gina's garden center sells many kinds of plants. Unusual plants are her specialty. It takes Gina a long time to start new plants. So, she is very careful to explain how a plant must be taken care of before selling it to a customer. Gina says she feels bad when someone buys a plant from her and then returns it in a month to tell her the plant has died. Gina thinks that most plants die because they have not been taken care of properly.

The garden center does a lot of business during the winter months. It seems that people enjoy the beauty of indoor plants most during the winter time. Whether it is winter or spring, no plant leaves Gina's garden center without a plastic sign stuck in the soil. The sign tells how to take care of the plant. It gives information about when to water and how much water the plant needs, how much sunlight it needs, and whether or not the plant is poisonous. Why might a customer need to know if a plant is poisonous?

You cannot take a plant from Gina's garden center without reading the plastic sign out loud. Gina wants to be sure each customer knows what he or she is buying and that her plants are going to have a good home.

Chapter 1 Review

Summary

1. Green plants can produce their own food.   1:1
2. Photosynthesis is the process by which green plants produce food.   1:1
3. Respiration is the process that breaks down food and releases energy.   1:1
4. Living things use energy for all of life's activities.   1:1
5. The roots, stems, leaves, flowers, and seeds of different plants are used for food.   1:2
6. Plants provide raw materials that can be made into useful products.   1:2
7. Plants prevent soil erosion and are used to beautify our environment.   1:2

Science Words

photosynthesis	**raw material**	**dye**	**latex**
chlorophyll	**wood pulp**	**cork**	**fiber**
respiration	**tannic acid**	**resin**	**erosion**

Understanding Science Words

Complete each of the following sentences with a word or words from the Science Words that will make the sentence correct.

1. Any matter that can be made into useful products is a _____.
2. The process by which plants make food is _____.
3. A soft, spongy material made from combining wood chips, chemicals, and steam is _____.
4. The process that breaks down food and releases energy is _____.
5. The green substance in plants that traps light energy to produce food is _____.
6. The stems of many plants contain threadlike cells called _____.

7. A milky substance that comes from a rubber tree is _____.
8. A substance that is used for coloring is _____.
9. The removal of soil by wind and water is _____.
10. The tough, spongy bark of the cork oak tree is _____.
11. A raw material used to make turpentine is _____.
12. A chemical that comes from tannin taken from the bark of some trees and used to change animal hides into leather is _____.

Questions

A. Recalling Facts
Choose the word or phrase that correctly completes each of the following sentences.
1. Through photosynthesis plants make
   (a) food.   (c) chlorophyll.
   (b) water.   (d) carbon dioxide.
2. All living things need
   (a) seed.   (b) energy.   (c) soil.   (d) leaves.
3. Matter that can be made into useful products is called
   (a) stored food.   (c) light.
   (b) raw material.   (d) energy.

B. Understanding Concepts
Answer each of the following questions using complete sentences.
1. Explain photosynthesis and respiration.
2. How do plants prevent erosion?
3. Name five plant raw materials and products made from these materials.

C. Applying Concepts
Think about what you have learned in this chapter. Answer each of the following questions using complete sentences.
1. How are photosynthesis and respiration different?
2. How do we depend on plants?

Chapter 2
More About Plants

Think of plants in your environment. Many have flowers. Some do not. Plants grow and eventually die. New plants grow in their place. How do you think new plants start growing?

Plants are part of our environment

Flowers and Seeds   2:1

LESSON GOALS

In this lesson you will learn
- about the structure of flowers.
- how flowers are pollinated.
- how fertilization takes place.

Earth is covered with many different kinds of plants. Most plants grow outdoors. Some grow in gardens or on farms. Some grow indoors in pots. Imagine how the area around your home or school would look if there were no plants.

Plants from Plants

Large numbers of plants are eaten or destroyed every day. We still have plants on Earth because plants are able to produce more of their own kind. Different kinds of plants produce new plants in different ways. Many plants produce seeds. These seeds can grow into new plants. Most of the plants around your home and school produce seeds. Some plants produce spores. Ferns and mosses produce spores. Many plants can grow from other parts of plants. The leaves, stems, and roots of different plants can break away and grow into new plants.

Figure 2-1. Plants grow from seeds (a), spores (b), and plant parts (c).

a

b

c

Figure 2-2. Some flowers have brightly colored petals (a), some have joined petals (b), and others have many separate petals (c).

Flowers

Many plants produce flowers. The **flower** is the plant part in which seeds are formed. Some flowers are large and brightly colored. Others are small and green. Some flowers have a pleasant smell and others have an unpleasant smell or no smell at all. Flowers grow in all sizes and shapes, but all flowers are very important parts of plants because they produce seeds.

The flower in Figure 2-2a has showy petals. **Petals** are the parts of the flower that are usually brightly colored. Petals have many different shapes, colors, and sizes. The flower shown in Figure 2-2b has joined petals. The flower in Figure 2-2c has separate petals. The petals surround the inside parts of a flower. Many of the flowers we use for decorations have large brightly colored petals. Some flowers have no petals at all. Flowers of oak trees and grasses have no petals.

Flower Parts

Some of the parts of the flower in Figure 2-3 have been taken away to show the inside of the flower. On the outside of the flower are green sepals (SEE pulz). **Sepals** are the outer parts of the flower that protect the bud before it opens.

Inside the petals of most flowers is a flower part called the pistil (PIHS tul). The **pistil** is the female part of the flower that contains the ovary (OHV ree). Find the pistil in Figure 2-3. The top of the pistil is narrow. The tip is sticky. The ovary is at the bottom. The **ovary** is the part of a plant that contains egg cells. The egg cells can become seeds. Find the ovary in Figure 2–3.

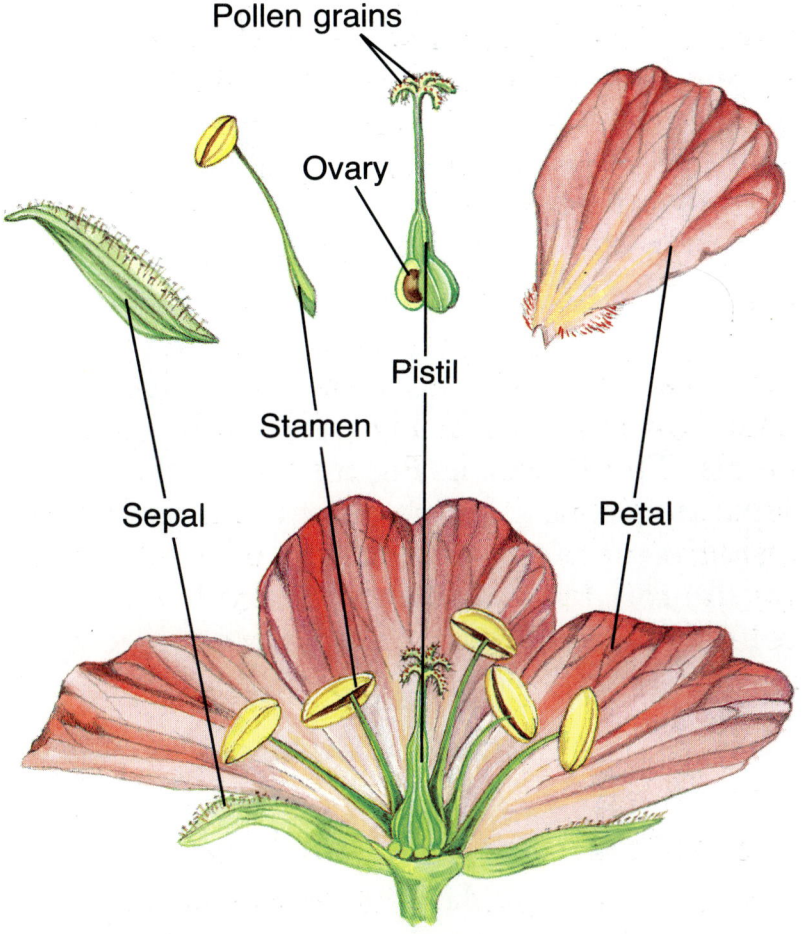

Figure 2-3. The parts of a flower.

Most flowers have other parts called stamens (STAY munz). The **stamens** are the male parts of the flower that produce a powdery material called pollen. At the top of the stamens are pollen sacs. These contain millions of pollen grains. **Pollen grains** are the parts of a plant that contain sperm cells. Find the stamens with their pollen sacs in Figure 2–3.

What are the male parts of a flower?

Pollination and Fertilization

What is pollination?

Pollination (pahl uh NAY shun) is the transfer of pollen grains to the sticky part of the pistil. Insects such as the honeybee often aid in pollination. Honeybees move from flower to flower gathering pollen. Pollen grains from the stamen stick to the hair on the bee's body. The honeybee moves to other flowers. The pollen grains may brush off onto the pistil of the other flowers. Where is the pollen on the honeybee in Figure 2-4?

Figure 2-4. A honeybee transfers pollen as it moves from flower to flower.

Pollination can occur in other ways. Often pollen grains are blown by the wind. The pollen grains may land on the pistil of a flower. The flowers of most trees and grasses are pollinated by the wind.

Pollination occurs when pollen grains stick to the top of the pistil of the same kind of flower. Once there, a tube begins to grow from each pollen grain. The tubes grow downward through the narrow part of the pistil until they reach the ovary. Find a pollen tube in Figure 2-5. The tubes enter the ovary. Sperm cells are released from the tube into the ovary. The sperm cells and egg cells join.

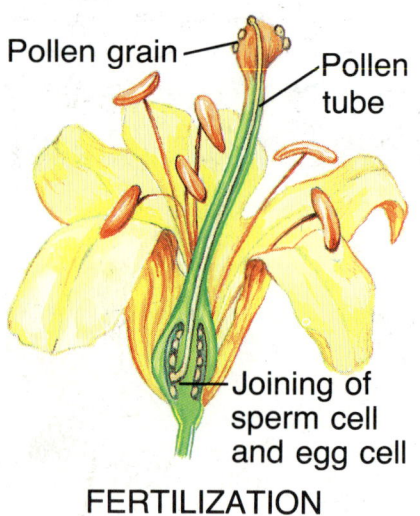

Figure 2-5. Fertilization is the joining of an egg cell and a sperm cell.

Fertilization (furt ul uh ZAY shun) is the joining of an egg cell and a sperm cell. In plants, the fertilized eggs grow into seeds. Pollination and fertilization must take place to produce seeds that will grow into new plants.

Seeds and Fruit

After pollination and fertilization, seeds are formed in the ovary of a plant. If four egg cells are fertilized, then four seeds are formed. As seeds form, other changes take place in the flower. The top parts of the pistil and stamens, petals, and sepals begin to dry. Then, as the seeds grow, the ovary gets larger and the ovary becomes a fruit. A **fruit** is an enlarged ovary. The fruit contains the seeds.

What does the fruit of a plant contain?

Figure 2-6. After fertilization, seeds are formed in the ovary of a plant.

25

Fruits can be dry, as in the winged maple. They can also be fleshy, as in many of the fruits we eat. Figure 2–7 shows the cross section of a tomato. Inside the fleshy fruit are small yellow seeds. Each seed can be planted to produce a new tomato plant.

Figure 2–7. Each tomato seed can be planted to produce a new plant.

Lesson Summary

- Most flowers have sepals, petals, a pistil, and stamens.
- Flowers are pollinated when pollen grains are transferred from stamens to the top of the pistil.
- Pollen grains have sperm cells that join with egg cells in the ovary. The joining of the sperm cell and the egg cell is called fertilization.

Lesson Review

Review the lesson to answer these questions.
1. Why are flowers important in some plants?
2. Name four parts of a flower.
3. What are two ways pollen can be transferred from flower to flower?
4. What is a fruit?

Activity 2-1 Flowers

QUESTION What are the different parts of a flower?

Materials
flower with petals
sheet of black paper
paper with names of flower parts
toothpick
hand lens
pencil and paper

What to do

1. Remove the sepals and petals of the flower.
2. Remove a stamen and brush the top against the black paper.
3. Use a hand lens to observe the matter that rubbed off the stamen.
4. Brush the stamen over the pistil.
5. Open the ovary with the toothpick.
6. Place the flower parts next to their names on the paper.

What did you learn?
1. What material rubbed off the stamen?
2. What happened when you touched the top of the stamen to the pistil?
3. What did you see inside the ovary?

Using what you learned
1. Why must the pistil be sticky?
2. How might pollen grains get to the pistil?
3. What would happen if no pollination occurred?

2:2 Plants Produce New Plants

LESSON GOALS
In this lesson you will learn
- how different kinds of plants can make new plants.
- how plants produce new plants from seeds.
- how plants produce new plants from plant parts.

From what do most plants grow?

Different kinds of plants have different ways to start new plants. Most plants grow from seeds. A seed needs water and proper temperature to germinate. When conditions are right, the seed will begin to grow. The early growth of a plant from a seed is called **germination** (jur muh NAY shun). What conditions affect germination?

Figure 2-8. The early growth of a plant from a seed is germination.

28

Figure 2–8 shows the tiny plant inside a bean seed. It also shows the bean seed as it germinates and grows. The tiny plant in the seed gets larger and breaks through the seed coat. The tiny plant grows roots, stems, and leaves. Later, flowers and new seeds are formed. If water and temperature conditions are not right, the seed will not germinate and grow.

Other Ways of Growing Plants

Some plants can grow without seeds. They can grow from plant parts or cuttings. A **cutting** is a leaf or a stem cut from a plant that is used to start a new plant. Figure 2–9 shows how a cutting of a philodendron plant can grow new roots when placed in water. In tropical forests, such as those found in South America, there are many plants that can grow new plants from small pieces that break off.

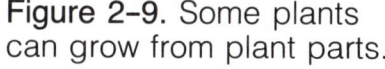

Figure 2-9. Some plants can grow from plant parts.

Figure 2-10. The stored food in a bulb is used by a plant when it grows.

What is a bulb?

Some plants, like onions, daffodils, and tulips, have underground bulbs. Look at the bulbs in Figure 2-10. A **bulb** is the underground part of a plant that has a very short stem surrounded by fleshy leaves. The bulbs shown in Figure 2-10 have thick parts that store food. The fleshy leaves have stored food. The stored food is used by the plant when it begins to grow.

Figure 2-11. Potato tubers have stored food.

The part of a white potato plant that you eat is a tuber. The **tuber** is a swollen underground root or stem. Potato stem tubers have stored foods. The "eyes" of the potato are buds. The buds form sprouts and develop into a completely new potato plant. Potato plants can also be grown from seeds. Many plants like potatoes can be grown in more than one way. Another underground stem that stores food is a **rhizome** (RI zohm). Many kinds of grass produce new plants from rhizomes.

Figure 2-12. Ginger is an example of a rhizome.

Activity 2-2   Growing Plants from Parts of Plants

QUESTION   How can you grow new plants without using seeds?

Materials

flower pot
carrot
saucer
tulip bulb
potting soil

ivy plant
jar
water
pencil and paper

What to do

1. Have your teacher cut about one inch off the top of a carrot. Do not remove the old leaves. Set the carrot top in a small saucer of water. Never let the saucer get dry.
2. Plant the bulb in a pot and keep the soil damp and warm.
3. Have your teacher cut off a small branch of ivy at a point just below where a leaf joins the stem. Place this in a jar of water.
4. Observe what happens to each of the plantings over the next 4 weeks or more.

What did you learn?

1. What changes did you observe with the carrot? The bulb?
2. What happened to the ivy?

Using what you learned

1. Why might gardeners prefer to start plants from parts of another plant rather than from seeds?
2. Where do the carrot and bulb get food to grow before they grow leaves?

Figure 2-13. A strawberry plant has thin stems that grow along the ground.

What is a runner?

A strawberry plant has thin stems that grow along the ground. These stems of the strawberry plant can form new plants at their tips. A stem that grows close to the ground and forms a new plant is called a **runner.** New plants will grow where the tip of the runner touches the ground.

Lesson Summary

- Different kinds of plants make new plants in different ways.
- Seeds contain tiny plants that will grow when they have the proper temperature and water.
- Some kinds of plants produce new plants from cuttings, bulbs, tubers, rhizomes, or runners.

Lesson Review

Review the lesson to answer these questions.
1. What happens when a seed germinates?
2. Name one plant that will grow from cuttings.
3. Name four plants that will grow from underground stems.
4. How do new plants start from runners?

Language Arts Skills

Using a Glossary

As you read, you often come across words that you do not know. Sometimes you can tell what the word means by the way it is used in the sentence or paragraph that you are reading. At other times you may need to look up the word in a dictionary. A dictionary not only lists the meanings for the word but also tells other facts about the word. It will tell how the word is pronounced, its part of speech, and other facts. Some books that you read have their own dictionaries. These dictionaries are called glossaries.

- How many entry words are listed in the sample glossary?
- In what kinds of order are the entry words listed?
- Compare a glossary and dictionary. How are they alike?

Each page in a dictionary has guide words at the top. The guide word on the left side tells what the first entry word is. The guide word on the right tells the last entry word on the page.

- How can the guide words be used to find a word in a glossary or dictionary?

Most books have the glossary at the back. It almost always comes before the index. Some glossaries are made to look exactly like a dictionary. Others just list the words and their meanings.

- Why might drawings be included in a glossary?
- What kind of glossary does your science book have?

---

petal   **pollination**

petal   part of a flower that is usually brightly colored

photosynthesis   process by which plants make food

pistil   female part of a flower that contains the ovary

pollen grain   part of a plant that contains sperm cells

pollination   the transfer of pollen grains to the top, sticky part of the pistil in a flower

Chapter 2 Review

Summary

1. The flower has parts for forming seeds. 2:1
2. Pollination is the transfer of pollen to the sticky part of the pistil. 2:1
3. The joining of an egg cell and a sperm cell is called fertilization. 2:1
4. Plants are able to produce more plants. 2:2
5. Most plants start from seeds. 2:2
6. Some plants can be grown from cuttings, bulbs, tubers, rhizomes, or runners. 2:2

Science Words

flower	ovary	fertilization	bulb
petals	stamens	fruit	tuber
sepals	pollen grains	germination	rhizome
pistil	pollination	cutting	runner

Understanding Science Words

Complete each of the following sentences with a word or words from the Science Words that will make the sentence correct.

1. The parts of the flower that contain cells called sperm cells are _____.
2. The flower part that contains the ovary is the _____.
3. The transfer of pollen grains to the sticky part of the pistil is _____.
4. The plant part where male and female parts are formed is the _____.
5. The joining of an egg cell and a sperm cell is called _____.
6. A leaf or a stem cut from a plant that is used to start a new plant is called a _____.
7. An enlarged ovary is called a _____.
8. The part of a white potato you eat is a _____.
9. The plant part that contains the egg cells is called the _____.
10. The flower part that produces pollen is called the _____.

11. The outer parts of flowers that protect the buds are _____.
12. A stem that grows close to the ground and forms a new plant is called a _____.
13. The parts of flowers that are usually brightly colored are _____.
14. Many grasses produce new plants from an underground stem called a _____.
15. The plant part from which onions, daffodils, and tulips are grown is called a _____.
16. The early growth of a plant from a seed is _____.

Questions

A. Recalling Facts
Choose the word or phrase that correctly completes each of the following sentences.
1. Seeds develop in a part of a plant called a
   (a) root. (b) stem. (c) leaf. (d) flower.
2. In pollination, pollen is transferred from the pollen sacs to the
   (a) pistil. (b) petals. (c) leaves (d) stamens.
3. The early growth of a plant from a seed is called
   (a) pollination. (c) germination.
   (b) fertilization. (d) cutting.

B. Understanding Concepts
Answer each of the following questions using complete sentences.
1. Other than seeds, how do plants reproduce?
2. Draw, label, and describe the parts of a flower.

C. Applying Concepts
Think about what you have learned in this chapter. Answer each of the following questions using complete sentences.
1. What is the difference between fertilization and germination?
2. Why will seeds not germinate when dry?

UNIT 1 REVIEW

CHECKING YOURSELF

Answer these questions on a sheet of paper.
1. What four things are necessary for photosynthesis to take place?
2. What two substances combine in photosynthesis?
3. What do plants do with the excess food they produce but do not use right away in respiration?
4. How is photosynthesis different from respiration?
5. What are four raw materials obtained from plants?
6. How do plants help prevent erosion?
7. Name four ways that plants reproduce.
8. Name four parts of a flower.
9. Where are seeds produced in a flower?
10. How does fertilization take place?

RECALLING ACTIVITIES

Think about the activities you did in this unit. Answer the questions about these activities.
1. How can you show that photosynthesis produces starch?   1–1
2. How can you observe plants producing a gas?   1–2
3. What are the different parts of a flower?   2–1
4. How can you grow new plants without using seeds?   2–2

IDEAS TO EXPLORE

1. Test the various parts of plants you eat to see if they contain starch.

2. Make a list of all the products you use in a day and check to see how many of them come from raw materials of plants.
3. Make a list of as many plants as you can that you see in your environment. For each: 1) name the plant; 2) tell whether you think it is a flowering plant or not and why; 3) tell what benefits it has for people—food, raw material, beauty, prevents erosion; and 4) tell how it reproduces.

CHALLENGING PROJECT

Collect and label different kinds of seeds. Find a book in the library that will help you identify these and other seeds in your collection. Observe the shape and structure of each seed. Prepare a report and a display that tells how each seed may be scattered away from the parent plant. Tell how some of the seeds will end up in conditions where they will germinate and grow into new plants. Also, tell why some seeds may not grow into new plants.

BOOKS TO READ

A Book of Vegetables by Harriet L. Sobol, Dodd, Mead & Co.: New York, © 1984.
   Learn how your favorite vegetables grow.

Tiger Lilies and other Beastly Plants by Elizabeth Ring, Walker & Co.: New York, © 1984.
   Animal plants! Read about tiger lilies, snapdragons, and others.

Tree Flowers by Millicent E. Selsam, William Morrow & Co.: New York, © 1984.
   Discover the beauty of twelve flowering trees.

UNIT 2
Light, Color, and Sight

In 1826, a French inventor, Joseph Nicéphore Niépce, made the world's first photograph. He did this by placing a specially coated metal plate inside a camera-like box. He then exposed the plate to sunlight for about eight hours. The resulting photograph shows the view from the inventor's window. Today you can see the results of your picture taking almost instantly. All you need is light, a camera with film, and a smile!

The world's first photograph—1826

Photography today

Chapter 3
Light and Color

Imagine what it would be like to live in a world without light. You would not be able to see the size, shape, or color of anything around you. How else might your life be different without light? Why is light important to your life?

Light and color in nature

Light 3:1

LESSON GOALS

In this lesson you will learn
- light is a kind of energy.
- light travels through most gases and liquids, and some solids.
- light can be reflected and refracted.
- transparent, translucent, and opaque objects affect light differently.

Some objects like our sun and other stars produce their own light. They are sources of naturally produced light. These sources of light cannot be directly controlled by people. You cannot turn the sun "on" or "off." You cannot make the light from our sun or other stars brighter or dimmer.

Some living things are sources of naturally produced light. A firefly is one example. It produces light by means of chemical changes. The chemical changes take place within the body of the firefly.

Figure 3-1. Three light sources are the sun, a firefly, and a flashlight.

41

What light sources are made and controlled by people?

Sources of artificially produced light are made and controlled by people. These light sources are very useful. A flashlight is one source of artificially produced light. A flashlight is used to give light when there is no source of naturally produced light. See Figure 3-1. How is light from a flashlight controlled?

An electric light bulb is another source of artificially produced light. Think of all the electric light bulbs that are used in your home. Where are they located? Why are they located there?

Figure 3-2. Electric bulbs are an important light source for our homes.

A Kind of Energy

Light is a kind of energy. The atoms that make up matter can take on extra energy. Taking on extra energy causes atoms to become more active. Some of the extra energy may be released as light.

Figure 3-3. Metal heated to a high temperature gives off light.

Look at Figure 3-3. The metal has been heated to a very high temperature. This causes the atoms that make up the metal to become more active. Its atoms have taken on extra energy. You can see that some of this energy is being given off as light. A light bulb works in a similar way. When the bulb is turned on, the filament becomes very hot. Some of this energy is given off as light.

How does a light bulb work?

Behavior of Light

Light travels at very high speeds. Light travels much faster than sound. Sometimes we can *see* something happen before we can *hear* it happen. You may notice this during a baseball game. You can see the bat strike the baseball before you hear the sound. This happens because the light reflected from the batter, the bat, and the ball travels to your eyes faster than the sound travels to your ears.

Which travels faster, light or sound?

43

Through what does light travel?

Light travels through most gases and liquids, and through some solids. Light can also travel through empty space. We would not be able to see any objects in space, such as the moon, if light could not travel through space. Light from the sun could not reach Earth if light could not travel through empty space.

Figure 3-4. Great Nebula in Orion

Reflection

Some of the light that strikes matter bounces off its surface. This bouncing back of light from a surface is called **reflection** (rih FLEK shun). Light reflects from a smooth surface without changing its pattern. See Figure 3-5a. Light from your face bounces off a mirror in a regular pattern. You are able to see a reflection of the light from your face in a mirror.

Light reflected from a rough surface scatters in different directions. See Figure 3-5b. Light from your face does not bounce off concrete in a regular pattern. This is why you cannot see a reflection of your face in a concrete wall.

What is reflection?

How does light reflect from rough surfaces?

Figure 3-5. Light reflected from a smooth surface (a) and a rough surface (b)

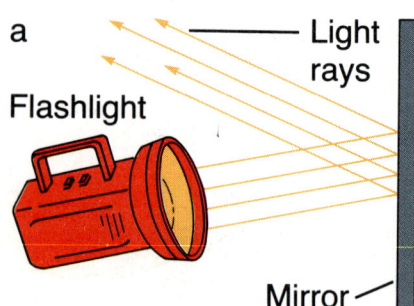
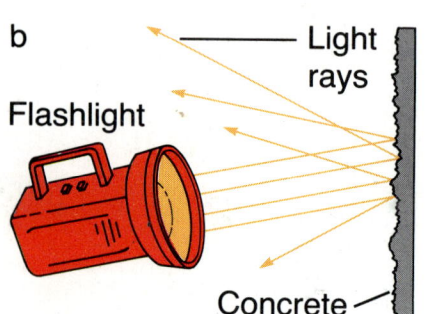

44

Refraction

Sometimes light bends when it passes between two different types of matter. This bending of light is called **refraction** (rih FRAK shun). This bending of light or refraction happens because the speed of light is not the same in all types of matter. Light is refracted only if it passes between two different types of matter at an angle. It is not bent if it passes straight through two different types of matter.

Why is light refracted in this way? Think about the boy skating along the sidewalk as shown in Figure 3-6a. As long as both of his skates are on the sidewalk, he will go straight. If one skate hits the grass he will turn into the grass. See Figure 3-6b. He turns because the grass slows him down. In a way, the boy's path or direction is refracted in much the same way as light is refracted. If the boy skates straight into the grass as shown in Figure 3-6c he is slowed down, but he is not turned because both skates hit the grass at the same time.

Figure 3-6. Observe the path of the boy skating on the sidewalk (a), on the sidewalk and the grass (b), on the grass (c).

Skating on sidewalk

Skating on sidewalk and grass

Skating on grass

Light is refracted in much the same way. When light passes through different matter at an angle, it is bent or refracted. Light is refracted because it travels at different speeds in different matter. Light is not refracted when it passes straight through different types of matter.

Figure 3-7. The fishnet handle appears bent because light is refracted as it passes from the water to the air.

Look at Figure 3-7. The handle of the fishnet appears to be bent. The handle is not really bent. The light is being refracted as it passes from the water to the air. Look at Figure 3-8. When the girl is standing in the water, her legs look shorter. This is also because of the refraction of light. The light is bent when it passes from the water to the air. Where else have you seen the effects of refracted light?

Matter Affects Light

Light passes straight through **transparent** (trans PER unt) **matter.** We can see objects clearly through matter that is transparent. Most windows and eyeglass lenses are made of transparent glass or plastic. Name some other kinds of transparent matter.

Figure 3-8. The girl's legs look shorter because of the refraction of light.

a b c

Figure 3-9. An apple wrapped in transparent (a), translucent (b), and opaque matter (c)

Some kinds of matter let light pass through but scatter the light in many directions. **Translucent** (trans LEWS unt) **matter** scatters light. A lamp shade, frosted glass, and waxed paper are translucent. You cannot see a light bulb clearly through a lamp shade. You cannot see objects clearly through frosted glass or waxed paper.

What is translucent matter?

Some matter blocks light completely. Light cannot pass through **opaque** (oh PAYK) **matter.** You cannot see through opaque matter at all. Your classroom wall is opaque. The floor of your classroom is opaque. Most of your body is opaque!

What is opaque matter?

Lesson Summary

- Light is a kind of energy.
- Light travels through most gases and liquids and some solids.
- Light can be reflected and refracted.
- Transparent, translucent, and opaque objects affect light differently.

Lesson Review

Review the lesson to answer these questions.
1. Give two examples of naturally produced light.
2. What is the difference between reflection and refraction?
3. Waxed paper is an example of what kind of matter?

Activity 3-1 Refracting Light

QUESTION How can you bend light?

Materials
flashlight
tape
black construction paper
water
clear plastic container
milk
scissors
dropper
pencil and paper

What to do

1. Fill the container nearly full of water. Add 2 drops of milk.
2. Make a narrow slit in the black paper. Tape the paper with the slit over the end of the flashlight.
3. Shine the beam of light straight at the container. Record your observations.
4. Shine the beam of light through the container at an angle. Record your observations.

What did you learn?
1. What happened to the light in step 3?
2. What happened to the light in step 4?

Using what you learned
1. How did you get the light to bend?
2. Imagine that you are fishing. Why is it important to know that light bends?

People and Science

A Real Shutterbug

The championship basketball game had just ended. The next morning, the sports page of the newspaper would have a color picture of an exciting moment in the game. It is Arleen McDonald's job to bring the sports editor photographs of the game. Arleen is a photojournalist. During the basketball game, or any other sporting or news event, Arleen takes pictures of the action. Arleen tells stories using pictures.

Arleen explains that light is very important in taking and developing pictures. Each time she opens the shutter of her camera, light enters it through the lens. When light hits the film in the camera, chemicals on the film cause an image to form. The proper amount of light is necessary for a clear picture.

After Arleen takes the pictures, she develops the film in a darkroom. A darkroom is a workshop where no light enters from the outside. Since outside light affects the chemicals on the film, the light would destroy the image. Arleen places the film in a container, turns on special lights, and begins to develop the film.

First, Arleen adds a series of chemicals to the roll of film. Then she washes the film with water. A roll of negatives is produced. Now she turns off the special lights, because outside light does not hurt the negatives. She dries the film and cuts it into strips. Arleen produces color photographs by using a process involving light-sensitive paper and chemical baths. Her pictures are worth a thousand words.

49

3:2 Color

LESSON GOALS

In this lesson you will learn
- white light is a mixture of many colors.
- a prism is a transparent object that refracts light.
- colored glass lets only some light pass through it.
- colored objects do not reflect all of the colors of the spectrum.

Sunlight is white light. **White light** is a mixture of many colors. White light can be separated into a band of colors. The band of colors that makes up white light is called the **visible spectrum.** Red, orange, yellow, green, blue, and violet are the main colors of the visible spectrum. These colors form many shades within the spectrum, such as the many shades of red.

White light separates into a visible spectrum when it is refracted. As you know, light is sometimes refracted when it passes from one kind of matter into another. Light is refracted when it passes from air through a prism (PRIHZ um). A **prism** is a transparent object that refracts light. The separate colors of the spectrum can be seen with a prism. This is possible because each spectrum color refracts or bends at a different angle. Blue light refracts at a greater angle than red light. Green light refracts at a greater angle than red light but at a lesser angle than blue light.

What is the visible spectrum?

Figure 3-10. A prism separates white light into the visible spectrum.

What is a prism?

Activity 3-2 Seeing Colors

QUESTION How can the color of an object appear to be changed?

Materials

colored construction paper
plastic rings
colored cellophane
pencil and paper
stapler
yarn
scissors

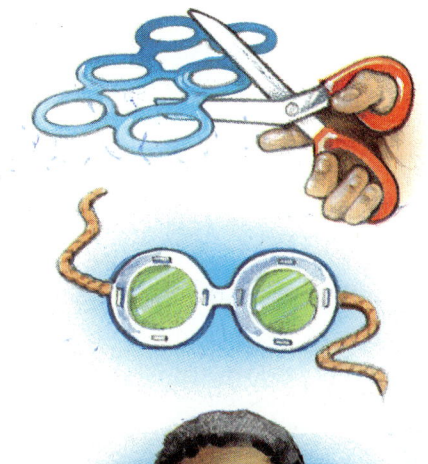

What to do

1. Cut the rings as shown.
2. Cover the holes with 2 or 3 layers of cellophane. Staple the cellophane to the plastic. Make a pair of red, blue, and green glasses. Use yarn to make ties for your glasses.
3. Put on a pair of glasses. Do not look while your partner sets out three sheets of different colored paper.
4. Look at the papers. Write down the colors you see in a chart like the one shown. Repeat steps 3 and 4 using glasses of different colors.

What did you learn?

1. How many color choices were correct?
2. What did the colors look like through the glasses?

Using what you learned

1. Which colors appeared to change?
2. Why does the color seem to change?

Color Observations		
Glasses	Color Sample	Color Observed
Red	1	
	2	
	3	
Blue	1	
	2	
	3	
Green	1	
	2	
	3	

How are raindrops like a prism?

We can also see the visible spectrum in a rainbow. Tiny drops of water in the air act as prisms and refract sunlight. The colors in the rainbow are in the same pattern as the colors made by a prism.

Figure 3-11. The visible spectrum can be seen in a rainbow.

Seeing Color

Looking through colored glass is different from looking through clear glass. Clear glass allows all the colors of light to pass through it. Colored glass lets only some colors of the light pass through it. Red glass lets mostly red light pass through it. Green glass lets mostly green light pass through it. Looking at objects through colored glass can make their colors appear to change. If you look at a red apple through green glass, the apple will appear black. What color would green grapes appear to be if you looked at them through a red glass?

We see objects when they reflect light to our eyes. If an object in white light reflects almost all the light to our eyes, the object

Figure 3-12. A red apple seen through a green glass

52

will look white. Red apples look red because they reflect more red light than other colors. The other colors of the spectrum are absorbed or taken in by the apples. Some grapes look green because they absorb most of the other spectrum colors. The light reflected to your eyes from the grapes has more green than other colors.

The zebra in Figure 3-13 has both black and white hair. The white hair looks white because it reflects almost all the colors of the visible spectrum. Remember: white light is made of all colors. The black hair looks black because it absorbs almost all the colors of the visible spectrum. Very little visible light is reflected to our eyes.

Figure 3-13. African zebra

Using Color

Colors are useful and important. We use colors in many ways. Colors may be helpful when you try to find your coat among others. Look at Figure 3-14a and b. Imagine that yours is the red coat. It is easy to find the red coat in picture a. Why is it difficult to find the red coat in picture b?

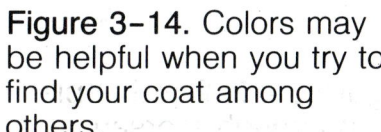

Figure 3-14. Colors may be helpful when you try to find your coat among others.

a

b

People use color to warn of danger. Red traffic lights mean "Stop!" Flashing yellow traffic lights usually mean "Proceed with caution." Most people are familiar with brightly colored fire engines and ambulances. Where have you seen color used to warn of danger?

Figure 3-15. Emergency vehicle

Lesson Summary

- White light is a mixture of many colors.
- A prism is a transparent object that refracts light.
- Colored glass lets only some light pass through it.
- Colored objects do not reflect all of the colors of the spectrum.

Lesson Review

Review the lesson to answer these questions.
1. What happens when white light is refracted?
2. Why can we see the visible spectrum in a rainbow?
3. Give one example of how the use of color is important.

Science and Technology

The Eyes Have It

A security guard walks up to the door of a top secret area. A pair of binoculars are mounted next to the door. The guard looks into them for a few seconds, and then turns back to the door. The door swings open. Does this sound like a scene from a science fiction movie? This kind of security system is being used today! This system is called a biometric (bi oh MEH trikh) security system.

Biometrics is a new type of security system. The word *biometric* means to measure living things. Biometrics differ from other security systems in one important way. Most security systems check for some special "thing" like an entrance card or a key. Biometrics checks you against earlier measurements made from your body.

There are four main types of biometrics. These systems may measure fingerprints, voice, palm of the hand, or vein patterns in the eye. The patterns made from fingerprints, voice, palm, or eye are different for each person. It is very difficult to make false copies of these patterns. Biometric systems are hard to fool.

One big problem with the eye scanners is that they are very expensive. Scientists are working to build less expensive systems. Someday biometrics may be used to protect your home.

Chapter 3 Review

Summary

1. Light is a kind of energy. 3:1
2. Light travels through most gases and liquids, and some solids. 3:1
3. Light can be reflected and refracted. 3:1
4. Transparent, translucent, and opaque objects affect light differently. 3:1
5. White light is a mixture of many colors. 3:2
6. A prism is a transparent object that refracts light. 3:2
7. Colored glass lets only some light pass through it. 3:2
8. Colored objects absorb all of the visible spectrum except the color of the object which is reflected. 3:2

Science Words

reflection   **translucent matter**   **visible spectrum**
refraction   **opaque matter**   **prism**
transparent matter **white light**

Understanding Science Words

Complete each of the following sentences with a word or words from the Science Words that will make the sentence correct.

1. Light that is a mixture of all colors is called _____.
2. Light passes straight through _____.
3. The bouncing of light off matter is called _____.
4. A device that is used to separate light into the spectrum is a _____.
5. The bending of light as it passes through different matter is called _____.
6. Light scatters in many directions as it passes through _____.
7. The separated colors of white light are called the _____.
8. Light cannot pass through _____.

Questions

A. Recalling Facts

Choose the word or phrase that correctly completes each of the following sentences.

1. When metal is heated, some of its extra energy is given off as
   (a) sound.   (b) color.   (c) matter.   (d) light.
2. You are able to see yourself in a mirror due to
   (a) refraction.   (b) absorption.   (c) spectrum.   (d) reflection.
3. What color light is reflected by a red object?
   (a) blue   (b) white   (c) red   (d) all
4. What causes a rainbow?
   (a) reflected light   (c) artificial light
   (b) refracted light   (d) absorbed light

B. Understanding Concepts

Answer each of the following questions using complete sentences.

1. Give an example of transparent, translucent, and opaque matter.
2. How is artificially produced light different from naturally produced light? Give an example of each.
3. What are the colors of the visible spectrum?
4. (a) Why do some objects appear white?
   (b) Why do some objects appear black?
5. How is color useful and important to us?

C. Applying Concepts

Think about what you have learned in this chapter. Answer each of the following questions using complete sentences.

1. Why is it sometimes difficult to tell the depth of water even if you can see the bottom?
2. How does a prism separate white light?
3. A brick wall and a mirror both reflect light. Why are you not able to see your face in a brick wall?

Chapter 4
The Sense of Sight

Your eyes are very important. You use your eyes in order to do most things every day. You are using your eyes right now as you read this book. How else have you used your eyes today?

The importance of vision

How We See 4:1

LESSON GOALS

In this lesson you will learn
- we see an opaque object because of the light it reflects to our eyes.
- the main parts of the eye are the iris, pupil, lens, retina, and optic nerve.

Remember, you cannot see without light. You see an opaque object because of the light that is reflected from the object to your eyes. You see color because a colored object reflects colored light to your eyes.

What is needed in order to see?

a

b

It is difficult to see in dim light. In dim light you cannot see the shapes of objects clearly. Objects may appear as shadows rather than real things. Also, in dim light objects may not appear to be their true colors. In dim light an apple may appear gray. You may have entered a darkened room and noticed how the shapes and colors of objects changed after you turned on the lights. Remember that you are able to see because of the light that is reflected from objects.

Figure 4-1. Objects seen in dim light (a), objects seen in bright light (b)

Figure 4-2. The pupil in bright light (a), the pupil in dim light (b)

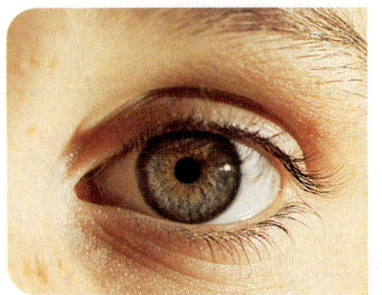 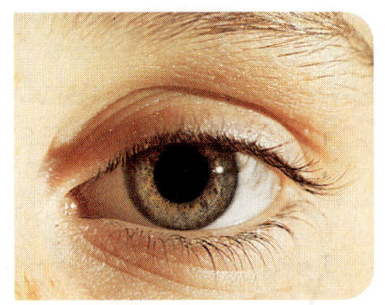

What is the pupil?

What happens to the pupil in bright light?

Light enters your eyes through the pupils. The **pupil** is a clear opening in the center of the iris of the eye. It looks black. The amount of light that enters the eye changes when the size of the pupil changes. The size of the pupil is changed by the movement of the iris. The **iris** is the colored part of the eye. The iris has a set of muscles. The muscles open and close the iris. This movement causes the size of the pupil to change. In bright light, the iris makes the pupil small to reduce the amount of light entering the eye. In dim light or darkness, the iris makes the pupil large to allow more light to enter the eye.

Activity 4-1   Observing the Iris

QUESTION How does light affect the iris?

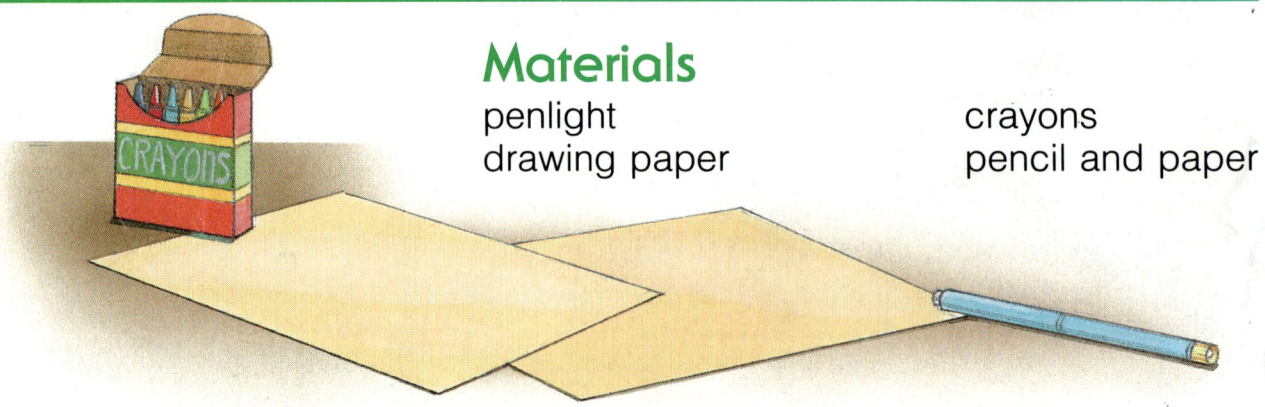

Materials

penlight
drawing paper

crayons
pencil and paper

60

What to do

1. Have your partner look away from any light source. Observe the size of your partner's pupils. Draw a picture of your partner's pupils and irises.
2. Draw a picture after your partner's eyes have been closed for one minute and then reopened.
3. Turn on the penlight. Hold it about 50 centimeters from your partner's eyes. Do not shine the light directly into your partner's eyes.
4. Draw another picture of your partner's pupils and irises after using the penlight.

Observations			
Pupils before looking at light	Pupils after looking at light	Pupils after eyes have been closed	Pupils after using penlight

What did you learn?

1. When were your partner's pupils smallest?
2. When were they largest?

Using what you learned

1. What effect does light have on the iris?
2. Imagine that you walk into a dark room after being in bright light. What happens to your irises?

What is a lens?

What is the optic nerve?

Behind the pupil of each eye is a lens. A **lens** is a transparent object with at least one curved surface. The lens refracts the light that comes into the eye. The refracted light comes together and forms a picture or **image** on the back of the eye. The part of the eye where the image forms is the **retina** (RET nuh). The retina is made of nerve endings. Light causes the nerve endings to send signals to the brain. The signals are sent along the optic nerve. The **optic nerve** is a path for nerve signals between the eye and the brain. The brain receives the signals and helps you understand what is seen. What would happen if the brain did not receive signals from the optic nerve?

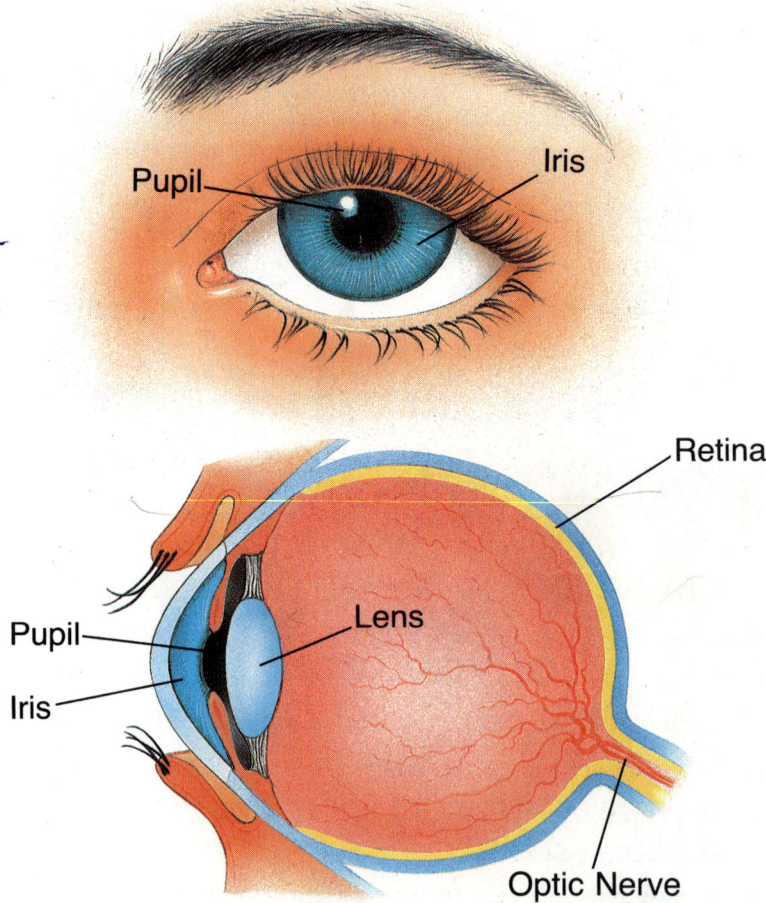

Figure 4-3. The parts of the eye

62

Study Figure 4-4. Notice that the image of the leaf is upside down. Images are formed upside down on the retina. When the brain receives the signals from the optic nerve, it "turns" the image right side up. We are able to "understand" what we see.

Figure 4-4. Light from the leaf is refracted by the lens to form an upside down image on the retina.

More time is needed to read about how we see than is needed to actually see an object. It took you a while to read these words. During that time, many images were formed on your retina and sent to your brain by way of the optic nerve.

Lesson Summary
- We see an opaque object because of the light it reflects to our eyes.
- The main parts of the eye are the iris, pupil, lens, retina, and optic nerve.

Lesson Review
Review the lesson to answer these questions.
1. What controls the amount of light that enters your eyes?
2. What is the retina?
3. What is the pathway between the eye and the brain?

4:2　Problems and Proper Care

LESSON GOALS

In this lesson you will learn
- many people have problems with their eyesight.
- some visual problems, or impairments, can be corrected by using concave or convex lenses.
- proper eye care is very important.

Many people have problems with their eyesight. Sometimes there is a problem because of the shape of parts of the eye. At other times, the lens may not focus or bring images together correctly on the retina. For some people, the visual problem, or impairment, is such that they must develop other body senses to help them live in their environment.

The boy in Figure 4-5 and the girl in Figure 4-7 are visually impaired. They have learned to read and move from place to place without using their eyes. The boy is using his fingers to read a book. The book

Figure 4-5. Reading from a Braille book

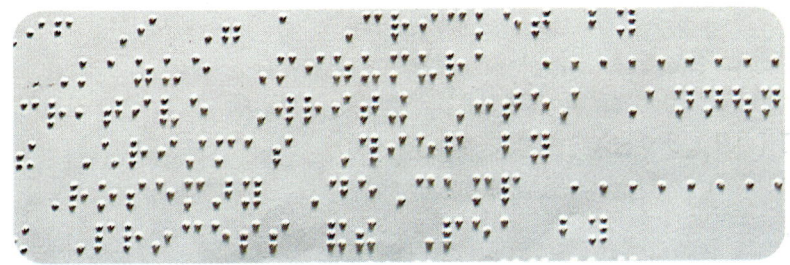

Figure 4–6. A sample of Braille writing

is written in Braille. **Braille** is a way of writing that uses letters made of raised dots. Different patterns of dots stand for different letters. This method of writing was invented by a teacher of visually impaired children in France. His name was Louis Braille. Louis Braille was also visually impaired.

What is Braille?

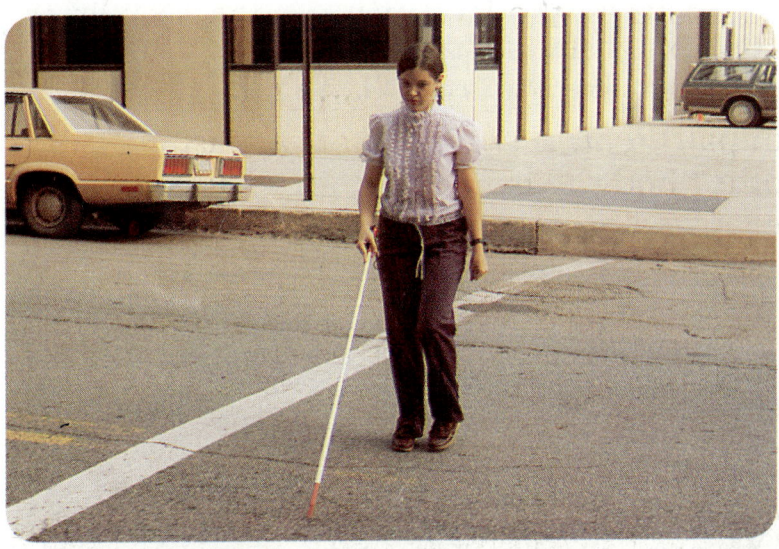

Figure 4–7. A cane is used by some visually impaired people to guide them as they walk.

Some visual impairments can be corrected with eyeglasses or contact lenses. The lenses in the eyeglasses or contact lenses combine with the lens in each eye to correctly focus images on each eye's retina. Remember that light is refracted when it passes through a lens. Lenses are used to magnify or reduce the appearance of objects. There are two basic kinds of lenses: concave and convex.

For what are concave lenses used?

A **concave lens** is thinner at its middle and thicker at the edge. Concave lenses are used mostly to reduce the appearance of an object. Concave lenses can cause light rays to spread apart. See Figure 4–8.

Figure 4–8. A concave lens

What is a convex lens?

A **convex lens** is thicker at its middle and thinner at the edge. Convex lenses are used mostly to magnify the appearance of objects. Convex lenses can cause light rays to come together. See Figure 4–9.

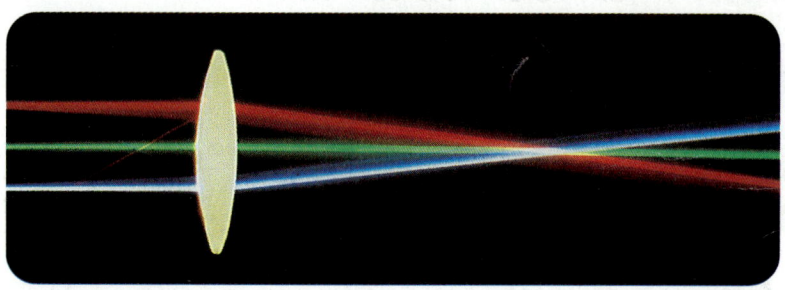

Figure 4–9. A convex lens

Nearsightedness

People whose eyes are nearsighted focus images of distant objects in front of the retina. That is why the image formed by faraway objects is not clear. This problem can be corrected by using eyeglasses or contact lenses made with concave lenses. The concave lenses cause light to spread apart. This allows the nearsighted eye to focus the image on the retina and not in front of it. See Figure 4–10a.

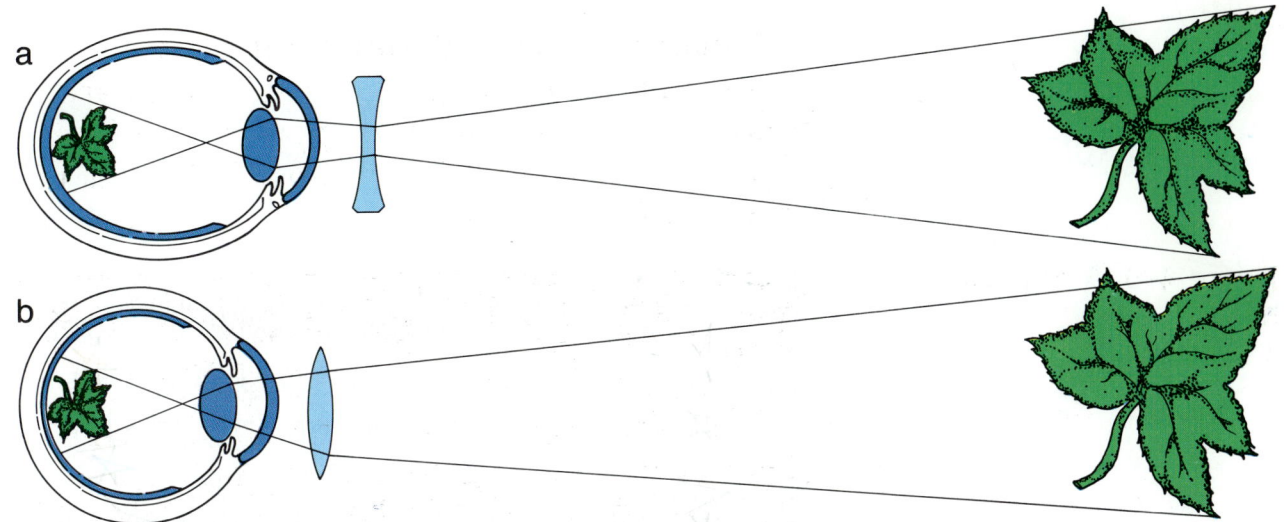

Figure 4-10. A nearsighted eye with glasses (a), a farsighted eye with glasses (b)

Farsightedness

People whose eyes are farsighted focus images of close objects behind the retina. Once again, unclear images are seen. People whose eyes are farsighted can wear eyeglasses or contact lenses made with convex lenses. Convex lenses cause light rays to come together. This allows the farsighted eye to focus the image on the retina and not in back of it. See Figure 4-10b.

An eye doctor who is either an **ophthalmologist** (ahf thuh MAHL uh just) or **optometrist** (ahp TAHM uh trust) examines a person's eyes to find out what type of lens may be needed. The doctor also decides how much the lenses should be curved. The doctor then writes a prescription for lenses. A prescription tells how the lenses should be made. A specially trained person called an **optician** (ahp TIHSH un) grinds and shapes the lenses according to the doctor's prescription. When a person uses the lenses, images appear sharper and clearer.

How can convex lenses help farsighted people?

Activity 4-2 Making a Water Drop Lens

QUESTION How can you make a simple magnifying lens?

Materials

glass microscope slides   water
dropper   small objects
grease pencil   pencil and paper

What to do

1. Make a small circle on the glass slide with the grease pencil. **CAUTION:** *Handle the slide very carefully.*
2. Put a drop of water in the circle as shown.
3. Carefully pick up the glass and water drop. Look through the drop at some small objects. Use the chart to record your observations.
4. Add another drop of water to change the shape of your lens. Look at the small objects again. Use the chart to record your observations.
5. Clean your slide and repeat steps 1 to 4. Use circles of different sizes.

WATER DROP LENS	
Shape of Lens	Observations

What did you learn?

1. What is the shape of the lens you made?
2. How did the objects appear under your lens?

Using what you learned

1. Which lens magnified the most?
2. Through which lens could you see most clearly?

Eye Infections

The tissue that lines the eyelid and covers the eye can become infected. The infection may cause the eyes to become bloodshot and teary. You may have heard of this infection. It is often called "pinkeye." Pinkeye can be passed easily from person to person.

Some people have the habit of rubbing their eyes with their hands. Many times their hands may not be clean. An infection can start in one of the glands near the eyelid. This infection of the glands is called a "sty." How might you care for your eyes so that eye infections do not become a problem?

Care of the Eyes

It is very important to take good care of your eyes. You should have your vision checked regularly. If you must squint to see clearly, you should have a doctor examine your eyes. A doctor should also check the eyes of people who get headaches when they read.

It is also important to protect your eyes in other ways. Always wear safety goggles if you are working with material that could get into your eyes. Figure 4–11 shows a person wearing safety goggles. For what other activities do you think safety goggles should be worn?

Why is it important to wear safety goggles?

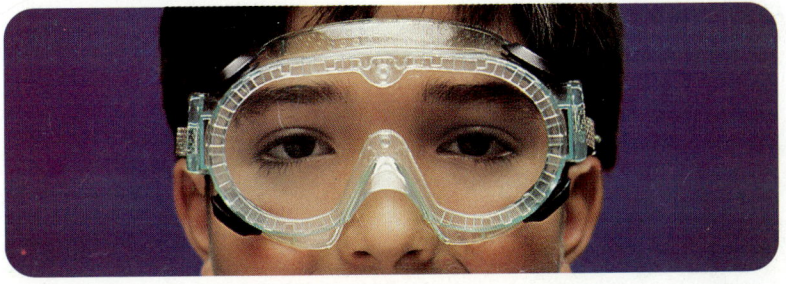

Figure 4–11. Safety goggles protect your eyes.

You can also protect your eyes by being careful with light. You should never look directly at very bright lights. Bright lights can permanently damage the eyes. You can protect your eyes by wearing sunglasses or a hat with a sun visor. Never look directly at a bright light source, such as the sun. Table 4-1 shows some simple rules for eye care.

Table 4-1 Eye Care

1. Have your eyes checked regularly by an eye doctor.
2. Report any eye or vision problems to a responsible adult.
3. Prevent eye infections with good personal hygiene habits.
4. Wear safety goggles to protect your eyes.
5. Never look directly at bright lights, such as the sun.

Lesson Summary

- Many people have problems with their eyesight.
- Some visual impairments can be corrected by using concave or convex lenses.
- Proper eye care is very important.

Lesson Review

Review the lesson to answer these questions.

1. How can nearsightedness and farsightedness be corrected?
2. Describe a concave lens and a convex lens.
3. Why are regular vision checks important?

Language Arts Skills

Understanding an Outline

Everything you read is made of parts. Words make up sentences. Sentences make up paragraphs. Each paragraph is more than just a group of words or a group of sentences. Paragraphs are also groups of ideas. Together the words, sentences, paragraphs, and ideas try to explain a main point. The main point is called the main idea.

An outline is a way of putting ideas into a form that makes them easy to understand. The outline at the bottom of this page lists the most important ideas about the sense of sight. It also lists some details that help readers understand the main ideas. This list of ideas is numbered. Different numbers and letters help to show how the ideas go together. Two main ideas make up the two main parts of this outline.

- What are the two main ideas?
- How are these main ideas numbered?

Details are used to explain each main idea. In this outline, there are two main ideas. There are at least two details that explain each main idea. Outlines should have two or more main ideas. There should be two or more details to explain each main idea.

- How many details explain the first main idea? The second main idea?
- How are they numbered?

```
                The Sense of Sight
     I. How We See
        A. See an object by the light it reflects to our eyes
        B. Main parts of the eye
           1. iris
           2. pupil
           3. lens
           4. retina
           5. optic nerve
    II. Problems and Proper Care
        A. Different problems with eyesight
        B. Can correct problems with lenses
           1. concave lenses
           2. convex lenses
        C. Importance of proper eye care
```

Chapter 4 Review

Summary

1. We see an opaque object because of the light it reflects to our eyes.   4:1
2. The iris controls the size of the pupil.   4:1
3. The lens refracts the light that comes into the eye.   4:1
4. The image of what we see is formed on the retina.   4:1
5. The optic nerve is a path between eye and brain.   4:1
6. Many people have problems with their eyesight.   4:2
7. Some visual problems can be corrected by using concave or convex lenses.   4:2
8. Proper eye care is very important.   4:2

Science Words

pupil   image   Braille   ophthalmologist
iris   retina   concave lens   optometrist
lens   optic nerve   convex lens   optician

Understanding Science Words

Complete each of the following sentences with a word or words from the Science Words that will make the sentence correct.

1. The part of the eye where an image is formed is the _____.
2. Lenses that are thicker in the middle are called _____.
3. Lenses that are thinner in the middle are called _____.
4. A way of writing that uses letters made of raised dots is _____.
5. The path between the eye and the brain is the _____.
6. A specially trained person who grinds and shapes lenses according to a prescription is an _____.
7. In the eye, light comes together to form a picture or an _____.

8. Light that comes into the eye is refracted by the _____.
9. The clear opening in the center of the eye is the _____.
10. The colored part of each eye is called the _____.
11. A person's eyes may be examined by a doctor who is either an _____ or an _____.

Questions

A. Recalling Facts

Choose the word or phrase that correctly completes each of the following sentences.
1. What type of lens makes objects appear larger?
   (a) convex   (b) concave   (c) flat   (d) colored
2. Light enters the eye through the
   (a) iris.   (b) pupil.   (c) retina.   (d) optic nerve.
3. What part of the eye controls how much light can enter?
   (a) optic nerve   (b) lens   (c) retina   (d) iris
4. In bright light, the iris makes the pupil
   (a) become smaller.   (c) stay the same.
   (b) close completely.   (d) become larger.

B. Understanding Concepts

Answer each of the following questions using complete sentences.
1. Why is the brain an important part of our ability to see?
2. What are some common eye problems?
3. Name and describe two common eye infections.

C. Applying Concepts

Think about what you have learned in this chapter. Answer each of the following questions using complete sentences.
1. Explain how concave and convex lenses are used to correct some vision problems.
2. Why is eye care important?

UNIT 2 REVIEW

CHECKING YOURSELF

Answer these questions on a sheet of paper.
1. What is light?
2. What is the difference between sources of naturally and artificially produced light?
3. What happens to light reflected from a smooth surface? A rough surface?
4. When is light refracted?
5. Give one example of each: transparent, translucent, and opaque matter.
6. What is the visible spectrum?
7. Give two examples of how color is used in everyday living.
8. What is the difference between nearsightedness and farsightedness?
9. What are two rules for proper eye care?
10. What kind of lens is used to correct nearsightedness? Farsightedness?
11. How does a prism separate white light?
12. Give two examples of naturally produced and artificially produced light.

RECALLING ACTIVITIES

Think about the activities you did in this unit. Answer the questions about these activities.
1. How can you bend light? 3–1
2. How can the color of an object appear to be changed? 3–2
3. How does light affect the iris? 4–1
4. How can you make a simple magnifying lens? 4–2

IDEAS TO EXPLORE

1. Gather pictures to make a story of light sources under the words: Naturally Produced   Artificially Produced
2. Sometimes words can be written so they look like their meaning. Try this idea with the following words: Reflect, Refract, Rainbow.
3. Find out how a camera works. Write a report comparing a camera to the eye.

PROBLEM SOLVING

Why are two eyes better than one? Find out about depth perception with this activity. Balance a small ball on top of a plastic bottle set on a table 15 centimeters from its edge. Walk 3 meters away. Cover one eye. Walk toward the bottle and try to flick the ball away. What happened? Try this again with the other eye and then again with both eyes. Let some of your classmates try this and record the results. Use the information to prepare a report about depth perception. Ask an ophthalmologist for more information. What kinds of work would be difficult with only one eye? What is meant by a dominant eye? Can practice improve your ability to perceive depth in the activity? Your report should answer each of these questions.

BOOKS TO READ

Exploring with Lasers by Brent Filson, Julian Messner: New York, © 1984.
   Explore the exciting world of lasers.

The Invisible World of the Infrared by Jack B. White, Dodd, Mead & Co.: New York, © 1984.
   Learn about the fantastic world of infrared rays.

Sun and Light by Neil Ardley, Franklin Watts: Danbury, CT, © 1983.
   Find out how light behaves and how we see things.

UNIT 3
Our Solar System

Alfonso X of Castile was a king of Spain who lived in the thirteenth century. He is remembered most for his respect for learning. King Alfonso encouraged people to study, not only the world around them, but also the members of our solar system. Imagine how excited and interested King Alfonso would be if he were able to study the pictures sent back to Earth by deep space probes such as *Voyager 2*.

Alfonso X—King of Spain

Voyager 2 flies by Neptune—1989

Chapter 5
Our Star

A star is the center of our solar system. That star is our sun. The sun is very important to us. How does life on Earth depend on the sun? How do scientists study the sun? What facts do you know about the sun?

The sun—our star

Comparing Stars   5:1

LESSON GOALS

In this lesson you will learn
- stars can be compared by size and color.
- energy is produced in the sun's core.
- sunspots and solar flares affect Earth.

Look at the sky on a clear night. You can see many twinkling lights. You know some of these lights come from objects in space called stars. Stars seem tiny because they are so far away. The sun looks big because it is so close. Astronomers say that our sun is just average in size. Some stars are much larger. Many other stars are smaller than our sun.

There are stars that appear to be very bright. Others look very dim. There are two reasons for these differences in appearance. The first reason is that stars give off different amounts of energy. The more energy given off, the brighter the star. The second reason is that stars are different distances from Earth. Stars closer to Earth appear brighter than those farther away even if the farther star gives off more energy.

Stars are even different colors. With a telescope you can see stars that have slight shades of red, orange, blue, white, and yellow. The sun is a yellow star. Its surface temperature is about 6,000°C. The sun is many times hotter in its center. White and blue stars are both hotter than the sun. Orange and red stars are cooler.

Figure 5-1. Observing stars on a clear night

What different colors are stars?

What stars are hotter than our sun?

79

Energy Maker

The sun, like other stars, is a sphere of glowing gases. A **sphere** (SFIHR) is an object shaped like a ball. The sun is composed mostly of hydrogen. In the core, or center of the sun, hydrogen atoms join together, or fuse, into atoms of helium. This joining together of hydrogen atoms to form helium is called **fusion** (FYEW zhun). The process of fusion releases energy in the sun's core. Energy produced in the core slowly works its way out through the sun. Then the energy is radiated out into space through the sun's surface.

What are the two main gases that make up the sun?

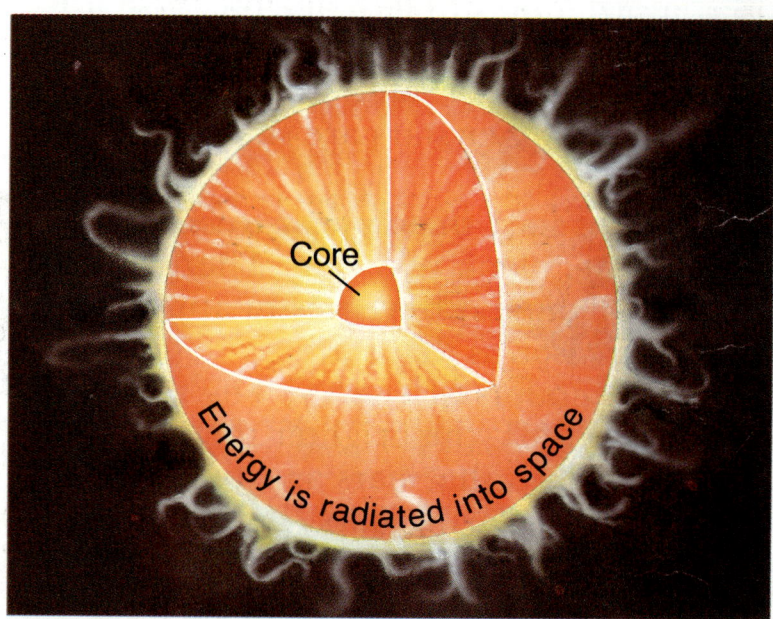

Figure 5-2. Energy from the sun's core is radiated into space.

Astronomers think our sun has produced energy for about 5 billion years. They say it will continue to do so for another 5 billion years. What might happen then is a topic of study for astronomers. Astronomers think the sun will swell in size. It may become so large it will absorb Mercury and Venus. Earth would become extremely hot. Life on Earth could not continue.

How long do scientists think the sun will produce energy?

Solar Activity

Astronomers know that our sun is active. Some of the sun's activities affect Earth. Studying the sun gives scientists an understanding of how its activities affected Earth in the past. Astronomers may be able to predict how activities on the sun might affect Earth in the future. Studying the sun helps them learn about other stars.

Sunspots are dark spots that appear on the surface of the sun. The surface temperature of the sun is about 6,000°C. The temperature of a sunspot is about 5,000°C. Because they are cooler, sunspots appear very dark or black against the surface of the sun. Sunspots seem to move across the sun's surface because the sun rotates.

What are sunspots?

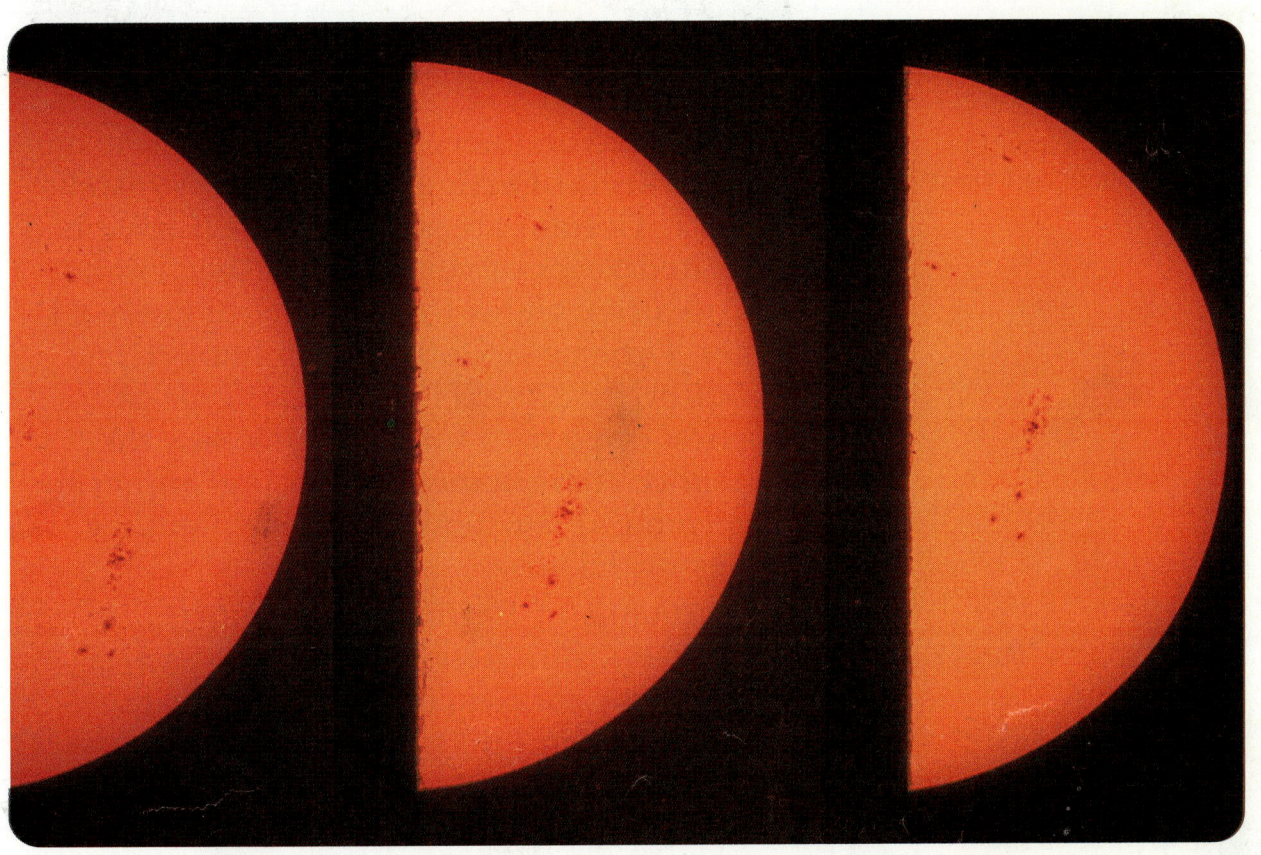

Figure 5-3. Sunspots moving across the sun's surface

81

How long is a sunspot cycle?

Pictures of sunspots are taken through telescopes. Information from the pictures is added to sunspot records. Sunspot records have been kept for over 300 years. Much can be learned about the sun from these records. In some years there were many sunspots. In other years there were very few. The numbers form a pattern. The pattern shows a cycle. The cycle is about 11 years long. Study the graph in Figure 5-4. What years since 1860 had more than 120 sunspots? How many sunspots were observed in each of these years?

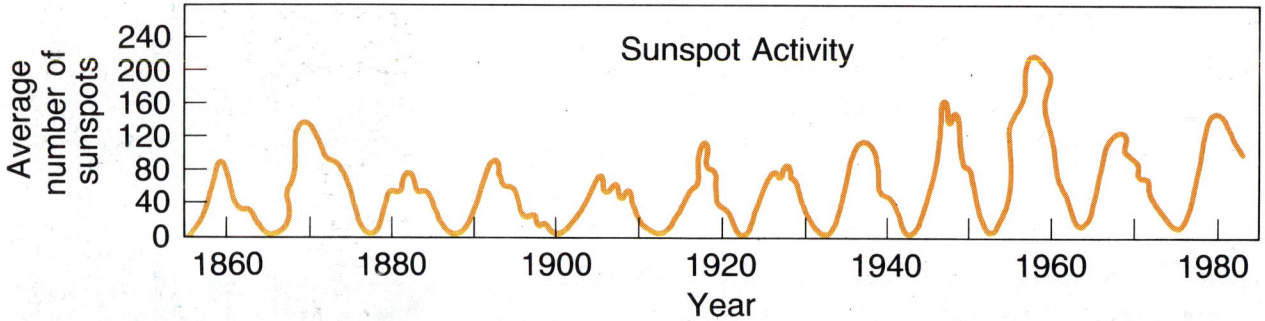

Figure 5-4. Sunspot activity observed since 1860

Some astronomers think that certain conditions on Earth are related to sunspot activity. Certain areas of the world have had repeated years of very dry weather. Some dry weather seems to occur about every 11 years. Other years of dry weather occur about every 22 years. These periods of dryness appear to follow a cycle like the sunspots. Astronomers are doing studies to determine if sunspots affect dry weather cycles on Earth.

What are solar flares?

Fountains of flowing gases sometimes shoot out from the sun. **Solar flares** are storms that spray mainly hydrogen and helium far out into space. Parts of this solar spray reach Earth and collect near the north and south poles of Earth.

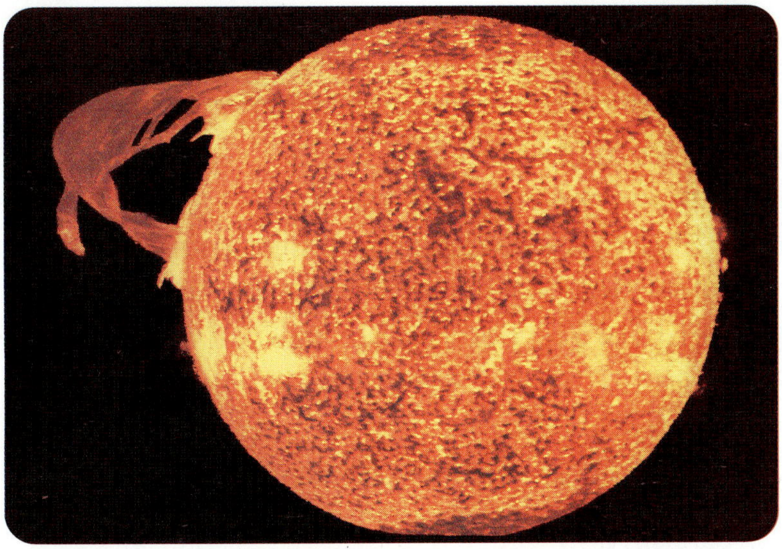

Figure 5-5. Solar flares

Solar flares cause several changes on Earth. They often cause static in long distance radio broadcasts. Solar flares may also make the night sky glow with brightly colored lights. These brightly colored lights seen in the night sky are called **auroras** (uh ROR uhz). Auroras are seen mostly near Earth's north and south poles.

Figure 5-6. Brightly colored lights called auroras

Lesson Summary

- Stars can be compared by size and color. Our sun is a yellow star.
- Energy is produced by fusion in the sun's core.
- Solar activity, such as sunspots and solar flares, affects weather and radio broadcasts on Earth.

Lesson Review

Review the lesson to answer these questions.

1. How is energy produced in the sun's core?
2. How do solar flares affect Earth?
3. How is star brightness related to energy?

5:2 Solar Eclipse

LESSON GOALS

In this lesson you will learn
- a solar eclipse happens when the moon comes directly between Earth and the sun.
- scientists are better able to study the sun's corona during a solar eclipse.

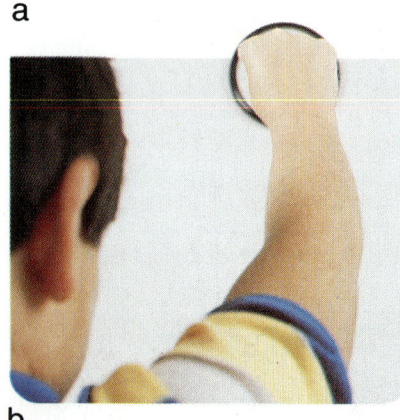

Figure 5-7. The clock is larger (a) the fist appears larger (b)

Figure 5-8. A solar eclipse

Find a large clock or picture on the wall. Which is larger, your fist or the object on the wall? Close one of your eyes. Move your fist directly between your open eye and the object. What happened? Something like this happens to the moon, Earth, and sun during an eclipse (ih KLIHPS) of the sun.

The moon is like your fist. It is much smaller than the sun. However, the moon appears larger because it is closer to Earth. During a solar eclipse, the moon moves directly between Earth and the sun. The moon then blocks out, or eclipses, the light from the sun. A **solar eclipse** is an event during which the moon comes directly between Earth and the sun. Look at Figure 5-8. In what positions are Earth, moon, and the sun during a solar eclipse?

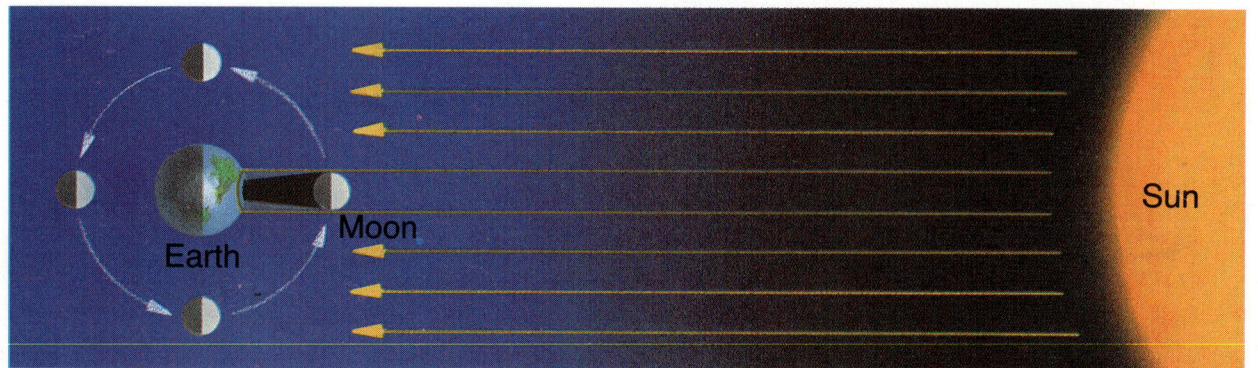

Activity 5-1 Making a Model of an Eclipse

QUESTION What causes an eclipse?

Materials
flashlight
ball
globe
pencil and paper

What to do
1. In a darkened room, arrange the flashlight, ball, and globe as shown.
2. Shine the flashlight on the globe. Let the flashlight represent the sun.
3. Move the ball between the light and the globe.
4. Record your observations.

What did you learn?
1. What do the ball and the globe represent?
2. Find the center of the shadow on the globe. What would you see if you were standing there?
3. What does this model represent?

Using what you learned
1. How would you arrange the globe, light, and ball to make an eclipse of the moon? Try this lunar eclipse and observe your results.
2. Draw a picture showing:
   a. a solar eclipse.
   b. a lunar eclipse.

Figure 5-9. Two views of the solar corona.

Astronomers study solar eclipses. They take many pictures that show the unlighted side of the moon. These photos also show the atmosphere around the sun. **Atmosphere** (AT muh sfihr) is the gases that surround a space object.

The **corona** (kuh ROH nuh) is the very outermost part of the sun's atmosphere. The solar corona is only about as bright as the full moon. So, the corona can only be seen during a solar eclipse. Other times the sun is too bright, and the corona is hidden. The corona is very active. Its shape changes all the time. During a solar flare, solar spray is shot far out into space from the corona.

Table 5-1 lists information about solar eclipses. When will the next solar eclipse take place? From where will you be able to view the next eclipse?

Table 5-1
Total Solar Eclipses
1990 July 22   Finland, Arctic

1991 July 11
    Hawaii, Brazil,
    Central America

1992 June 30   South Atlantic
1994 November 3   South America
1995 October 24   Southern Asia

Lesson Summary

- A solar eclipse is an event during which the moon comes directly between Earth and the sun.
- During a solar eclipse, scientists take pictures of the sun's corona. Scientists study the pictures to learn about the sun.

Lesson Review

Review the lesson to answer these questions.
1. What happens during a solar eclipse?
2. What is the corona?
3. How can the moon, which is smaller than the sun, block out the sun's light during a solar eclipse?

People and Science

Designing a Satellite

Edward is an engineer who works in a laboratory where satellites are designed. Satellites are spacecraft that are used for research, observation, or for sending messages. Edward designs satellite instruments that will send accurate information back to Earth.

The satellite he is designing now will orbit Earth. It will follow a path over the north and south poles. The satellite will send back information about large areas of Earth's oceans. Measurements will be taken of surface water temperature, the direction and speed of the wind, wave height, tides, and ocean currents. The satellite will also carry a camera. The camera will take many small pictures. These pictures will be recorded on tape. On Earth they will be put together into one large picture and studied by scientists.

Who will use the information gathered by the instruments? Ship navigators will be able to travel by the safest routes and save time and fuel. Because they will know ocean currents and temperatures, fishermen will be able to find areas where many fish may be caught. Meteorologists will be able to gather data for long-range weather forecasts. People who work on offshore oil-drilling platforms will have more advanced notice of hurricanes.

Engineers like Edward do important work when they design accurate instruments for satellites. On Earth, the information from these satellites is used to make our lives and work safer.

Chapter 5 Review

Summary

1. Stars can be compared by size and color. 5:1
2. Our sun is a yellow star. 5:1
3. Energy is produced by fusion of hydrogen in the sun's core. 5:1
4. Sunspots and solar flares are two kinds of solar activity. 5:1
5. Astronomers study how solar activity affects Earth. 5:1
6. A solar eclipse is an event during which the moon comes directly between Earth and the sun. 5:2
7. The sun's outer atmosphere, or corona, can be observed only during a solar eclipse. 5:2

Science Words

sphere   **sunspots**   **auroras**   **atmosphere**
fusion   **solar flares**   **solar eclipse**   **corona**

Understanding Science Words

Complete each of the following sentences with a word or words from the Science Words that will make the sentence correct.

1. An event during which the moon moves directly between Earth and the sun and blocks out the sun's light is called a _____.
2. Solar activities that spray atoms of hydrogen and helium into space are _____.
3. The very outermost part of the sun's atmosphere is the _____.
4. Dark spots that appear on the surface of the sun are called _____.
5. Gases that surround a space object make up the object's _____.
6. The joining together of hydrogen atoms to form helium in the sun's core is a process called _____.

7. An object shaped like a ball is a _____.
8. The brightly colored lights most often seen in the night sky and caused by solar flares are called _____.

Questions

A. Recalling Facts

Choose the word or phrase that best completes each of the following sentences.
1. Stars can be compared by size and
    (a) shape.   (c) distance from Earth.
    (b) color.   (d) distance from each other.
2. A solar eclipse occurs when the moon comes directly between
    (a) Earth and sun.   (c) the sun's corona and core.
    (b) Earth and Mars. (d) moon and Earth.
3. Energy is produced in the sun's core by a process called
    (a) fission.   (b) sphere.   (c) fusion.   (d) melting.
4. Solar activities that may affect Earth's weather are
    (a) auroras.   (b) eclipses.   (c) spheres.   (d) sunspots.
5. The sun is hottest at its
    (a) corona.   (b) center.   (c) surface.   (d) sunspots.

B. Understanding Concepts

Answer each of the following questions using complete sentences.
1. How might sunspots affect Earth?
2. How do solar flares affect Earth?
3. What are some properties of the sun?
4. How do white and blue stars compare with the sun?

C. Applying Concepts

Think about what you have learned in this chapter. Answer each of the following questions using complete sentences.
1. Why is the sun important to us?
2. Why can the sun be called an energy maker?
3. Why do astronomers study solar activity?

Chapter 6
Members of Our Solar System

Our solar system is just one small part of a large star group called a galaxy. The entire universe is filled with many galaxies. The picture below shows a neighboring galaxy. It is composed of many stars and many solar systems.

A neighboring galaxy

Planets and Orbits 6:1

LESSON GOALS

In this lesson you will learn
- the solar system is our sun and all the space objects traveling around it.
- the force of gravity keeps planets in orbit around the sun.

The sun is the center of our solar system. **Solar system** is the sun and all the space objects traveling around it. Without a telescope, planets and stars look alike. Ancient astronomers learned to tell them apart by their motions. They observed that some space objects appeared to keep the same positions in the sky night after night. Other objects slowly but visibly changed their positions. These objects were the planets traveling around the sun.

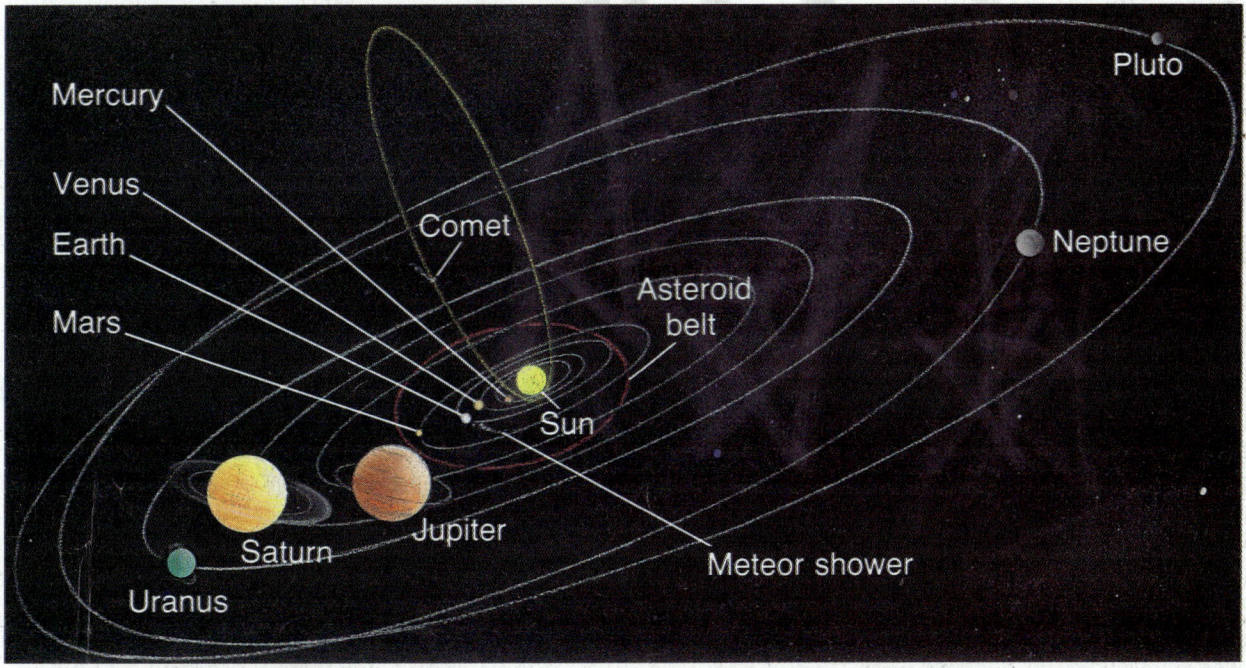

Figure 6-1. Our solar system

What is a planet?

A **planet** is a large space object that moves around the sun. Ancient people called these moving objects planets. The word meant wanderer. This word "planet" is still used today.

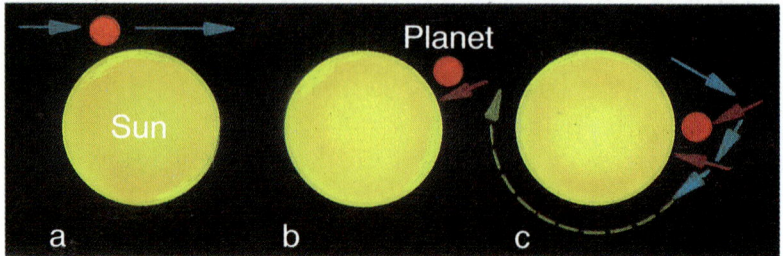

Figure 6–2. A planet moving in a straight line (a), is affected by the pull of gravity (b), and remains in orbit around the sun (c).

Planets travel around the sun in paths called orbits. An **orbit** is the path an object follows when it revolves around a larger object. A planet is kept in its orbit by the force of gravity. If there were no force of gravity, a planet would move in a straight line in space. The pull of the sun's gravity affects the direction of the motion of a planet. See Figure 6–2. Because of the sun's pulling force, a planet orbits the sun in an almost football-shaped pathway. This football-shaped pathway is called an **ellipse** (ee LIHPS). The sun is NOT located at the center of a planet's orbit. Figure 6–3 shows that the sun is slightly off-center.

What keeps planets in orbit around the sun?

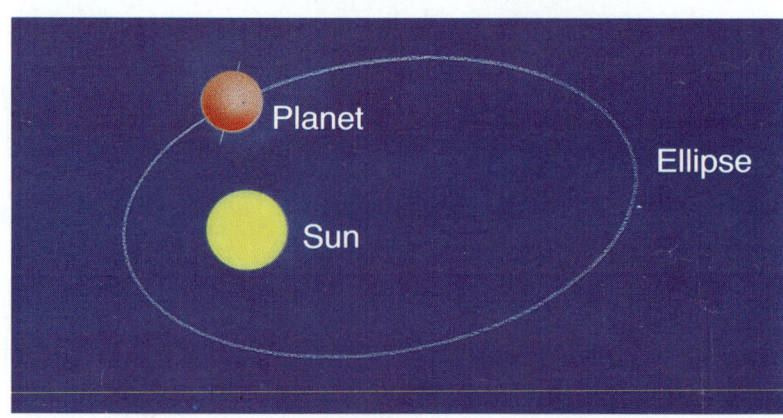

Figure 6–3. A planet orbits the sun in a path called an ellipse.

92

The size and shape of each planet's ellipse is different. Figure 6-4 shows examples of the ellipses formed by the orbits of two planets: Mercury and Jupiter. Mercury is closer to the sun than Jupiter. The ellipse formed by Mercury's orbit is smaller than Jupiter's ellipse. The speed of a planet also changes as it goes around the sun. A planet speeds up when it is closer to the sun. It slows down when it is farther away. A planet whose ellipse is more round travels at almost the same speed throughout its orbit. Which planet shown in Figure 6-4 travels at about the same speed throughout its orbit?

When in its orbit does a planet travel fastest?

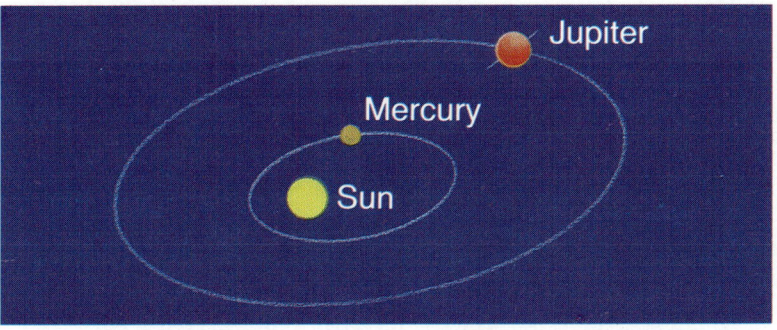

Figure 6-4. The orbits of Mercury and Jupiter

Lesson Summary

- The solar system is our sun and all the space objects traveling around it.
- The force of gravity keeps planets in orbit around the sun. Planets orbit the sun in football-shaped pathways called ellipses.

Lesson Review

Review the lesson to answer these questions.
1. What does the word *planet* mean?
2. What would happen to a planet if there were no force of gravity?
3. What is an orbit?

93

Activity 6-1 Sun, Planets, and Gravity

QUESTION How can you observe the effects of gravity?

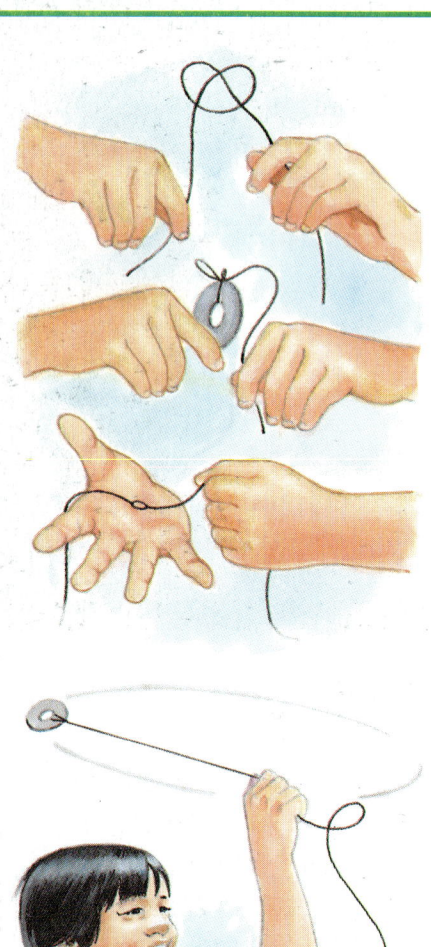

Materials
string
1 metal washer
pencil and paper

What to do

1. Tie a knot in the middle of the piece of string.
2. Tie the washer to the end of the string. **CAUTION:** *Do this activity in an open area.*
3. Hold the free end of the string in one hand. Center the knot in the other hand.
4. Swing the tied washer in a circle. Increase the speed until the string is taut.

What did you learn?
1. What object used in the activity represented a planet?
2. What object used in the activity represented the sun?

Using what you learned
1. The inward force acting on the washer through the string represents what force?
2. In what direction is the force of the sun's gravity on the planet?

Science and Technology

Giotto Meets Comet Halley

Comet Halley visited our part of the solar system in 1986. It will not return until 2061. Scientists wanted to get a close look at the comet while it was near. Spacecraft were sent into space to observe the comet.

The closest view of Comet Halley was recorded by the European spacecraft, *Giotto*. It came within 500 kilometers of the head of the comet. *Giotto* sent thousands of photographs back to Earth.

The photographs were used by scientists to get important information about the shape and size of the head of the comet. The head of Comet Halley looked like a "lumpy, dirty snowball" anywhere from five to eight kilometers in diameter.

Along with photographs, *Giotto* sent back information about the comet's make-up. Instruments on the *Giotto* discovered oxygen, carbon, and other materials. The mission was considered a great success. It gave scientists a lot of new information about comets.

While spacecraft were meeting Comet Halley in space, scientists from many countries were meeting on Earth. One of the best results of the space probe program was the cooperation and sharing among people from around the world.

6:2 The Inner Planets

LESSON GOALS

In this lesson you will learn
- Mercury, Venus, Earth, and Mars are called the inner planets.
- surface features, temperatures, and orbits differ from planet to planet.

Suppose your class could blast off right now and take a tour of the solar system. Your tour would begin with the inner planets: Mercury, Venus, Earth, and Mars. These planets can be described as small, rocky bodies that get energy from the sun. What would you like to learn about each of the planets you visit?

Mercury

You would probably want to visit Mercury for a very short time because of the extreme temperature differences. There is a total difference of over 400°C between day and night temperatures. During the day, the temperature on Mercury can become as hot as an oven broiler!

Figure 6-5. The surface of Mercury

Mercury is hard to study from Earth because it is so close to the sun. Spacecraft *Mariner* photos taken in 1974 show that Mercury looks a lot like our moon. It is covered with craters. Also, Mercury has a unique pattern of ridges and cracks. Most astronomers believe that the pattern is due to the shrinkage of Mercury shortly after it formed.

Mercury has a high surface temperature because it is so close to the sun. Mercury also has a low surface gravity. For these reasons, Mercury has a very thin atmosphere. Sodium and helium have been found in Mercury's atmosphere.

Figure 6-6. *Mariner* spacecraft

Venus

Earth and Venus are nearly the same size and mass. Venus is often called Earth's twin. At one time, people imagined Venus to have water and plant life. Its surface is hidden by thick clouds and has never been seen through telescopes.

Both radar and space probes have given us new information. We now know that Venus has a very unpleasant environment. The clouds are swirling mists of acid droplets. The atmosphere is very thick and hot. Temperatures on the surface of Venus reach over 400°C. The surface appears to be covered with rolling hills, mountains, valleys, and several large volcanoes.

Venus is one of the brightest objects in the night sky. As with Mercury, we on Earth must look near the sun to see Venus. From Earth, part of the time Venus appears low in the western sky in early evening. The rest of the time it is low in the eastern sky just before sunrise.

Why has no one ever seen the surface of Venus through a telescope?

Figure 6-7. Venus

Where in the sky must you look to see Venus?

Earth

From space, what could you see on Earth?

On your tour, you could get a good look at Earth from space. You could see some of the continents, feathery clouds, and lots of water. Then you could see why Earth is called the "watery" planet.

What important gas is found in Earth's atmosphere?

Earth is the only planet in our solar system known to have life. Water is found in the atmosphere and on the surface. The atmosphere contains an important gas called oxygen. Why are water and oxygen important?

Earth's surface has mountains, canyons, deserts, and even a few craters. Mountains form and are worn away. Volcanoes erupt. Lakes form and then dry up. Earth is always changing.

Earth has one natural satellite, the moon. It has an orbit around Earth. The moon's weak gravity cannot hold an atmosphere. That is why you would not see clouds or oceans on its surface.

Figure 6-8. Earth as seen from the moon

Mars

Mars is often called the "red" planet because of the reddish colored soil on its surface. Scientists have sent spacecraft to Mars. Recent pictures of the surface show rocks and soil. Mars also has mountains, valleys, craters, and ancient volcanoes.

Mars has a thin atmosphere that is mainly carbon dioxide. There is also a small amount of water vapor. Thin ice crystal clouds form on Mars in the afternoon. There is little or no oxygen in the atmosphere of Mars. Mars sometimes has strong winds. The winds blow soil into the atmosphere causing large dust storms. These large dust storms cause changes in seasons on Mars.

Mars is visible from Earth without a telescope. Astronomers have determined the length of its day to be 24 hours 37 minutes Earth time. Its year is 687 Earth days.

Mars has two satellites. One of these moons, Deimos, orbits Mars once every 30 Earth hours. The other moon, Phobos, makes one orbit in less than 8 Earth hours. As an observer on Mars, how many times would you see Phobos rise and set in one day?

Figure 6-9. The surface of Mars

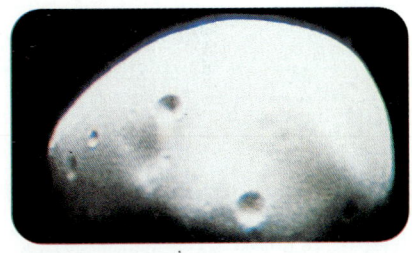

Figure 6-10. Deimos.

What gas makes up most of the atmosphere of Mars?

How many moons does Mars have?

Lesson Summary

- Mercury, Venus, Earth, and Mars are called the inner planets.
- The inner planets can be compared and contrasted using surface features, temperatures, and lengths of orbits.

Lesson Review

Review the lesson to answer these questions.

1. Which planet takes the least time to orbit the sun?
2. Which planet has clouds of swirling acid droplets?
3. Why is Mars called the "red" planet?

99

6:3 The Outer Planets

LESSON GOALS
In this lesson you will learn
- Jupiter, Saturn, Uranus, Neptune, and Pluto are the outer planets.
- Jupiter, Saturn, Uranus, and Neptune are sometimes called the gas giants.
- space probes have taken pictures of several outer planets.

Which planets are known as the gas giants?

Jupiter's diameter is how much larger than Earth's?

Figure 6-11. Jupiter's moon, Io

The second part of your tour will take you to the outer planets. Four of them, Jupiter, Saturn, Uranus, and Neptune are called the gas giants. They are more like stars than planets. The gas giants have little, if any, solid surface. These planets are mostly gas. The outermost planet, Pluto, is more like the inner planets.

Jupiter

As you approach Jupiter, two words will come to mind: enormous and colorful. Jupiter's diameter is 11 times larger than Earth's, and its mass is 300 times greater. Jupiter has a thin ring around it and at least 16 natural satellites. Four of the moons are very large and can be seen through binoculars. Two of these moons are about the size of Earth's moon. The other two are as large as Mercury.

Astronomers believe Jupiter is made mostly of the gases hydrogen and helium. Its upper atmosphere has brightly colored bands made of gases that mix and change.

Figure 6-12. Jupiter

Jupiter is famous for its Great Red Spot. The red spot is over three times the size of Earth! It changes shape and appearance. Scientists think the spot is a giant storm in Jupiter's atmosphere.

It takes Jupiter 12 Earth years to make one orbit around the sun. But a day on Jupiter lasts only about 10 Earth hours. How does that compare with the length of a day on Earth?

Saturn

If you and your classmates could really take of tour of the planets, you would not want to miss Saturn. Saturn is the second largest planet. Like Jupiter, it is made of hydrogen, helium, and a few other gases.

What is Jupiter's Great Red Spot?

How long is a day on Jupiter?

Of what is Saturn made?

101

How many rings does Saturn have?

Saturn is special because of its many rings. The rings have long been seen through Earth-based telescopes. Recently, close-up pictures of the rings were taken by *Voyager* spacecraft. *Voyager* sent signals back to Earth. The signals were put into a computer and changed to TV pictures. The pictures show more rings than you can count. Over 1,000 rings have been discovered around Saturn. However, only three or four rings are visible from most Earth-based telescopes. The rings are made of millions of small particles of ice and rock.

Figure 6-13. Saturn

From your spacecraft, you could observe that Saturn rotates once in just over 10 Earth hours. You would also discover that Saturn has many moons. So far scientists have discovered over 20. Because of its distance from the sun, a year on Saturn is about 29½ Earth years.

How many moons does Saturn have?

Uranus

In January of 1986, *Voyager 2* explored Uranus from space. *Voyager's* cameras took many pictures and sent them to Earth. The pictures were used by scientists to get a better look at Uranus's rings. Scientists also discovered many more moons orbiting the blue-green planet. Uranus appears to have at least 15 moons.

Uranus is also made of gases such as hydrogen, helium, methane, and cloud layers of ammonia ice. Very few markings appear on the planet. It looks like a large, smooth blue-green ball. One fact that makes Uranus interesting is the position in which it revolves around the sun. It revolves on its side. Because of this position, each pole of Uranus will point toward the sun for some time as it orbits the sun.

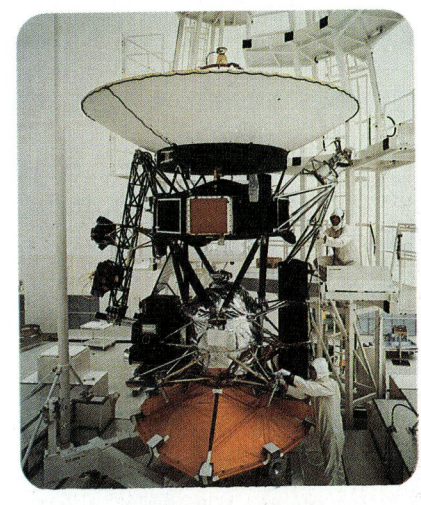

Figure 6–14. *Voyager 2*

How did scientists get a better look at Uranus?

Neptune

Neptune appears to be much like Uranus. This planet appears pale blue in color. It too is made of hydrogen, helium, and other gases. Neptune has broken rings called arcs. These arcs are made of particles separated by empty space. This makes the rings appear broken.

Neptune's orbit is very large. A Neptune year is equal to 165 years on Earth. In 1989, *Voyager 2* will explore Neptune from space. Much more will be learned from the pictures taken by *Voyager's* special cameras. Scientists are anxious to learn more about this outer planet.

When will *Voyager 2* observe Neptune from space?

Activity 6-2 Comparing Planets

QUESTION How can you compare sizes of planets?

Materials
construction paper
metric ruler
scissors
pencil and paper

What to do
1. Draw a circle on the construction paper to represent each planet. Check the chart to make sure each circle has the correct diameter.
2. Cut out and label each model planet.
3. Place the model planets in order by size.
4. Rearrange the model planets so they are in the correct position from the sun.

Object	Diameter
Mercury	.5 cm
Venus	1.2 cm
Earth	1.3 cm
Mars	.7 cm
Jupiter	14.6 cm
Saturn	12.2 cm
Uranus	5.2 cm
Neptune	5.0 cm
Pluto	.3 cm

What did you learn?
1. How did the order of the planets by size compare to their positions from the sun?
2. Which planet is about the same size as Earth?
3. About how many Earths does it take to stretch across Jupiter?

Using what you learned
1. Tell how the sizes of the model planets compare to the size of the model sun.
2. How is your model different from our solar system? How are the model and our solar system alike?

Pluto

Pluto is called the ninth planet. It, however, is not always the ninth planet from the sun. Sometimes, Pluto's orbit brings it closer to the sun than the planet Neptune. In 1979, Pluto orbited inside the orbit of Neptune. It will remain closer to the sun than Neptune until 1999. Then it will again become the farthest planet from the sun.

Because of its great distance from the sun, Pluto is a cold, dark planet. It appears Pluto is made of ice and gases. Pluto has one moon. Pluto takes 248 Earth years to complete one orbit.

Astronomers know very little else about Pluto. Some scientists have asked these questions: Are Pluto and its moon really twin planets? Was Pluto once a moon of Neptune? It will be a while before astronomers answer all of their questions about Pluto.

Figure 6-15. Pluto

When will Pluto again be the most distant planet?

What is it like on Pluto?

Lesson Summary

- The outer planets are Jupiter, Saturn, Uranus, Neptune, and Pluto.
- Jupiter, Saturn, Uranus, and Neptune are called the gas giants.
- Space probes have taken pictures of some of the outer planets.

Lesson Review

Review the lesson to answer these questions.
1. What are the outer planets?
2. What planet is known for its Great Red Spot?
3. Why is Pluto not always the ninth planet from the sun?

6:4 Other Members

What other members are found in the solar system?

LESSON GOALS

In this lesson you will learn
- asteroids orbit the sun between Mars and Jupiter.
- a comet is a space object made of ice particles and dust.
- a meteoroid is a space object made of metal or rock that orbits the sun.

Other members of our solar system are asteroids, comets, and meteoroids. Some can be seen from Earth. Some are too small to be seen from Earth. Others come near enough to be seen without a telescope.

Figure 6-16. The asteroid belt is located between the orbits of Mars and Jupiter.

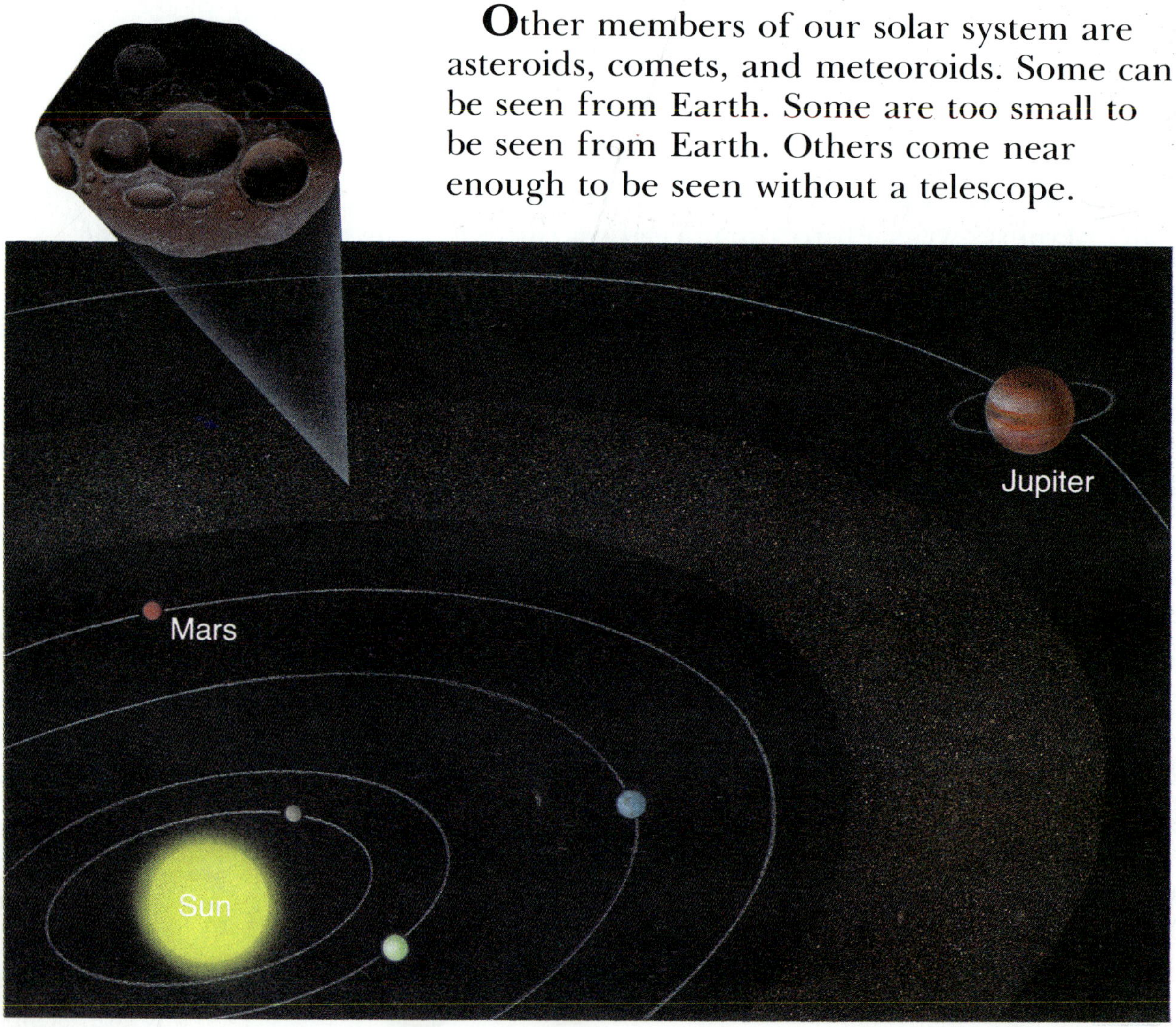

Somewhere between the orbits of Mars and Jupiter there are many thousands of space objects made of rock, metal, or minerals. An **asteroid** (AS tuh royd) is a space object that orbits the sun between Mars and Jupiter. Most asteroids orbit the sun in a wide band called the asteroid belt. Most asteroids take five Earth years to complete one orbit around the sun.

Asteroids come in all shapes and sizes. They range in size from less than 16 to more than 160 kilometers in diameter. Ceres (SIHR eez) is the largest known asteroid. It is about 770 kilometers in diameter. Another asteroid, Vesta, is half the size of Ceres. Both can be seen from Earth without a telescope.

Some astronomers think that the asteroids are leftover matter from the time the planets were being formed. Asteroids, then, may be pieces of the solar system that never formed a planet.

Comets

A long time ago people became frightened when they saw a comet. They thought a comet was a sign that an unpleasant event, such as an earthquake, would take place. Astronomers now know that such ideas are not correct.

A **comet** is a space object made of ice mixed with dust particles. Comets orbit the sun. Comets probably come from the far, outer edges of our solar system. Comets can be seen only when they are close enough to be heated by the sun. It is then that comets give off light.

Where is the asteroid belt found?

How large is Ceres?

How do scientists think asteroids were formed?

Figure 6-17. Throughout history, seeing a comet has been a special event.

A comet is like a dirty snowcone. A comet has three parts: a head, coma, and tail. The head is made of ice, gases, and particles of rock. The heads of most comets are only a few kilometers wide. As a comet nears the sun, gases escape from the head. A large, fuzzy, ball-shaped cloud is formed. This ball-shaped cloud is the coma. The tail is present only when the coma is heated by the sun. The tail is made of fine dust and gas. A comet's tail always points away from the sun. The tail can be millions of kilometers long.

Comets have very large orbits. It takes comets a very long time to go around the sun. During part of its orbit, a comet is very close to the sun. That is the only time we can see a comet. It then moves out into space far away from the sun. Some comets take many Earth years to complete one orbit. A person may see only two or three comets in a lifetime.

Figure 6-18. The three parts of a comet

What are comet tails made of?

When can comets be seen?

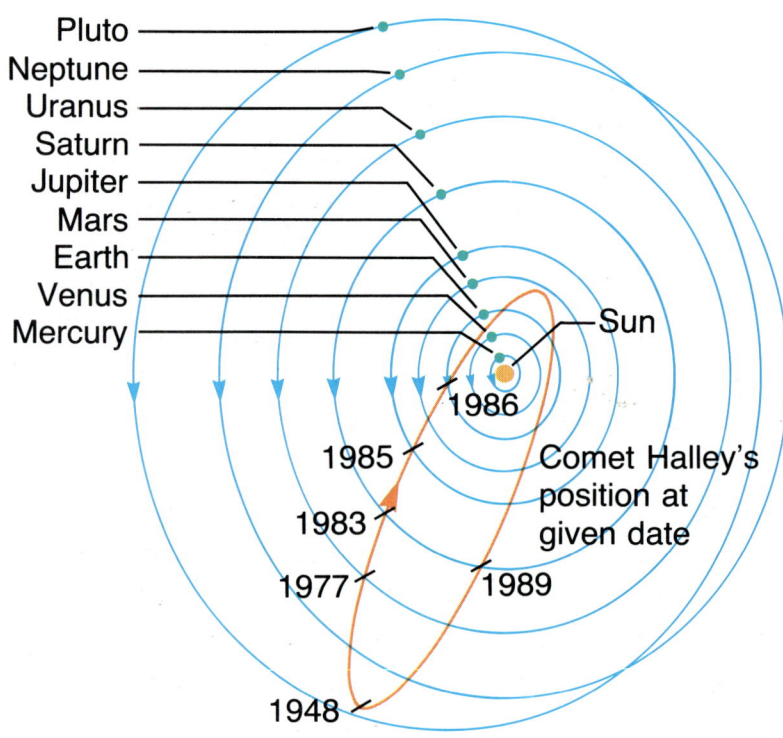

Figure 6-19. Comet Halley's orbit and position at a given date

The comet we know as Comet Halley was seen many times as far back as 240 B.C. An English astronomer, Edmond Halley, proved that all the sightings were really the same comet. Halley proved that the same comet appeared every 76 years. Scientists sent space probes to meet Comet Halley in 1985–1986. The European space probe, *Giotto*, came within 500 kilometers of the head. *Giotto* sent pictures of the comet back to Earth. The head of the comet appeared to be five to eight kilometers in diameter. It was black. *Giotto* was struck by particles of ice and dust as it moved through the coma of Comet Halley. When can we expect to see Comet Halley again?

Figure 6-20. *Giotto* space probe

How large is the head of Comet Halley?

Meteoroids

A **meteoroid** (MEET ee uh royd) is a piece of metal or rock that orbits the sun. There are many meteoroids in space. Many are too small to be seen from Earth. Meteoroids are scattered in different orbits in space. Sometimes their orbits bring them close to Earth. When they travel through the atmosphere we can see a trail of light.

If you can get far enough away from the glare of city lights, you can see about 20 to 30 meteors on a clear night. A **meteor** (MEET ee ur) is a stray particle from the asteroid belt that has entered Earth's atmosphere. Meteors are sometimes called falling stars, shooting stars, or fireballs.

Most meteors burn up in the atmosphere 50 to 100 kilometers above Earth's surface. Some reach Earth's surface as small particles of metal, rock, or dust. A few very large ones do strike Earth's surface.

Figure 6-21. A meteor or shooting star

What happens to most meteors?

Figure 6-22. Meteorite

Where is Barringer Crater located?

A meteor that strikes Earth's surface is a **meteorite** (MEET ee uh rite). The crater in Figure 6-23 was formed by a meteorite. The meteorite made a crater 1,200 meters in diameter and 180 meters deep. The crater is called Barringer Crater. It can be found in Arizona. Where else in the solar system can you see meteoroid craters?

Figure 6-23. Barringer Crater is 32 kilometers west of Winslow, Arizona.

Lesson Summary

- Somewhere between the orbits of Mars and Jupiter there are many thousands of space objects made of rock or metal. These objects are asteroids.
- Comets, space objects made of ice particles mixed with dust, come from the far, outer edges of our solar system.
- Meteoroids are space objects that orbit the sun.

Lesson Review

Review the lesson to answer these questions.
1. What is a meteoroid?
2. What are the three parts of a comet?
3. How might asteroids have formed?

Language Arts Skills

Understanding Graphs

A dictionary can help a reader understand new words. A picture can help a reader understand a new idea. Finding out how things are alike or different can help people understand new ideas, too. One kind of picture is a graph. Some graphs show how things are alike and different. Remember: in this graph the word *gravity* is being used to tell how each planet's gravity compares with Earth's gravity.

Look at the graphs at the bottom of this page.

- What does the title of the graph on the left tell a reader?

Look at the numbers at the left side of the graph. Put your finger on the number .5. Look at the names at the bottom of the graph. Slide your finger along the line beside .5 to the spot just above the name Venus. If Venus had a gravity of .5, a point would be drawn at this spot.

- What are the gravities of each of the inner planets?

This graph is a line graph. A line has been drawn to connect each point that was drawn on the graph. This line helps to show how the planet's gravities are alike and how they are different.

- Is the gravity of Mercury less than or greater than Earth's?
- What does the title of the graph on the right tell a reader?

This graph is called a bar graph. A bar is drawn for each planet. It shows what the gravity of each planet is. By seeing how the bars are alike and different, a reader can get an idea of how the gravities are alike and different.

- Which planet has the greatest gravity?
- Which outer planet has a gravity that is less than Earth's?

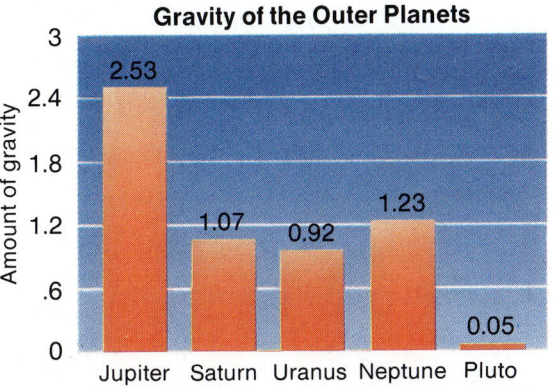

Chapter 6 Review

Summary

1. The solar system is the sun and all the space objects traveling around it. 6:1
2. The force of gravity keeps planets in orbit around the sun. 6:1
3. All the planets follow an orbit around the sun. 6:1
4. Mercury, Venus, Earth, and Mars are the inner planets. 6:2
5. Jupiter, Saturn, Uranus, Neptune, and Pluto are the outer planets. 6:3
6. There are nine known planets in our solar system. 6:3
7. Asteroids are space objects made of rock, metal, or minerals; most asteroids orbit the sun in a wide band called the asteroid belt. 6:4
8. A comet is a space object made of ice mixed with dust particles. 6:4
9. Meteoroids are pieces of metal or rock that are scattered in different orbits in space. 6:4

Science Words

solar system   orbit   asteroid   meteoroid   meteorite
planet   ellipse   comet   meteor

Understanding Science Words

Complete each of the following sentences with a word or words from the Science Words that will make the sentence correct.

1. The path Earth follows around the sun is its _____.
2. A football-shaped pathway is called an _____.
3. Ceres is the largest known _____.
4. A stray particle from an asteroid belt is called a _____.
5. The sun, nine planets, and other space objects make up the _____.
6. A space object made of ice and dust particles is a _____.

7. An ancient word meaning "wanderer" is _____.
8. A small piece of rock or metal orbiting the sun is called an _____.
9. A meteor that strikes Earth's surface is a _____.

Questions

A. Recalling Facts
Choose the word or phrase that correctly completes each of the following sentences.
1. The planet with the largest orbit is
   (a) Jupiter.   (b) Saturn.   (c) Mercury.   (d) Pluto.
2. The planet called Earth's twin is
   (a) Saturn.   (b) Mars.   (c) Mercury.   (d) Venus.
3. The asteroid belt is located between
   (a) Jupiter and Saturn.   (c) Earth and Mars.
   (b) Mars and Jupiter.   (d) Mercury and Venus.
4. The planets stay in orbit due to the force of
   (a) size.   (b) speed.   (c) atmosphere.   (d) gravity.

B. Understanding Concepts
Answer each of the following questions using complete sentences.
1. What are the names of the inner planets? The outer planets?
2. Which planet travels faster in its orbit, Mars or Jupiter?
3. What are the properties of a comet?
4. How does the length of a "year" compare between inner and outer planets?

C. Applying Concepts
Think about what you have learned in this chapter. Answer each of the following questions using complete sentences.
1. How does distance from the sun affect the surface temperature of a planet?
2. Other than size, how are Earth and the other planets different?

UNIT 3 REVIEW

CHECKING YOURSELF

Answer these questions on a sheet of paper.
1. Describe the color and temperature of the sun.
2. What happens when the moon comes directly between Earth and the sun?
3. Why is Pluto a cold, dark planet?
4. Where did the word "planet" originate?
5. How do the nine planets differ?
6. Why do scientists study the sun?
7. Why do some stars appear brighter than others?
8. Why is Mars called the "red" planet?
9. How do planets travel around the sun?
10. How does the sun produce energy?
11. Why can the corona be seen only during a solar eclipse?
12. What are sunspots and solar flares? How do they affect Earth?
13. How is each planet's ellipse different?
14. Name a special characteristic of Saturn.
15. What would happen to the planets if there were no force of gravity?

RECALLING ACTIVITIES

Think about the activities you did in this unit. Answer the questions about these activities.
1. What causes an eclipse? 5–1
2. How can you observe the effects of gravity? 6–1
3. How can you compare sizes of planets? 6–2

IDEAS TO EXPLORE

1. Draw a mural that shows all the members of the solar system.
2. Attend a planetarium show and write a short report about the program.
3. Use a pair of binoculars or a telescope. Observe and sketch the moon, Venus, or Jupiter for one week.

CHALLENGING PROJECT

Conduct an experiment to discover the relationship between light intensity and distance. You will need a 25 watt light bulb and socket, a light meter, and a meter stick. Mount the light bulb at the zero end of the meter stick that has been taped down onto a table. Darken the room completely. Place the light meter at the 20 cm mark on the meter stick. Record this distance and the light meter reading in a data table. Double the distance to 40 cm. Record the reading. Take and record readings at 60 cm, and then at 80 cm. Study the data. How is distance related to light intensity? How does this apply to light given off by stars? What would happen if Earth were closer to the sun? Further from the sun?

BOOKS TO READ

101 Questions and Answers About the Universe by Roy A. Gallant, Macmillan Publishers: New York, © 1984.
   Your questions about the world around you are answered.

The Moon by Seymour Simon, Four Winds Press: New York, © 1984.
   Read an introduction to our neighbor in space.

Space Voyager by Wendy Boase, Simon & Schuster: New York, © 1984.
   Take an imaginary trip through the solar system.

UNIT 4
Minerals, Rocks, and Fossils

Earth is always changing. Rocks and minerals you observe today, such as the volcanic columns, were formed many millions of years ago from hot liquid rock deep inside Earth. Sometimes hot liquid rock reaches Earth's surface very dramatically during the eruption of a volcano. Volcanic activity is one proof that Earth is constantly changing.

Volcanic columns

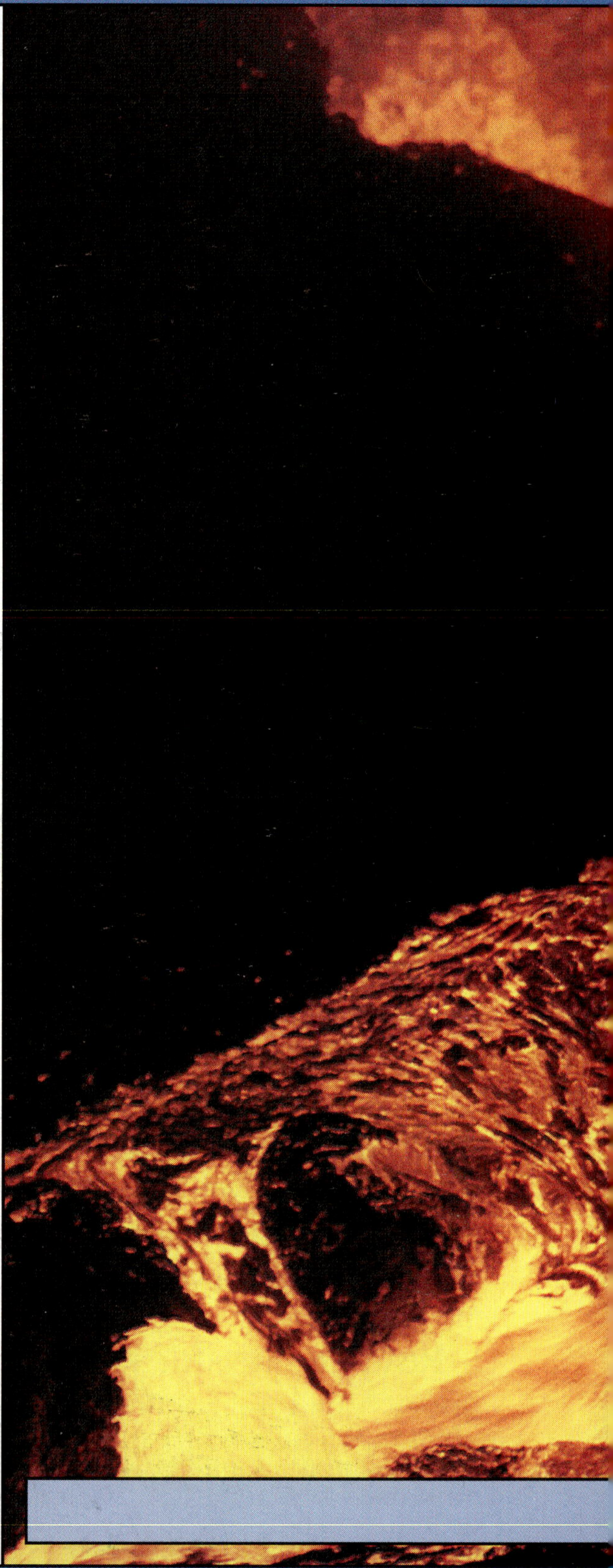

Active volcano

Chapter 7
Earth's Composition

The rocks shown are part of Earth's crust. From a distance they appear to be the same color. Look carefully at the close up view. Describe what you see. Is the rock made of one or more than one substance? How many different kinds of substances do you see?

Sierra Nevada Range—granite

Identifying Minerals 7:1

LESSON GOALS

In this lesson you will learn
- minerals are solid chemical matter formed in nature.
- minerals can be identified by physical properties.
- the visible shape of a mineral's atom pattern is a crystal.

The different colored substances you observed on page 118 are minerals. A **mineral** is solid chemical matter formed in nature by Earth processes. Minerals are not alive. They are not formed by living things. Each mineral has its own special combination of atoms. Each mineral has a definite pattern of atoms.

What is a mineral?

Figure 7-1. A geologist studying minerals

A **geologist** (jee AHL uh just) is a scientist who studies Earth. Some geologists collect and study minerals. They learn how different minerals form in Earth. They learn how to find minerals. Many minerals are useful to people.

What do geologists study?

119

How is hematite used?

Certain minerals are used in industry. One example is hematite, a mineral used in making steel. Hematite is a source of iron. Iron is used to make steel. Hematite forms in Earth's crust.

Diamonds are also minerals. Diamonds form deep in Earth's mantle. Heat and pressure make diamonds very hard. Some diamonds are valuable for their quality and beauty. These special diamonds are cut and polished for jewelry. However, diamonds of lesser quality and beauty are used in industry. Diamonds are used on cutting edges of some saws. Some phonograph needles are made of diamond. Some drills have diamond bits. Diamond bit drills can cut through rocks.

Figure 7-2. A diamond used in jewelry (a), diamond phonograph needle (b), talc (c), and hematite (d)

Talc is another mineral that has many uses. Talc is used in paints and some tableware such as bowls and plates. Very pure talc is used in talcum powders, lotions, and face creams.

Kim and Mark are learning to identify physical properties of minerals. A **physical property** is a characteristic that can be observed. Some physical properties are color, hardness, streak, luster, and crystal pattern. Kim and Mark have been able to identify three minerals so far. See Figure 7-3. How are each of these minerals different? What properties do you think Kim and Mark used to identify the minerals?

What are some physical properties?

Figure 7-3. Identifying minerals using physical properties

Color is a physical property of minerals. Study the minerals in Figure 7-4. What do you observe about their colors? Color alone is not enough to help you identify a mineral because many different minerals can be the same color. The very same mineral can also be different colors.

Figure 7-4. Amethyst, clear, and smokey quartz can be identified by color

Some minerals are hard and others soft. Some appear glassy and others look like metal. You will learn how to use these and other physical properties to help you identify minerals.

Mohs' Scale	
1	talc
2	gypsum
3	calcite
4	fluorite
5	apatite
6	orthoclase
7	quartz
8	topaz
9	corundum
10	diamond

What does the hardness of a mineral mean?

Hardness

Hardness is a physical property of minerals. **Hardness** is the measure of how easily a mineral can be scratched. The hardness scale is based on 10 minerals. These minerals are called Mohs' minerals. Mohs was a scientist who invented this scale. Soft minerals are given lower numbers. Hard minerals are given higher numbers.

If Mohs' minerals are not available, common objects can be used to test the hardness of mineral samples. Your fingernail has a hardness of about 2. Which minerals can you scratch with your fingernail? A glass plate has a hardness of about 5. Will diamond scratch the glass plate? A steel file has a hardness of 6. Why will quartz scratch the steel file?

Streak

A streak test is a color test. **Streak** is the color of the powdered mineral. To see the streak, a mineral is scratched across a tile. The powdered trail left by a mineral is its streak. However, a streak is not always helpful when trying to identify a mineral. Some minerals have the same color streak. Others are harder than the tile and thus leave no streak. Table 7-1 shows some common minerals and their streak colors.

What is a streak test?

Table 7-1 Streak Test	
Mineral	Streak Color
Pyrite	Greenish-black
Galena	Gray
Hematite	Reddish-brown
Limonite	Yellow-brown

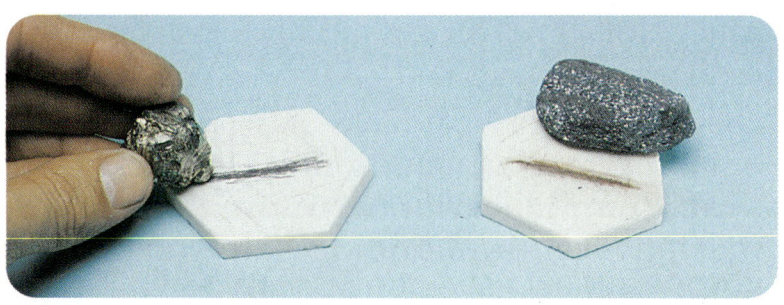

Figure 7-5. Streak test

Activity 7-1 Mineral Properties

QUESTION How can you group minerals?

Materials
poster paper
color marker
10 mineral samples
pencil and paper

What to do

1. Place all samples in one pile at the top of the paper. Draw a circle around the pile.
2. Separate the light and dark-colored samples into two piles. Draw a circle around each pile.
3. Observe the dark-colored samples. Choose a physical property that will allow you to divide the samples into 2 piles. Draw a circle around each pile. Write the property you used next to each circle.
4. Repeat step 3 using the light-colored samples.
5. Keep dividing the piles until each mineral is by itself.

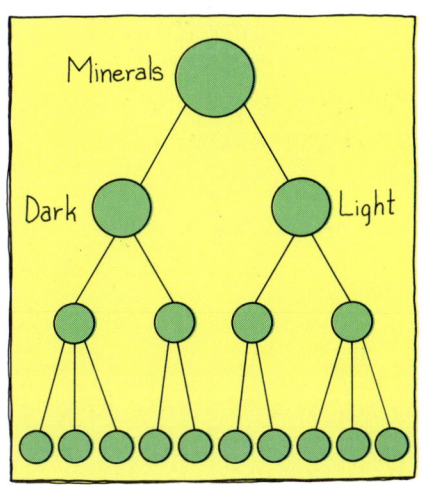

What did you learn?

1. What properties did you use to divide the light-colored samples?
2. What properties did you use to divide the dark-colored samples?

Using what you learned

1. How might a mineral property chart be used?
2. Is any one property enough to identify a mineral? Why or why not?

What is luster?

Luster

Luster is the kind of shine a mineral has when light strikes it. Certain minerals shine like metals. They have a metallic luster. Other minerals appear dull or shine like glass. They have a nonmetallic luster. Which of the minerals in Figure 7–6 show a metallic luster? Which look nonmetallic?

Figure 7–6. Pyrite (a) and galena (c) have metallic lusters. Quartz (b) and hematite (d) have nonmetallic lusters.

Crystal Shape

Atoms are tiny particles that make up minerals. Atoms in minerals are arranged in patterns. The patterns may be repeated. When the pattern is repeated enough, it makes a shape. The shapes have smooth, flat surfaces. They also have corners and sharp edges. The visible shape of a mineral's atom pattern is called a **crystal** (KRIHS tul). Many minerals have a special crystal shape. Crystals grow by adding on to their atom patterns.

Crystals form from liquids and gases. Crystals form when the matter becomes a solid under special conditions. There must be enough space for crystals to grow. Crystals must not be disturbed while they are growing. Crystals that grow slowly and have plenty of room grow to be large.

The crystals of a certain mineral always have the same shape. This shape is due to a mineral's atom pattern. Figure 7-8 shows table salt crystals that have been photographed many times larger than true size. Table salt crystals always have the same shape. How do you think crystal shapes are used to identify minerals?

Figure 7-7. Amethyst crystal

From what do mineral crystals form?

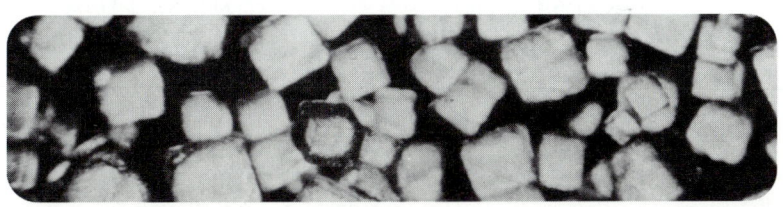

Figure 7-8. Table salt crystals magnified 50 times.

Lesson Summary

- Minerals are solid chemical matter formed in nature.
- Minerals can be identified by physical properties.
- The visible shape of a mineral's atom pattern is a crystal.

Lesson Review

Review the lesson to answer these questions.
1. What is a geologist?
2. Name one mineral and explain how it is used in industry.
3. What physical properties can be used to identify minerals?
4. How do crystals form?

7:2 Rocks: Mineral Mixtures

LESSON GOALS

In this lesson you will learn
- rocks are made of one or more minerals.
- igneous, sedimentary, and metamorphic are the three groups of rocks.
- one group of rocks forms from melted rock, one from sediment deposits, and one from heat and pressure.

What is a rock?

A solid mixture of one or more different minerals is a **rock**. Figure 7-9 shows Kim looking at a rock with a hand lens. The smaller picture shows what she sees. How many different substances do you see? Each of these is a mineral. Kim can tell them apart by their physical properties.

Figure 7-9. Observing minerals in a rock sample

Geologists study and compare rocks. They identify minerals in rocks and study their general appearances. This helps them decide how the rocks formed. They classify rocks into three main groups. They group rocks by the way they form. One group forms from melted rock. The second group of rocks form from deposits of sediments. Rocks in the third group were changed by heat and pressure. Study the photos below. To which group might Kim's rock belong? What clues did you use?

How do geologists group rocks?

a b c

Figure 7-10. Rock formed from melted rock (a), rock formed from sediment deposits (b), and rock formed by heat and pressure (c)

Igneous Rocks

Magma is hot liquid material. All magmas must form deep within Earth where temperatures are high. Sometimes magma cools slowly deep within Earth. Other times it flows out onto the surface and cools quickly. An **igneous** (IHG nee us) **rock** forms when magma cools.

How are igneous rocks formed?

Figure 7-11. A lava flow

127

Figure 7-12. Granite—an intrusive igneous rock

Magma that cools deep in Earth forms **intrusive** (ihn TREW sihv) **igneous rock.** Because it cools slowly, large crystals grow. Crystals in intrusive rocks are easy to see.

Figure 7-12 shows granite. Granite is an intrusive igneous rock. Granite is used in buildings and monuments. It is very strong and attractive in appearance. Mount Rushmore is made of granite. Where did Mount Rushmore's granite form?

Figure 7-13. Mount Rushmore is located in South Dakota.

Magma that reaches Earth's surface is called lava. Lava cools fast on Earth's surface. Lava cools so quickly there is little time for crystals to grow. Rocks that form on the surface from lava are called **extrusive** (ihk STREW sihv) **igneous rocks.** Where might you go to see extrusive igneous rocks forming today?

How do extrusive rocks form?

Basalt is an extrusive igneous rock. It forms when certain volcanoes erupt lava. The lava flows out of the volcano. The lava cools forming basalt. Obsidian is also an extrusive igneous rock. It forms from very quick-cooling lava. Obsidian is used for jewelry and art. Some arrowheads were made from it. Study the rocks in Figures 7-12 and 7-14. Which rock cooled fastest?[4] Which rock is intrusive?

Figure 7-14. Obsidian—an extrusive igneous rock

Sedimentary Rocks

All rocks on Earth's surface are slowly broken down into small pieces. The pieces are called sediments. Sediments can be as large as gravel or as fine as powder.

What are sediments?

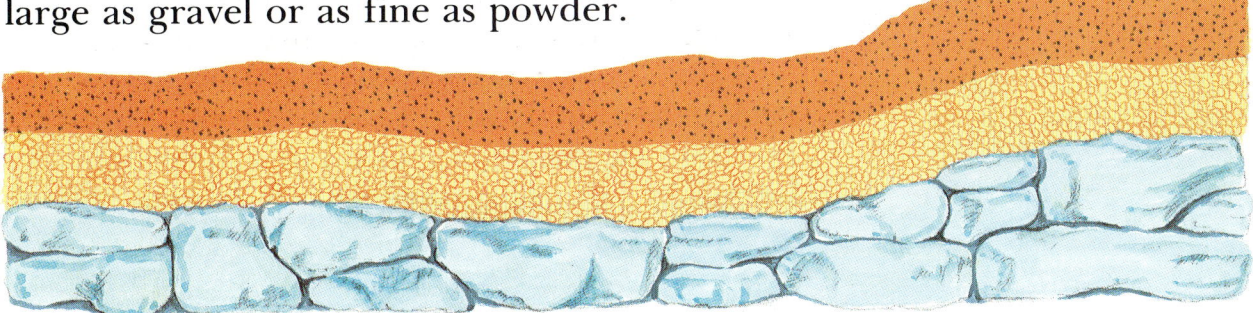

Sediments are often moved far from where they form. They can be moved by running water, ice, wind, waves, and gravity. They collect in layers at the bottoms of lakes, rivers, and oceans. Layers of sediment become cemented together to form **sedimentary** (sed uh MENT uh ree) **rock.**

Figure 7-15. Layers of sediments

One layer becomes buried under other layers. The buildup of layers becomes heavy. The weight squeezes the layers of sediment. Minerals dissolved in water cement the sediments together. Pressure and cementing change sediments to sedimentary rock. How does the word *sedimentary* help you remember how these rocks were formed?

What is the most common sedimentary rock?

There are different kinds of sedimentary rocks. Gravel and pebbles are deposited in fast flowing rivers. They form a rock called conglomerate. Large amounts of sand are found in deserts and on beaches. This sand can become a sedimentary rock called sandstone. Mud is carried into lakes and oceans. Layers of mud slowly change to shale. Shale is the most common sedimentary rock.

Figure 7-16. Conglomerate and shale

129

Another group of sedimentary rocks forms chemically. Some minerals form in ocean water. Thick deposits of these minerals and sea animal shells may slowly collect on the floors of warm, shallow oceans. Slowly these shells and minerals become cemented to form a sedimentary rock called limestone. Limestone is found on the land in places like Ohio and Kentucky. Scientists say there once was an ocean covering parts of these states. Why do they think these states were covered by an ocean?

a

b

Figure 7-17. Limestone (a) and coal (b)

From what does coal form?

The buried remains of plants may also form sedimentary rock. Thick deposits of plants in tropical swamps form coal. If you examine a piece of coal under a microscope or hand lens, you may observe plant parts. The plant parts have gone through a chemical change, but they can still be identified as having been leaves, bark, and so on. Coal is another kind of sedimentary rock.

Metamorphic Rocks

Heat and pressure can change rocks. **Metamorphic** (met uh MOR fihk) **rocks** are formed by heat and pressure. Heat causes the particles in rocks to move faster. Atoms may move from one crystal to another. This causes some crystals to grow larger. It can also cause particles of different kinds to change places. This movement of particles changes the structure of minerals and a new rock is formed. The new rock is a metamorphic rock.

Igneous, sedimentary, and other metamorphic rocks can be changed to metamorphic rocks. Heat and pressure can change shale, a sedimentary rock, into a metamorphic rock called slate. Heat and pressure can change granite, an igneous rock, into gneiss (NISE). Limestone, a sedimentary rock, can be changed into marble.

How are metamorphic rocks formed?

Figure 7-18. Heat and pressure change shale, granite, and limestone to slate, gneiss, and marble.

Figure 7-19. Marble table used for making fudge

How is marble used?

Metamorphic rocks can be put into two groups. The groups are banded and nonbanded. Gneiss and slate are banded. The bands in gneiss are easy to see. You may need a hand lens to see the bands in slate. Marble is a nonbanded metamorphic rock. Marble is used to make floors and table tops. It is often used to make statues. Some of the world's oldest and most beautiful buildings are made of marble.

Lesson Summary

- Rocks are made of one or more minerals.
- Igneous, sedimentary, and metamorphic are the three groups of rocks.
- One group of rocks forms from melted rock, one from sediment deposits, and one from heat and pressure.

Lesson Review

Review the lesson to answer these questions.
1. Where do all magmas form?
2. What is the difference between intrusive and extrusive igneous rock?
3. Into what two groups can metamorphic rocks be placed?

Activity 7-2 Identifying Rocks

QUESTION   What properties can be used to name rocks?

Materials
color marker
poster paper
rock samples
vinegar
hand lens
pencil and paper

What to do
1. On poster paper, draw the chart shown. Place all the rock samples in the top circle.
2. Use the hand lens. Divide the rocks into two groups using the property of mineral size. Test each rock with vinegar.
3. Divide these groups into two other groups. Use the chart to help you.
4. Continue until you have one rock in each of the bottom circles. Each circle has a name for that rock.

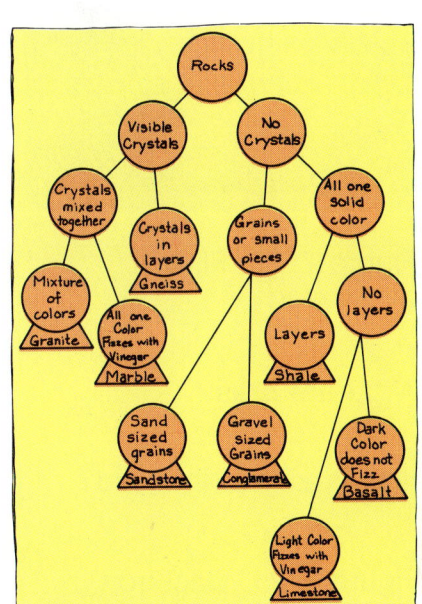

What did you learn?
1. What rocks have you named?
2. Which rocks have you seen before?

Using what you learned
1. Divide the rocks into the three groups.
2. Collect some rocks. Use the chart to name them. Make a list of the rocks you find.

7:3 Useful Rocks and Minerals

LESSON GOALS

In this lesson you will learn
- ores are rocks that contain useful metals.
- nonmetallic minerals are useful to people.
- ores and nonmetallic minerals form in different ways.

Figure 7-20. Flint arrowhead

What are ores?

How is aluminum used?

Figure 7-21. Cast iron, aluminum, and copper cookware

Many rocks and minerals are useful. Limestone and granite are used as building stones. Recall that diamonds, which are minerals, have many uses. Flint is the type of rock that was used many years ago to make arrowheads, scrapers, and knife blades. Sandstone was used to sharpen tools.

Some rocks contain useful metals. Useful metals are found in rocks called **ores.** Iron, aluminum, and copper are metals that occur as ores. Iron can be melted and shaped into useful tools. Many products we use are made on machines made of iron.

Aluminum is not a strong metal by itself. It is usually mixed with other metals. Aluminum is used for window frames, pots, pans, and zippers. What have you used today that is made of aluminum?

Nonmetallic minerals can also be useful. Clay is a mineral that was used by early people. Figure 7-22 shows some examples of ancient pottery. Clay was and still is used in bricks and modern pottery.

Figure 7-22. Ancient pottery

Rock salt is a mineral you probably see every day. Salt is added to many foods. Salt is also used in certain industries.

Sulfur is another nonmetallic mineral. It is bright yellow. Sulfur is used by almost every kind of industry in the world. Sulfur is used to make paper, plastic, dyes, and medicines. It is used in batteries and fertilizers.

Mica is another important mineral. Mica splits into thin sheets. Sheet mica is used in electronics. Radios, televisions, and some toasters use sheet mica. Most mica is ground into flakes or powder. This form of mica is used in wallpaper, plaster, paint, cosmetics, and some cements. Even some airplane spark plugs are made of mica.

Many rocks are used for building. Sandstone is cut into blocks and used like bricks. Slate is used as tile for roofs or entryways. Rocks are very useful.

How is mica used?

In what kind of rock do most ores form?

Figure 7-23. A sulfur mine

There are over 1,000 rocks and minerals that are useful to people. They form in many different ways. You have learned some of these ways. Ores are formed differently. Most ores form during the formation of igneous rocks. Sometimes the magma is rich in iron or copper. When the magma cools, the iron and other metals collect in the rock. Sometimes heat and pressure cause minerals to form. Diamonds are found in certain igneous rocks. These rocks form deep within Earth where it is very hot.

Most nonmetallic minerals are found in sedimentary rocks. Clay is often found in sandstones. Some rock salt was formed in ancient oceans.

Sulfur is a nonmetallic mineral that can form in many ways. Sulfur can be deposited around volcanoes. It is sometimes found with rock salt. Sulfur can also be deposited by hot springs. Some bacteria produce sulfur deposits.

Lesson Summary

- Ores are rocks that contain useful metals.
- Nonmetallic minerals are useful to people.
- Ores and nonmetallic minerals form in many ways.

Lesson Review

Review the lesson to answer these questions.
1. What is an ore?
2. What are two uses for clay?
3. Where are sulfur deposits found?

People and Science

Searching for Oil

Oil is a very important energy source. It is limited in supply and not always easy to find. Because so much oil is used every day, oil companies are interested in easier ways to find it.

Donald Minh is an exploration geologist. He works for an oil company. His job is to decide where to drill when his company explores for oil. The company cannot afford to drill just anywhere. Donald has been trained to look for certain clues above ground. He knows that oil is usually found where a river bottom, lake, or small sea existed millions of years ago. Certain rock formations may also help him decide whether or not oil might be underground.

Since the 1970s, exploration geologists have used satellite photographs to help with their field work. Cameras on the satellites use a special film called infrared film. Different types of rock appear in different colors on infrared film. By studying the satellite photographs of Earth, Donald can determine where oil might be found underground. For example, he looks for patterns of cracks in Earth's crust. These cracks may be signs of oil deposits. Once Donald determines where oil might be located, a field crew makes many tests for oil at that spot.

Donald knows that oil is getting harder to find. Satellite photographs help make the search easier.

Chapter 7 Review

Summary

1. Minerals are solid chemical matter formed in nature. 7:1
2. Minerals can be identified by physical properties such as color, hardness, streak, luster, and crystal pattern. 7:1
3. A crystal is the visible shape of a mineral's atom pattern. 7:1
4. Rocks are made of one or more minerals. 7:2
5. Igneous, sedimentary, and metamorphic are the three kinds of rocks. 7:2
6. Useful metals are found in rocks called ores. 7:3

Science Words

mineral	luster	intrusive igneous rock
geologist	crystal	extrusive igneous rock
physical property	rock	sedimentary rock
hardness	magma	metamorphic rocks
streak	igneous rock	ores

Understanding Science Words

Complete each of the following sentences with a word or words from the Science Words that will make the sentence correct.

1. The way a mineral shines when light strikes is called its _____.
2. A scientist who studies Earth is called a _____.
3. The powder trail left by a mineral is its _____.
4. Solid chemical matter formed in nature by Earth processes is a _____.
5. The hardness of a mineral is an example of a _____.
6. The shape of a mineral's atom pattern is called a _____.
7. A measure of how easily a mineral scratches is its _____.
8. A solid mixture of one or more different minerals formed in Earth is a _____.

9. Sand and mud may become cemented together to form two different kinds of _____.
10. Magma that cools slowly inside Earth's crust forms _____ igneous rock.
11. Rocks changed by heat and pressure become _____.
12. Lava cooled at the surface of Earth forms _____ igneous rock.
13. The cooling of magma or lava forms _____.
14. Useful metals are found in rocks called _____.
15. Hot liquid material is called _____.

Questions

A. Recalling Facts
Choose the word or phrase that correctly completes each of the following sentences.
1. One example of an igneous rock is
   (a) granite.   (b) marble.   (c) sandstone.   (d) shale.
2. Deposits of mud can form a sedimentary rock called
   (a) grantite.   (b) marble.   (c) sandstone.   (d) shale.
3. Limestone is changed by heat and pressure to form a metamorphic rock called
   (a) granite.   (b) marble.   (c) sandstone.   (d) shale.

B. Understanding Concepts
Answer each of the following questions using complete sentences.
1. Name two rocks and two minerals and explain how they are used.
2. How are the three main groups of rocks formed?

C. Applying Concepts
Think about what you have learned in this chapter. Answer each of the following questions using complete sentences.
1. How do crystals grow?
2. Why are many ores found in igneous rock?

Chapter 8
Using Rock Records

Scientists are interested in Earth's history. They can learn about Earth's history by studying its rocks. The history of Earth is recorded in its rocks. The rock shown contains the fossil of a reptile. Where are fossils found?

Mesosaurus

Fossil Records   8:1

LESSON GOALS

In this lesson you will learn
- fossils are found in many sedimentary rocks.
- fossils are found in many forms.
- fossils form in different ways.

Fossils are found in many sedimentary rocks. A **fossil** is a record of ancient life on Earth. Fossils are found in many forms. Some fossils are the real bones and shells of animals or parts of plants. Others are prints of plants or animals. Geologists use fossils to learn about life in the past. Limestone, sandstone, and shale often contain fossils. Look at Figure 8-1. Which fossil is the actual parts of a plant or animal? Which is a print?

What is a fossil?

How do geologists use fossils?

Figure 8-1. Fossil starfish and crinoids

Not all living things that die become fossils. Most are destroyed before they can become fossils. Some are buried quickly and left undisturbed. These may become fossils. Living things in the ocean become fossils more often than living things on land. Why do you think this happens?

141

How were the fossils of some mammoths preserved?

Kinds of Fossils

Some fossils are found in their true form. Animals called mammoths have been found frozen solid in ice. These frozen bodies are fossils. Mammoths looked a lot like elephants do today. Mammoths lived during the ice age. They are extinct. They no longer live on Earth. Where might fossils be formed in this way today?

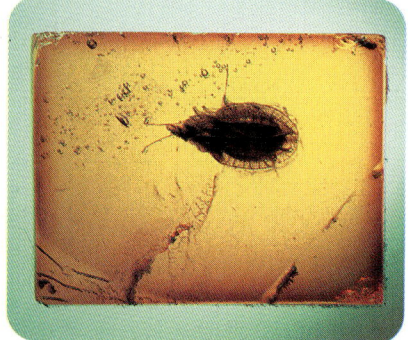

Figure 8-2. Insect in amber

Some ancient plants and animals became stuck in tree sap. They were covered by the sap. Later, the sap hardened and was changed to a plasticlike substance. The substance is called amber. The plants or animals were preserved in the amber. What is preserved in the amber in Figure 8-2?

Sometimes, climate has an effect on what kinds of fossils are formed. In some places, animal bodies became dried before they decayed. These dried bodies became mummies. The drying process is called **mummification.** In what kind of climate would fossils form by mummification?

Finding a complete body of a plant or animal does not happen often. The fossil shown is often mistaken for a complete body. It is a mold and cast fossil. Mold and cast fossils are formed in the following way. A plant or animal dies. It is covered with sediment. The sediment is hardened by pressure and cemented together. At the same time, the plant or animal body decays and dissolves. The hollow space left by the body is called the **mold.** Sediments fill the space and harden. The hardened sediments become the cast. The **cast** is the form or shape of the plant or animal.

Figure 8-3. Mold and cast fossil

Activity 8-1   Making a Fossil

QUESTION   How can you make a mold and cast fossil?

Materials

paper cup
plaster of paris
petroleum jelly
spoon

water
bowl
seashell
pencil and paper

What to do

1. Mix plaster of paris with water. Make it thick but runny like soft ice cream.
2. Fill the cup half full of the plaster.
3. Spread a thin layer of petroleum jelly all over the seashell.
4. Place the seashell on top of the plaster in the cup. Push the shell down lightly into the plaster. Allow it to set until hard.
5. Mix more plaster and cover the shell. Allow this to set until hard. Tear away the paper cup.
6. The two layers of plaster should come apart easily. Remove the shell.

What did you learn?

1. What was the mold in the activity?
2. What was the cast in the activity?

Using what you learned

1. Where might you find true fossils like the ones you made?
2. How are molds and casts made in nature?

What are petrified fossils?

Figure 8-4. Petrified wood

Some plants or animal bones become fossils because they are petrified. **Petrified** (PEH truh fide) **fossils** are once-living plants or animals that have been replaced by minerals. Wood and bone most often become petrified. Wood and bone become buried in sediment. Often these sediments are full of water. This water may contain many dissolved minerals. The minerals replace each particle of wood or bone. This process preserves the original texture and sometimes even the color of the wood or bone.

Figure 8-4 shows petrified wood from the Petrified Forest. The Petrified Forest is located in the Painted Desert in northern Arizona. It contains the greatest and most colorful examples of petrified wood in the world.

Would you expect to find fossil worms? Why or why not? Animals such as worms have no bones or hard parts. They are rarely preserved as fossils. But their tracks can be preserved as mold and cast fossils.

Lesson Summary

- Fossils are found in many sedimentary rocks.
- Fossils are found in many forms.
- Fossils form in different ways.

Lesson Review

Review the lesson to answer these questions.
1. What is mummification?
2. Where are many fossils formed?
3. Name three kinds of sedimentary rock that may contain fossils.

Science and Technology

Taking Care of Fossils and Artifacts

Do you know what cameras, paint brushes, and scuba gear have in common? These are tools used by a modern archeologist (ar kee AHL uh just) to find and preserve the past. Archeologists are scientists who study about past human life. They look for fossils and artifacts. An artifact (ART uh fakt) is an object such as a tool, pot, or statue.

Fossils or artifacts are usually dug from the ground. The place or site is called a "dig." Work at a dig must be done very carefully. Soft paint brushes are used to brush away layers of soil from around bones or tools. Each item that is found is recorded and photographed while it is still in the ground. The artifact may be removed from the ground, labeled, cleaned, and examined. Soil from the dig is put through fine screens to collect even the smallest broken piece of a fossil or artifact. It takes an archeologist many years to examine all the items from a dig.

Many people have found important archeological sites. School boys in France found caves with pre-historic paintings. In Mexico City, several large statues were uncovered while a building was being constructed. Since the laws of Mexico City protect artifacts, all construction was stopped!

Every country in the world has history waiting to be discovered and studied.

8:2 Using Fossils

LESSON GOALS

In this lesson you will learn
- fossils are records of change preserved in Earth's crust.
- scientists can learn about ancient animals, plants, and people from fossils.

Fossils tell us much about Earth. They are records of change preserved in Earth's crust. Corals have been found in Michigan. Where do corals live today? What does this tell you about Michigan in the ancient past?

Figure 8-5. Coral fossil and underwater coral reef

Coal forms in warm, swampy regions. Coal has been found in Antarctica. How can you explain this? What does this tell you about the climate of Antarctica in the past?

Tree trunk fossils have been found. They are used to learn about climates long ago. Each year a tree adds a new ring to its trunk. The rings are wide when there is much rainfall. The rings are narrow when there is little rainfall. What can scientists learn about the climate long ago by studying fossil tree trunks?

Earth has changed very much since it formed. It is still changing today. In the ancient past, warm shallow oceans covered much of Earth. This can explain why ocean fossils are found in Michigan.

Slowly, the oceans left the lands they covered. Swamps formed. Decaying swamp plants formed a soft, brown material called peat. Heat and pressure over a long period of time changed the peat to coal. Much later, Earth was covered by glaciers. This is why mammoths have been found frozen in the ground. Most of the glaciers melted and Earth became much like it is today.

Other changes occurred in Earth's past. Pieces of Earth called plates moved around through time. Antarctica was once near the equator. North America and Africa were joined near Florida in the ancient past. Why might fossils found in Florida be like fossils found in Africa?

Figure 8-6. Glacier

What two continents were joined together in the ancient past?

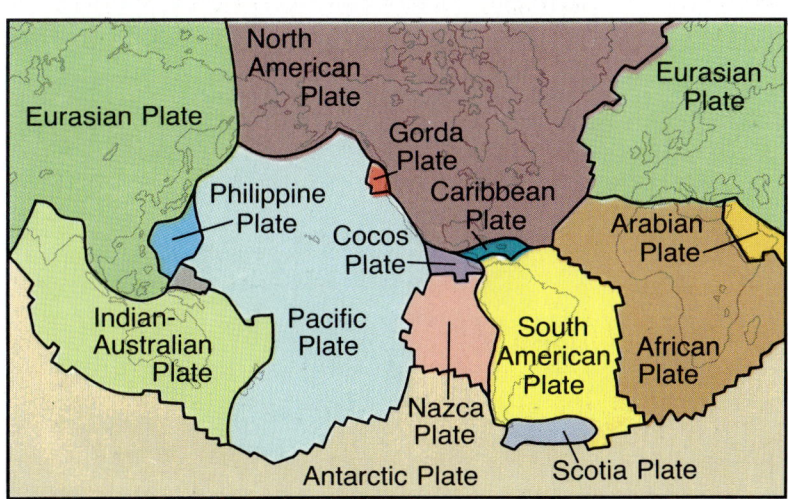

Figure 8-7. Earth's plates

Fossils are clues to Earth's past climate. Fossils can also give clues to Earth movements. Why might fossils be a clue to where your state was located long ago?

147

How can scientists build a model of an animal?

Scientists can learn much about ancient animals by studying their fossils. By observing and studying a few bones, scientists can build a model of an animal. They can study the teeth and find out what the animal ate. Some ate only plants. Others ate only meat. How can they tell what dinosaurs ate from studying their teeth?

Figure 8-8. Much can be learned by studying fossils.

Activity 8-2 Making Footprints

QUESTION What can you learn from footprints?

Materials
clay
waxed paper
roller
small rocks
pencil and paper

What to do
1. Place your clay on the waxed paper.
2. Roll the clay into a pancake shape.
3. Use a small rock to make imaginary animal footprints in the clay.
4. Make footprints to show your imaginary animal walking, running, or jumping.

What did you learn?
1. How could you tell the direction of the imaginary animal's tracks?
2. How were the running footprints different from walking prints?
3. How could you tell a heavy animal from a light animal?
4. How could footprints give clues to an animal's size?

Using what you learned
1. How are the footprints you made like fossil prints?
2. What can scientists learn from fossil footprints?

What are clues to how ancient people looked?

Scientists can learn about ancient people by studying their fossils. The shapes of skulls and bones are clues to how ancient people looked. The shapes of their teeth are clues to what they ate. Scientists study cave drawings and other ancient records. They study ancient tools. These are all clues to how ancient people lived.

Figure 8-9. Ancient records are clues to how people lived.

Fossils are like books. Scientists have learned to read them. From fossils, they have learned about ancient plants and animals. They have learned about ancient people. Fossils are being formed today.

Lesson Summary
- Fossils are records of change preserved in Earth's crust.
- Scientists can learn about ancient plants, animals, and people from fossils.

Lesson Review
Review the lesson to answer these questions.
1. How can scientists learn about the climate on Earth long ago?
2. How do scientists build models of ancient animals?
3. How can scientists tell what ancient people looked like?
4. What other clues do scientists use to study ancient people?

Language Arts Skills

Classifying

A group is a set of things, people, animals, ideas, or any other kind of item you can think of. To belong to a group, its members must be alike in some way. The ways they are alike are called their characteristics.

Characteristics for a group might be nine members, uniforms, bats, and ball gloves.
- What kind of group is this?
- What other characteristics might this group have?

If you know to what group something belongs, you know some of its characteristics. The characteristics tell you how the members of the group are alike.
- What kinds of characteristics might ocean animals have?

If you know the characteristics of a thing, you can tell to what group it belongs.

Think about sharks and whales. Sharks are fish that breathe through gills. Whales are mammals that breathe with lungs. Even though they are both sea creatures, they are different.

Think about how the following are alike and different: octopus, camel, alligator, dragonfly, starfish, cactus, lizard, and Spanish moss.
- Which live in the ocean?
- Which live in the desert?
- Which live in the swamp?
- Which can live in more than one kind of place?
- What characteristic was used to decide to which group each belonged?
- What other characteristics do you know about these plants and animals now that you know to which group they belong?

Chapter 8 Review

Summary

1. Fossils are found in many sedimentary rocks. 8:1
2. Fossils are records of past life on Earth. 8:1
3. Some fossils are the actual body parts of once-living plants, animals, or people. 8:1
4. Fossils may be prints or molds and casts of body parts. 8:1
5. Some fossils are formed when plant or animal bodies are replaced by minerals. 8:1
6. Fossils are records of change preserved in Earth's crust. 8:2
7. Scientists can learn about ancient plants, animals, and people from fossils. 8:2

Science Words

fossil **mold** **petrified fossils**
mummification **cast**

Understanding Science Words

Complete each of the following sentences with a word or words from the Science Words that will make the sentence correct.

1. Dry desert climates help fossils form by _____.
2. Once-living plants or animals that have been replaced by minerals are called _____.
3. The hollow space left from a dissolved plant or animal body is called a _____.
4. A record of ancient life preserved in Earth's crust is called a _____.
5. Sediments or minerals may fill a mold and harden, becoming a _____.

Questions

A. Recalling Facts

Choose the word or phrase that correctly completes each of the following sentences.

1. Fossils are most often found in
   - (a) igneous rocks.
   - (b) metamorphic rocks.
   - (c) sedimentary rocks.
   - (d) all kinds of rocks.
2. Some mammoths were preserved by
   - (a) being petrified.
   - (b) being frozen.
   - (c) mummification.
   - (d) cast and mold.
3. Some fossils have been found perserved in a plasticlike substance called
   - (a) coal.   (b) ice.   (c) limestone.   (d) amber.
4. Scientists learn what dinosaurs ate by studying their
   - (a) teeth.   (b) footprints.   (c) bones.   (d) size.

B. Understanding Concepts

Answer each of the following questions using complete sentences.

1. List five ways fossils can form.
2. How is a mold different from a cast?
3. How does a fossil give clues about climate?
4. Why are fossils called records of change?

C. Applying Concepts

Think about what you have learned in this chapter. Answer each of the following questions using complete sentences.

1. Suppose you found shark teeth in a shale layer near your house. What does that tell you about your area in the past?
2. What can scientists study to find out how ancient people got food and did work?

UNIT 4 REVIEW

CHECKING YOURSELF

Answer these questions on a sheet of paper.
1. What is a geologist?
2. What are three uses for diamonds?
3. Explain five ways fossils are formed.
4. Would you find fossils in granite? Why or why not?
5. What is the difference between a rock and a mineral?
6. Name five physical properties used to identify minerals.
7. How are intrusive igneous rocks formed?
8. What is an ore?
9. Heat and pressure can change limestone into what metamorphic rock?
10. Where are extrusive igneous rocks formed?

RECALLING ACTIVITIES

Think about the activities you did in this unit. Answer the questions about these activities.
1. How can you group minerals? 7–1
2. What properties can be used to name rocks? 7–2
3. How can you make a mold and cast fossil? 8–1
4. What can you learn from footprints? 8–2

IDEAS TO EXPLORE

1. Obtain information about economic rocks and minerals mined in your state. Make a display with samples of each. Write a brief description of the rock and/or mineral and its uses on an index card. Put this card next to each sample. Write a more detailed report to accompany the display.

2. Write to other fourth graders and ask them to send small rock and mineral samples from their states. Do not ask them to identify the samples. With the help of reference books, your textbook, and your teacher, identify the various samples sent to you. Make a chart listing all the properties you used to identify the samples.
3. You have learned that Earth has changed much since it formed. About 40,000 years ago, much of North America was covered by glaciers. Use reference books to learn more about the most recent ice age. Do a report about the kinds of plants and animals that lived during this time.

CHALLENGING PROJECT

Earth is always changing. You have learned that pieces of Earth called plates have moved around through time. These plates have carried continents to different locations. Use reference books to learn more about Earth's plates. Include figures that show the locations of different continents at different times in the ancient past. Compare these with the present locations of the seven continents. Find out how the plates move.

BOOKS TO READ

Discovering Fossils by Wendy Rydell, Troll Associates: Mahwah, NJ, © 1984.
   Learn how you can find fossils.
Fossils Tell of Long Ago by Aliki, Harper & Row Junior Books: New York, © 1983.
   What was life like millions of years ago? Fossils give us clues.
Rocks and Minerals by Elizabeth Marcus, Troll Associates: Mahwah, NJ, © 1983.
   Learn how to classify rocks and minerals.

UNIT 5
Animal Adaptations and Behavior

Even as a child, Konrad Lorenz was interested in animal behavior. As an adult and scientist, Dr. Lorenz continues to study the effects of environment on animal behavior. Scientists at a zoo are observing the behavior of the gorillas shown to determine whether animals taken from their natural environment can live together and raise their young as a family. Animal behavior is an interesting subject to study.

Konrad Lorenz and friends

Gorilla family—Modern zoo

Chapter 9
Adaptations for Survival

An animal must be able to find food and protect itself to survive in its environment. Describe your environment. How are you adapted to survive in your environment?

Building an igloo

Adaptation of Body Parts 9:1

LESSON GOALS
In this lesson you will learn
- how animals survive.
- what animal adaptations are.
- about specific adaptations of animals.

An animal must be able to protect itself and find food for it to live in its environment. When an animal is adapted to its environment, it is able to live successfully.

Adaptation

Any body part, body covering, or behavior that helps an animal live in its environment is called an **adaptation** (ad ap TAY shun). Body coverings help protect body organs. Look at the armadillo in Figure 9-1a. Notice that a hard, protective armor covers its upper body. Bands of the armor are hinged so that the armadillo can curl into a ball to protect its legs and belly if it is disturbed. The dog in Figure 9-1b has hair or fur to help keep it warm in cold weather.

What is an adaptation?

Figure 9-1. An armadillo has a hard outer body covering (a). A dog has hair or fur as an outer body covering (b).

159

Figure 9-2. An eagle uses its talons to capture food.

Some body parts are used for food getting. The eagle in Figure 9-2 has sharp talons and strong claw feet to catch prey for food.

Skin

Adaptations in body coverings are important to survival in animals. **Skin** is the outer covering of an animal's body. Skin makes up a body system that protects the organs of the body. It also helps to keep the correct body temperature of some animals. Skin is sensitive to changes in temperature and touch. Skin can hold or release water as needed by an animal.

Figure 9-3. Many animals have another layer of body covering over the skin.

Many animals have another layer of body covering over the skin. This layer may be scales, feathers, or hair. Although scales, feathers, and hair look different from each other, they are all parts of the skin tissue. The extra layer of body covering gives more protection to an animal.

Some animals do not have an extra layer of body covering. Their skins provide all the protection they need. A frog's skin gives off a fluid that makes its body moist and slimy. Some toads have poison glands in their skins. These glands give off a whitish fluid that may be harmful to the animals that try to eat them.

Scales

Scales are small thin plates that cover the skin of most fish and all reptiles. There are different kinds of scales. In fish, scales can be smooth, rough, or pointed. Fish scales are slippery. They help fish glide through the water.

Snakes have scales that are dry. Most snakes have scales that overlap and stretch apart when the snake moves. Snakes shed their scaly skins as they grow. They usually crawl out of their old skins, leaving them in one piece. Why do you think a snake needs to shed its skin as it grows?

a

b

Figure 9-4. A frog's skin is moist and slimy (a). The American toad's poisonous glands are an adaptation for protection (b).

What are scales?

Figure 9-5. Snakes shed their skins.

Activity 9-1   Fish Scales

QUESTION   How do fish scales look viewed under a microscope?

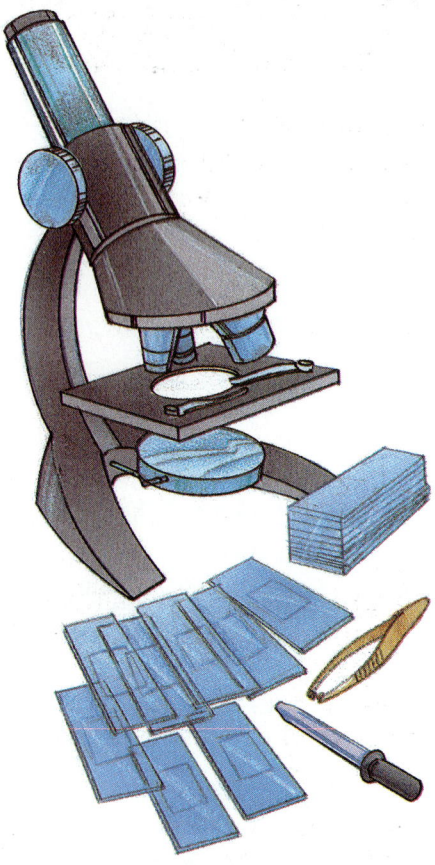

Materials
fish scales   cover slip
microscope   tweezers
glass slide   pencil and paper

What to do
1. Make two slides, one for scales from the upper body and one for scales from the lower body of each fish.
2. Put two drops of water on a glass slide. Use the tweezers to put a fish scale in the water and hold it in place on the slide with a cover slip.
3. Observe each slide under the microscope, first under low power and then under high power.
4. After each viewing, make a drawing of what you saw.

What did you learn?
1. How do the scales look different under the microscope compared to seeing them with the unaided eye?
2. Compare upper and lower scales from the same fish.

Using what you learned
1. Compare the scales of the two different fish you observed.
2. How are scales an adaptation for survival?

Feathers

Feathers are a strong, lightweight outer covering of birds. Figure 9-6 shows what a feather looks like up close. Notice how the parts of the feather lock together, something like a zipper. Very little air can pass through a feather.

You may have seen baby chicks covered with soft, fluffy feathers called down. In older birds, down feathers are found close to the skin. Down feathers keep the bird's body at the correct temperature, even if it flies through very cold air. The body temperature of a bird is often five or six degrees higher than a mammal's. Feathers are better than hair for controlling body temperature. The insulating quality of feathers also helps birds keep their eggs warm. Keeping eggs warm is important to the hatching process.

Many birds must dive or swim in water to find food. Their feathers are covered with a layer of body oil. Oil makes the feathers waterproof. These feathers keep a bird's skin dry, control its body temperature, and keep it afloat in water.

Figure 9-6. The parts of a feather lock together so very little air can pass through.

What is the purpose of down feathers?

Figure 9-7. Down feathers are soft and fluffy (a); they keep a bird warm even when it flies through cold air (b); oil makes feathers waterproof (c).

a

b

c

What do all mammals have in common?

Fur

All mammals have hair. In some mammals the hair is a thick covering of soft hairs called fur. A polar bear is one example. A polar bear lives in a very cold environment where temperatures are often below zero. The thick fur of a polar bear traps air. The trapped air is warmed by the body of the animal. This warmed air helps keep the polar bear's body at the correct temperature even when it dives into freezing water.

The fur of some animals changes at different seasons of the year. Hair may fall out in the spring and grow back into a heavier coat in the fall.

Figure 9-8. A polar bear needs thick fur to live in a cold environment (a). A lion's thick mane is an adaptation for protection (b).

a

b

Fur also protects animals from bumps and scratches. Animals such as lions and caribou have long, thick growths of hair around their necks where injuries would be especially serious. Some animals, such as cats, can make their hair stand out so that they look larger to any other animal that threatens them.

Feet and Wings

To survive in an environment, an animal must protect itself as well as find and catch food. The feet and wings of animals may be adapted for food getting and protection. Some animals crawl around searching for food. Other animals walk, run, or hop. There are animals that fly in the air and some that dive and swim in water.

Some body parts that are adapted for protection may also be used for food getting. For example, an animal might use sharp claws and teeth to protect itself. The animal may also use its claws and teeth for food getting. Look at the sharp claws and the teeth of the badger in Figure 9-9.

Some animals such as the lynx, the arctic fox, and the snowshoe hare grow extra long thick hair on their feet. This increases the size of their feet and helps them move about easily on soft snow to escape their enemies. Notice the extra growth of long hair on the snowshoe hare in Figure 9-10a.

Figure 9-9. A badger uses its sharp teeth and claws for food getting.

What two things must an animal do to survive?

Figure 9-10. A snowshoe hare (a) and an arctic fox (b) have thick fur on their feet so they can move about on soft snow.

a

b

Figure 9–11. Seagulls move from place to place in search of food.

Figure 9–12. The webbed feet of a duck are adapted for swimming.

Figure 9–13. Woodpeckers are able to chisel into tree bark in order to find food.

An animal must find its food before it can eat. Most animals find food by moving from place to place. A seagull glides over the water looking for shellfish. A swallow is able to make quick moves in the air in order to catch a flying insect. An egret wades into a stream on its long legs to catch a fish. Figure 9–12 shows how the feet of a duck are particularly well adapted to swimming in water in search of food.

Mouthparts

Some animals, such as a sea lion, swallow their food whole. Others have mouthparts for tearing, grinding, or spearing food. The mouthpart of a bird is called a bill. Woodpeckers have hard, pointed bills that they use to chisel or cut into the bark of a tree. Woodpeckers also have long tongues to reach into small openings for insects beneath the bark. Some finches have short, hard, cone-shaped, pointed bills. The size, shape, and strength of their bills help these finches eat seeds.

Some birds, like ducks, eat water plants and animals. These birds have bills with strainers to sift food from the mud and water. Look at Figures 9-13 and 9-14. Try to decide from the shapes of the bills which birds are seed eaters, chiselers, spearers, fish eaters, and water plant eaters.

a

b

c

Figure 9-14. The shape of a bird's bill is an adaptation for food getting; shown are a finch (a), shoveler duck (b), heron (c), and pelican (d).

d

Teeth

Teeth are mouthparts that are used to bite, tear, crush, and grind food. Chisel-shaped teeth at the front of the mouth are found in animals such as mice and squirrels. These teeth are used for biting and gnawing. A few animals, such as the beaver, have front gnawing teeth that keep growing longer. A beaver wears away its teeth as it gnaws down trees to eat leaves and branches. Cats, wolves, and dogs have long pointed teeth to stab and tear the meat they eat. Giraffes, horses, and sheep have flat teeth for crushing and grinding plants. What types of teeth do you have?

Figure 9-15. A beaver has chisel-shaped teeth for food getting.

How is a snake able to swallow food whole?

A snake has teeth that curve toward the back of its mouth. The curved teeth hold the food in the snake's mouth until food is swallowed. The snake does not chew its food. A snake can open its jaws very wide to swallow its food whole. A snake is able to swallow food that is about three times the size of its own head.

Figure 9–16. A snake's teeth and jaws are specially adapted for food getting.

Lesson Summary

- Animals must be able to protect themselves and find food in order to survive in their environment.
- An adaptation is anything that helps an animal live in its environment.
- Adaptations include body coverings and body parts.

Lesson Review

Review the lesson to answer these questions.
1. What are three ways adaptations help animals survive?
2. Name three types of body coverings that come from skin tissue.
3. How do feathers keep birds warm?
4. How are the teeth and jaws of a snake adapted for eating?

Science and Technology

Elk Arrive 400 Years Early

Roosevelt elk usually live at the edge of a forest. In the forest, elk can find protection from severe weather and hide from predators. The elk feed on plants in open areas beyond the forest. For centuries, Roosevelt elk lived on Mount St. Helens.

In May of 1980 something happened that destroyed many of the elk and their home. Mount St. Helens erupted. About 1,500 elk were killed as a result of the eruption. The fields and forests within 406 square kilometers (156 square miles) of the volcano were destroyed. Scientists thought that it would take 400 years for the forests to grow back. They also thought the elk would not return until the forests had grown back.

Recently, some scientists visited the Mount St. Helens area. Much to their surprise they found Roosevelt elk living on the volcanic mountain. Some of the elk that had escaped the volcanic blast returned.

Scientists are concerned that the elk may not be able to survive in the open area on Mount St. Helens. Some of these scientists are watching the elk carefully to see how they will adapt to the changes in their environment. In order to follow the elk, scientists have placed collars around the elks' necks. The collars contain radio transmitters. Scientists can track the radio signals made by the transmitters. These signals lead them to the elk. The transmitters work over long distances so the scientists can make observations without disturbing the elk.

By watching how the elk adapt, scientists may be able to help the elk and other animals adjust to changes in their environments.

9:2 Special Adaptations

LESSON GOALS
In this lesson you will learn
- about animal camouflage.
- about different kinds of camouflage.

Some animals are the same color as their environment. They are hard to see because their body coloring blends into the surrounding coloring. Some animals blend in because they look like objects in their environment.

Camouflage

Being able to blend into the environment is an adaptation called **camouflage** (KAM uh flahj). Camouflage helps an animal hide from predators or from prey.

What is camouflage?

Figure 9-17. Camouflage helps an animal hide from predators or from prey.

a

b
c

170

In Figure 9–17a the praying mantis is hidden from predators because it looks like the stems and leaves of the plant. When the mantis hunts other insects the prey may not see the mantis because of its camouflage. Notice how the walking stick in Figure 9–17b looks like a twig. When it is not moving, it has the same color, shape, and position as a twig. Find the butterfly in Figure 9–17c. Notice how it resembles a dead leaf when its wings are closed.

In summer and early fall a ptarmigan (TAR muh gun) has brown and gray feathers. These colors allow the bird to blend into the colors of the surrounding rocks and plants. In late fall and winter, the bird changes color from brown and gray to white. The white feathers allow the bird to blend into a snowy background. The ptarmigan as well as other animals, such as frogs, chameleons, and fish, use the color of body covering to blend in with their surroundings.

Figure 9–18. The color of its body covering allows a ptarmigan to blend into its surroundings.

Countershading

Countershading is also a form of camouflage. **Countershading** is an adaptation in which the top side of an animal is a different color from the bottom side. Most fish have countershading. When seen from above, the fish blend with the bottom of the lake, river, or ocean. The bottom sides of the fish are silver white. When seen from below, the fish blend with the water's surface and the sky. Notice the countershading of the shark shown in Figure 9–19.

What is countershading?

Figure 9–19. A shark's body has countershading.

171

Figure 9-20. Some birds have countershading.

Some land animals have countershading also. The underside of the animal is lighter than the top side. Look at the two birds in Figure 9-20. Notice how the outline of the bird's body is camouflaged in the second drawing. The bird with the dark underside would be easier to see from below. The bird with the light-colored underside would be more difficult to see from below. Why do you think this is so?

Warning Colorations

Some animals do not blend in with their surroundings. They have bright colors and patterns that make them stand out. The bright coloration in some animals acts as a warning to predators. Animals with this adaptation have ways to protect themselves. The bright colors warn predators that the animal may be dangerous.

Figure 9-21. A monarch butterfly (a) and a viceroy butterfly (b) look alike.

Mimicry

In **mimicry** (MIHM ih kree), one animal looks like another animal. A harmless animal will look like a more dangerous animal that has adaptations for protecting itself. Predators avoid the harmless animal because it appears dangerous. The viceroy butterfly mimics the monarch butterfly. Predators avoid the viceroy because it looks like the monarch. The monarch butterfly is bitter to taste.

Figure 9-22a shows an animal that looks like a bumblebee. Bumblebees can sting, so predators keep away from them. The animal in the picture is a robber fly. The

Figure 9-22. A harmless robber fly (a) is often mistaken for a bumblebee (b).

robber fly is not eaten by predators because it looks like a bumblebee. The snake in Figure 9-23a is a king snake. Figure 9-23b shows a coral snake. Notice how the king snake looks like a coral snake. The coral snake is poisonous so predators leave it alone. Predators avoid the king snake because its brightly colored bands resemble those of the coral snake. Observe both snakes. How would you be able to tell the difference between a king snake and a coral snake?

a

b

Figure 9-23. The harmless king snake (a) is often mistaken for a poisonous coral snake (b).

Lesson Summary

- Camouflage is an adaptation animals use to avoid their predators and hide from their prey.
- Countershading and mimicry are two forms of camouflage.

Lesson Review

Review the lesson to answer these questions.
1. What is camouflage?
2. Describe the protective coloration of a ptarmigan.
3. How is mimicry helpful to an animal?

Activity 9-2 How an Animal Adapts to Its Environment

QUESTION What adaptations can you observe?

Materials
construction paper
index card
scissors
animal picture
paste
pencil and paper

What to do
1. Study the example shown.
2. Cut out and paste your animal picture to the construction paper.
3. Paste the index card to the construction paper.
4. Fill in the information on the index card.

What did you learn?
1. How does the body covering aid in an animal's adaptation to its environment?
2. What body parts does the animal use for food getting?

Using what you learned
1. What body parts are used for both food getting and protection?
2. Explain how your animal could or could not survive in another environment.

People and Science

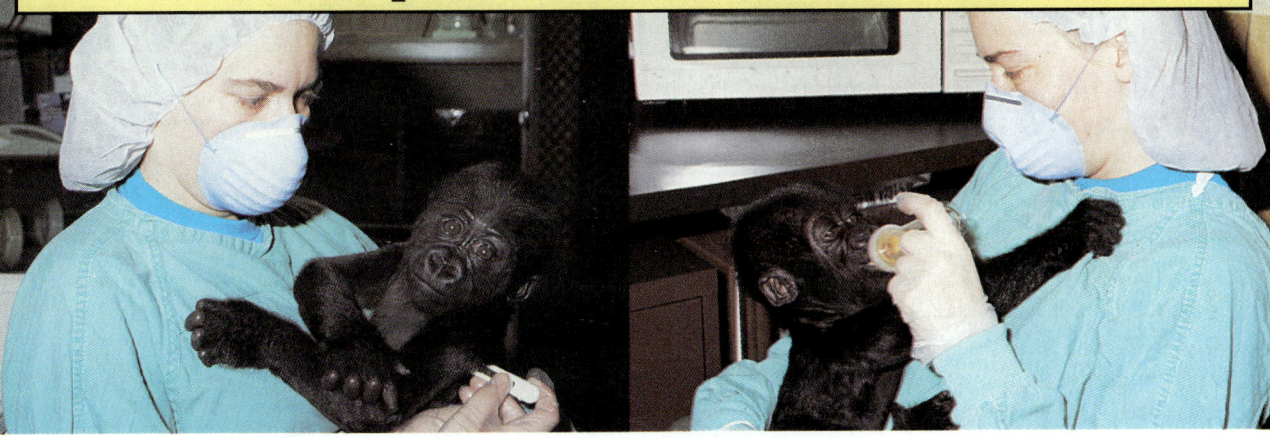

Dusty's Babies

It is the middle of the night. Dusty Lombardi gets up to give the baby its next feeding. There is something different about this baby. It is a gorilla! Dusty Lombardi is head nursery keeper at the Columbus Zoo. She is in charge of the general care for the zoo infants.

There are many jobs that Dusty must do as head nursery keeper. She works with the veterinarian to make sure the babies have healthy diets. Dusty keeps records on each baby. She watches for changes in their growth and behavior.

Dusty also trains the other nursery workers. She teaches the workers how to talk to the animals. To tell a baby gorilla "no" she makes a low grunt. She makes nice sounds to calm a baby gorilla.

Some baby animals must be fed every three hours just like human babies. Therefore, many different animals have gone home with Dusty to make sure they get fed on schedule. She has taken home cheetahs, cougars, goats, sheep, gorillas, and even a baby hippopotamus! Under Dusty's watchful eye, the animals can wander around her house until bedtime. Then they sleep in their carriers next to her bed.

The animal babies are fun to watch. But sometimes the animal babies get into trouble. Dusty raised twin gorillas in the nursery. One time she was fixing them hard-boiled eggs. While she was cooking, the twins opened the refrigerator and threw a whole bowl of raw eggs onto the floor.

Dusty enjoys watching the animals grow up. She knows she has done a good job when the baby animals can join their real families.

Chapter 9 Review

Summary

1. An animal must be able to protect itself and find food in order to live in its environment. 9:1
2. Anything that helps an animal live in its environment is called an adaptation. 9:1
3. Adaptations include body coverings and body parts. 9:1
4. Animals use camouflage as an adaptation for protection. 9:2
5. Warning coloration is an adaptation animals use to warn predators to stay away from them. 9:2

Science Words

adaptation   camouflage   mimicry
skin   countershading

Understanding Science Words

Complete each of the following sentences with a word or words from the Science Words that will make the sentence correct.

1. An adaptation in which the top side of an animal is a different color from the bottom side is _____.
2. Being able to blend into the environment is an adaptation called _____.
3. Anything that helps an animal live in its environment is called an _____.
4. The outer covering of an animal's body is called _____.
5. When one animal looks like another, it is called _____.

Questions

A. Recalling Facts

Choose the word or phrase that correctly completes each of the following sentences.

1. An animal that can live in its environment has
   (a) been absorbed.   (c) learned.
   (b) adapted.   (d) freedom.

2. When one animal looks like another, it has an adaptation called
   (a) protective coloration.
   (b) countershading.
   (c) mimicry.
   (d) warning coloration.
3. An added layer of covering some animals have on their skin is
   (a) bone. (b) feet. (c) wings. (d) scales.
4. Birds' bills are adapted for
   (a) flying.   (c) eating.
   (b) swimming.   (d) keeping warm.
5. A ptarmigan shows camouflage by
   (a) changing colors.
   (b) countershading.
   (c) mimicry.
   (d) warning coloration.
6. An animal with countershading is a
   (a) horse.   (c) bumblebee.
   (b) shark.   (d) monarch butterfly.

B. Understanding Concepts

Answer each of the following questions using complete sentences.
1. What are three extra layers of body covering that come from skin tissue?
2. What adaptation for protection does a walking stick insect have?
3. How does fur keep a polar bear warm?
4. Why is mimicry a helpful adaptation?

C. Applying Concepts

Think about what you have learned in this chapter. Answer each of the following questions using complete sentences.
1. How does a cat avoid predators?
2. Describe how one particular animal is adapted for food getting and protection.

Chapter 10
Animal Behavior

How do ducks know how to swim? How does a mother duck know how to take care of her young? How do ducklings learn to feed themselves?

Mother and ducklings

Reflex and Instinct 10:1

LESSON GOALS

In this lesson you will learn
- about animal behavior.
- about reflex behavior.
- about instinctive behavior.

A cat arches its back and hisses at a dog. A pet dog sits up and begs for food. You are reading this book. Your eyes blink. All of these actions are examples of behavior.

Figure 10-1. Everything an animal does is part of its behavior.

Behavior

Everything an animal does is part of its behavior. **Behavior** is a living thing's response to any stimulus in its environment. A **stimulus** (STIHM yuh lus) can be anything in the environment, such as light, sound, touch, smell, and so on, that causes a living thing to respond. There are two kinds of behavior. An animal is born with one kind. The other is behavior an animal learns. The behavior an animal is born with cannot easily be changed. The behavior an animal learns can be changed. Both kinds of behavior help an animal live in its environment.

What kind of behavior can be changed?

a

b

Figure 10-2. Nest building and tying shoelaces are two types of behavior.

Figure 10-2a shows a bird building a nest in a treetop where it is safe from predators. The bird does not have to learn how to build the nest. Figure 10-2b shows a girl tying her shoes. The girl had to learn this behavior.

Inborn Behavior

The behavior an animal is born with is called **inborn behavior.** Inborn behavior is not learned. An animal knows how to perform inborn behavior without being taught. Inborn behavior cannot be changed very easily.

Figure 10-3 shows ducklings hatching from their eggs. This is one example of inborn behavior. The mother duck does not tell the duckling when to break out of the shell. There is no way for the duck to teach her duckling how to break the shell. The duckling is able to peck its way out of the shell at the correct time. This is an inborn behavior.

Figure 10-3. Hatching and swimming are inborn behaviors.

Ducklings follow their mother. The mother duck leads the ducklings to water. The ducklings swim without being taught. Figure 10-3 also shows ducklings following their mother as they swim. Following and swimming are inborn behaviors for the ducklings.

Reflex

The **reflex** (REE fleks) is a simple type of inborn behavior. A reflex is an automatic action or response of an animal caused by a stimulus in the animal's environment.

What is a reflex?

a b

Figure 10-4. An owl's eyes in bright light (a) and dim light (b)

For example, when an animal moves from darkness into bright light, there is a change in the animal's eyes. In darkness, the colored parts, or irises, open wide to let in light. In bright light, the irises close and less light enters each eye. Figure 10-4 shows an owl's irises open and closed. The opening or closing action of the iris is a reflex. Light is the stimulus. The reflex action of the iris is the response.

Your eyes have this reflex also. The reflex happens without you thinking about it. You can see it happen by watching a classmate. Have a classmate close his or her eyes and hold their hands over their eyes for 30 seconds. When they remove their hands and open their eyes, you will see the irises close.

You have other reflexes. For example, you jerk your hand away if you touch a hot stove. The reflex protects you from getting burned. A reflex is usually very swift. Blinking your eyes to keep them moist is also a reflex action.

Activity 10-1 Reflex Behavior of a Sow Bug

QUESTION What is the behavior of a sow bug?

Materials
sow bug
hand lens
toothpick
paper towel
ruler
pencil and paper

What to do

1. Place the sow bug on a paper towel. Observe it with the hand lens.
2. Place the ruler in the path of the sow bug as it moves. Observe its behavior.
3. Very gently, touch the sow bug with the toothpick. Observe its behavior.

What did you learn?
1. Describe how the sow bug moves.
2. What happened when the sow bug touched the ruler?
3. What reflex actions does a sow bug show when it is touched?

Using what you learned
1. How do you know the behavior of the sow bug is inborn?
2. What kind of inborn behavior did you observe?

Instinct

Instinct (IHN stingt) is a complex type of inborn behavior. It is different from a reflex because an instinct includes more than one action.

Many songbirds spend the spring, summer, and fall in the United States and Canada. Food is plentiful during these seasons. When winter comes, food supplies are low and the birds migrate, or move, to warmer climates where there is more food.

Figure 10-5. Many songbirds migrate to warmer climates during the winter months.

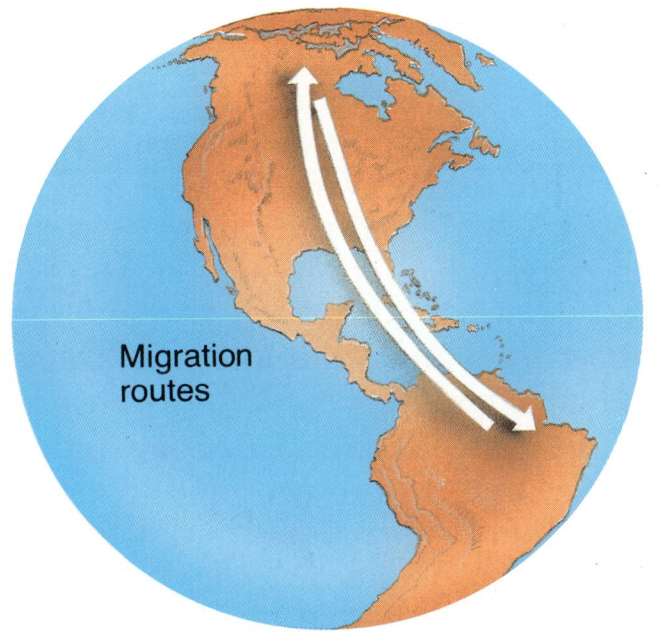

What is instinct?

Figure 10-6. The migration routes of some songbirds are thousands of kilometers long.

Migration is an example of a behavior that involves instinct. How do birds know when to fly south for the winter? Scientists are still studying bird movements to explain migration. Changes in the length of day, in temperature, or in the slant of the sun's rays are some factors that may cause migration. The lack of food may also be a cause for bird migration. Scientists study how these changes affect birds.

Figure 10-7. Canada geese migrate in a group.

Figure 10-8. Salmon migrate in search of food and a safe place to live.

Why do spiders spin webs?

Many birds migrate in groups or flocks. Figure 10-7 shows a flock of Canada geese flying in a V-shape formation. How do they know where to go? Birds may use landmarks, stars, and the sun to help them find their way. Other animals such as seals, whales, salmon, and caribou also migrate in search of food and a safe place to live and raise their young.

Spinning a web is an instinct in spiders. They spin webs to capture food to eat. Different kinds of spiders spin different kinds of webs. A spider does not learn to spin a web. Spiders spin perfect webs from the first time they try.

Figure 10-9. Spiders spin perfect webs from the first time they try.

Inborn behavior cannot easily be changed. Nest building in birds is an instinct. If a bird's nest is destroyed by wind or another animal during nest building, the bird will build a new nest in the same area. This action may be repeated many times until the young are raised. The bird does *not* learn to build the nest in a new and safer place.

Figure 10-10. Nest building is an instinct.

Lesson Summary

- An animal's behavior is everything an animal does. Some animal behavior is inborn; some is learned.
- Reflex behavior is a simple type of inborn behavior caused by a stimulus in the surroundings.
- Instinct is a complex type of inborn behavior that usually includes more than one action.

Lesson Review

Review the lesson to answer these questions.
1. What are two kinds of inborn behavior?
2. What are two animal reflex behaviors?
3. What are two animal instinct behaviors?

10:2 Learned Behavior and Social Behavior

LESSON GOALS

In this lesson you will learn
- about animal behavior that is learned.
- how some animals live together in groups.
- why some animals claim their own territories.

What is learned behavior?

Not all behavior is inborn. Some behavior is learned. **Learned behavior** is behavior that is caused by experience. Learned behavior can be changed. A dog may learn to sit up when its trainer gives a command. Because sitting up is learned behavior, it can be changed. The sitting up behavior can be "unlearned." The dog can then learn to do another action when the same command word is spoken. The dog could learn to roll over or put its paw in the trainer's hand to the old command. An animal learns a behavior by repeating the same action many times.

Figure 10-11. Learned behavior can be changed.

Think about teaching a dog to "shake hands." The learning involves three steps. First, the command word "shake" may be given. This is the signal. Second, the dog may give you its paw. At first the trainer may have to pick up the dog's paw to teach what is wanted. This is the response. Third, the desired action is rewarded by giving the dog food or praise. The dog learns to shake hands when these three steps are repeated many times. The three steps: signal, response, and reward are a pattern of learning.

Dogs can be taught much more complex behaviors. For example, they can learn to guide people who cannot see and help them avoid accidents. Learning complex behaviors takes much practice and a great deal of time.

What does it take to learn complex behaviors?

People have learned many complex behaviors. You learned to write your name and dress yourself. Playing a piano and riding a bicycle are learned behaviors. You have also learned to behave socially. What are some other difficult tasks you have learned?

Figure 10-12. Learning complex behaviors takes practice and a great deal of time.

Activity 10-2 Learning a New Behavior

QUESTION How can you learn to write with your opposite hand?

Materials
pencil and paper

What to do
1. Write your name at the top of a blank sheet of paper. Write all the letters of the alphabet across the page underneath your name.
2. If you are right-handed, try to repeat what you did in step 1 using your left hand. If you are left-handed, use your right hand.
3. Practice step 2 five minutes each day for 5 days.

What did you learn?
1. Why did you find it difficult to write with your opposite hand?
2. Why was it difficult for you to read what you wrote the first time you tried step 2?
3. Why did your writing improve after 5 days of practice?

Using what you learned
1. Why is it important to practice a new learned behavior?
2. Why would you need patience and time to teach an animal a new trick?

Social Behavior

Ants, termites, and some bees live with their own kind in groups. The group lives together in an organized way. Each member of the group performs certain jobs that are helpful to the whole group. The behavior of animals living together in an organized way is called **social behavior.** Social behavior is complex and includes both inborn and learned behavior.

Animals that live in groups have developed an effective way to protect themselves and their young. Animals that live in groups also help each other find and capture food to eat. An ant colony is a good example for the study of social behavior. The most important member of the colony is called the queen. Her task is to lay eggs. There are ants who feed and clean the queen. Other ants take care of the eggs in a kind of nursery. Some dig new tunnels and repair old ones. Some colonies have soldier ants that are specially adapted for protecting the colony. How are the ants in Figure 10-13 showing social behavior?

Prairie dogs live in groups called prairie dog colonies. Living together makes it easier for them to avoid predators. Certain animals called sentinels watch for predators. Others are free to gather food or perform different tasks. The underground tunnels in a prairie dog colony are interconnected. If a predator attacks a colony in one place, the prairie dogs can travel underground to a different place. The colony provides a safe place for prairie dogs to protect themselves and produce young.

Figure 10-13. Ants live with their own kind in groups called ant colonies.

What is social behavior?

Figure 10-14. Prairie dogs live in colonies.

Figure 10-15. Certain fish move about in groups called schools.

Certain ocean fish move about in groups called schools. A school of fish occupies a tiny area in a very large ocean. If the fish were scattered throughout the ocean, predators could eat them one by one until they were gone. The fish in the school can watch for predators in all directions and seek places where they are less likely to be attacked. If a predator does attack, it will probably only capture one or two fish while others in the school dart away to escape.

Some animals travel in herds for protection from predators. Musk oxen travel in groups to protect themselves against wolves. When wolves approach, the musk oxen form a circle. Young calves are kept inside the circle while stronger adults face out from the circle to fight off any wolves that try to attack.

Figure 10-16. Musk oxen travel in herds.

Animal Territories

Some animals live in an area they consider their own. The area within certain boundaries is considered to be their territories, and they defend it against rivals, or competitors. A **territory** is an area defended by one or more animals against rivals. Animals use their own territories as a safe place to reproduce and raise their young. Having their own territories may assure them of enough food to survive.

Some male birds take over and defend territories in order to attract a female. The songs of the male birds tell their rivals that a certain territory has been taken.

Figure 10-17. A male cardinal will take over a territory to attract a female.

What is a territory?

Figure 10-18. Wolf packs set up and defend territories.

Wolves in a pack set up territories and defend them against rival packs. A newcomer wolf that intrudes will be faced by the pack leader and forced to retreat. When an animal has a territory, or belongs to a pack, it will behave more confidently than the newcomer. The animals in the pack rarely fight among themselves. Having their own territories helps different animals survive.

Territories allow animals to extend their range over a wider area. The food in the area is then shared and more animals survive.

Figure 10-19. Territories allow animals to extend their range.

Lesson Summary

- Some animal behavior is not inborn but is learned. Learned behavior can be changed.
- Some animals live together in groups. The group is organized so that different members do different tasks for the good of the group.
- Some animals live in territories that they defend from rivals.

Lesson Review

Review the lesson to answer these questions.
1. How is learned behavior different from inborn behavior?
2. What are two reasons animals live in groups?
3. Name two different kinds of animals that live in groups.
4. How do animals that have territories keep their territories?

Language Arts Skills

Writing the Results

People who study animals spend a great deal of time just watching the animals. They take notes about everything the animals do. This helps them form general ideas of what animals are like. The ideas or answers that are found are the results of their work.

To find answers, it is necessary to have a way to measure what is observed, or seen. Knowing the different kinds of behavior aids in measuring animals' actions. The results help people understand why animals behave in certain ways.

- What are the kinds of inborn behavior?
- What is the difference between learned and social behavior?

This information tells you how to measure an animal's actions. Look at the picture at the bottom of the page. As you study the picture, answer the questions that follow.

- The beaver building the dam is showing what kind of behavior?
- Why is this action an instinct?
- Why might the buffalo be standing together in one group?
- What kind of behavior is this?

The answers to these questions tell general ideas about the actions of different animals. The answers are the results of your study.

Chapter 10 Review

Summary

1. Behavior is everything an animal does. 10:1
2. Behavior an animal is born with is called inborn behavior. 10:1
3. Inborn behavior cannot be changed very easily. 10:1
4. Reflexes and instincts are inborn behaviors. 10:1
5. Learned behavior is behavior that is not inborn. 10:2
6. Learned behavior is caused by experience; learned behavior can be changed. 10:2
7. The behavior of animals living together in an organized way is social behavior. 10:2
8. An area defended by one or more animals against rivals is called a territory. 10:2

Science Words

behavior **reflex** **social behavior**
stimulus **instinct** **territory**
inborn behavior **learned behavior**

Understanding Science Words

Complete each of the following sentences with a word or words from the Science Words that will make the sentence correct.

1. A complex type of inborn behavior is called _____.
2. The behavior of animals living together in an organized way is called _____.
3. A simple type of inborn behavior is a _____.
4. An area defended by one or more animals against rivals is called a _____.
5. Behavior an animal is born with is called _____.
6. Behavior that can be changed is called _____.
7. Everything an animal does is part of its _____.
8. Anything in the environment that causes a living thing to respond is a _____.

Questions

A. Recalling Facts
Choose the word or phrase that correctly completes each of the following sentences.
1. Animals that set up territories to defend their packs are
   (a) ants.   (b) wolves.   (c) prairie dogs.   (d) fish.
2. Behavior an animal is born with is
   (a) learned behavior.   (c) social behavior.
   (b) easily changed.   (d) inborn behavior.
3. Behavior that is learned can be
   (a) inborn.   (c) an instinct.
   (b) changed.   (d) a reflex.
4. A duckling breaking out of the shell is an example of
   (a) learned behavior.   (c) territory.
   (b) inborn behavior.   (d) social behavior.
5. The changing size of irises as you move from darkness into light is an example of
   (a) instinct.   (c) learned behavior.
   (b) reflex.   (d) social behavior.

B. Understanding Concepts
Answer each of the following questions using complete sentences.
1. Name two animals that live in groups. Name two that establish territories.
2. What is the difference between inborn and learned behavior?
3. Give two examples of reflex.
4. Give an example of an animal instinct.

C. Applying Concepts
Think about what you have learned in this chapter. Answer each of the following questions using complete sentences.
1. What might happen if a trainer tries to change an inborn behavior, such as an instinct, in an animal?
2. Describe some ways you have changed a behavior that you have learned.

UNIT 5 REVIEW

CHECKING YOURSELF

Answer these questions on a sheet of paper.
1. What are some things animals must have to live in their environment?
2. How does fur protect a polar bear in below zero temperature?
3. What is camouflage?
4. What is the difference between inborn and learned behavior?
5. What kind of behavior is shown by birds flying south for the winter?
6. What kind of inborn behavior happens when you jerk your hand away from a hot iron?

RECALLING ACTIVITIES

Think about the activities you did in this unit. Answer the questions about these activities.
1. How do fish scales look viewed under a microscope? 9–1
2. What adaptations can you observe? 9–2
3. What is the behavior of a sow bug? 10–1
4. How can you learn to write with your opposite hand? 10–2

IDEAS TO EXPLORE

1. Identify and name five different animals that you have observed or read about. For each animal, tell how it has adapted to survive in its environment.
2. Write a question you have about animals. Find the answer to your question by doing research in the library. Write the question and the answer.

3. Prepare a written or oral report about an example of animal learning. The example may be one you are familiar with because you have observed it or it may be one you have read about.

CHALLENGING PROJECT

An ant colony is an example of social behavior. Make an ant colony and observe how different ants behave in the colony. Use two glass containers so that one fits inside the other. Fill the space between them with soil. Place a plastic tube in the soil. Use it to keep the bottom soil damp. The top soil must be dry at all times. Anchor a string to the soil and let it hang to the bottom of the inner container. Place food—small pieces of lettuce, carrots, and bread crumbs—and a small dish of water in the inside container. Put ants in the new home for the colony, and fasten black paper around the outside. Remove the paper when you wish to observe the ants. Remove excess food before it spoils. Keep a record of your observations. Make drawings of the tunnels built by the ants.

BOOKS TO READ

All Kinds of Feet by Ron and Nancy Goor, Crowell Junior Books: New York, © 1984.
  This book describes how animals' feet are suited to their needs.

Fish Facts and Bird Brains: Animal Intelligence by Helen R. Sattler, Lodestar Books: New York, © 1984.
  Learn some interesting facts about the intelligence of many animals.

Orangutans: The Red Apes by Kay McDearnon, Dodd Mead: New York, © 1983.
  A book about orangutans and how they live.

UNIT 6
Sounds We Hear

The harpsichord is a keyboard instrument with strings and hammers. Musical sounds are produced when the strings are struck by hammers. Today, many musicians use a musical keyboard instrument that produces sounds electronically. A synthesizer can imitate the sounds of other instruments such as a piano, violins, and drums. It can also reproduce some natural sounds such as wind and thunder. Yesterday and today, musical instruments have been and are being used to produce pleasing sounds for us to hear.

Harpsichord—1581

Electronic music

Chapter 11
Making and Using Sound

Think about how you have used sounds today. How did you wake up? Perhaps you heard an alarm or someone calling you to get up. After you got to school you used sounds too. What sounds have you used at school today?

Sounds are useful every day.

Properties of Sound

11:1

LESSON GOALS

In this lesson you will learn
- sounds are caused by vibrations.
- volume is the loudness or softness of sound.
- pitch is the highness or lowness of sound.
- frequency is the speed of sound vibration.

There are sounds around you all the time. If you listen carefully, you can hear sounds around you right now. You can hear many sounds when you are very quiet.

Sounds can warn you of danger. The sound of a police officer's whistle warns you of possible danger. The sound of a fire alarm is a warning that there may be a fire. When you hear this warning sound, you need to leave your classroom, home, or any building by using the nearest fire exit.

How do we use sound?

Figure 11-1. Sounds can warn us of danger.

Figure 11–2. Waves crashing on a beach

Why are loud sounds harmful?

There are many different kinds of sounds. Many sounds are pleasant. Pleasant sounds can make you feel happy or relaxed. Most people would agree that music is a pleasant sound. Many people also like to listen to the sounds of nature. Some people like the sound of ocean waves crashing onto a beach. Others like the song of a bird or the sound of wind as it blows through the leaves of a tree. What kinds of sounds do you like?

Most people would agree that loud noise is an unpleasant sound. Besides being unpleasant, very loud sounds can damage your ears. This damage is sometimes lasting and can affect your sense of hearing. You should protect your ears when you are around loud sounds.

Sounds are around us all the time. We use sounds to communicate with one another. The radio, TV, telephone, and record player are some forms of communication that depend upon the use of sound. What other forms of communication use sound?

Making Sound

A **vibration** (vi BRAY shun) is the back and forth movement of particles of matter. Sounds are caused by vibrations. When you strum a guitar string, it moves back and forth. The vibrations of the guitar string make a sound. Sometimes you can see objects vibrate. The guitar string looks fuzzy as it vibrates. It looks fuzzy because it is moving. The tuning fork in Figure 11-3 makes sound by vibrating. How do you know the tuning fork is vibrating?

What causes sound?

Figure 11-3. Sounds are caused by vibrations.

You can also feel some vibrations. The sound of your voice is caused by vibrations. You can feel the vibrations if you place your fingers against your throat while speaking.

When an object vibrates back and forth, it pushes on small particles of air, or air molecules, causing the air to vibrate. These moving air molecules bump into other nearby air molecules, causing them to vibrate, too. In this way, the sound vibrations move through air or other matter.

As you may recall, energy can do work and work is done when anything is moved. You just learned that sound can cause matter to move. Since sound can cause matter to move, we know that sound is a form of energy.

203

Activity 11-1 Observing Vibrations

QUESTION What do sound vibrations look like?

Materials
small mirror tile
paste
rubber sheet
empty can
heavy rubber band
flashlight
drawing paper
pencil and paper

What to do

1. Stretch the rubber sheet over one end of the empty can as shown.
2. Attach the rubber sheet to the can with the rubber band.
3. Paste the mirror to the rubber sheet and set it aside to dry. Handle the mirror carefully. The mirror should be slightly off center.
4. Darken the room. Have your partner shine the flashlight on the mirror. Observe the reflection on the wall.
5. Sing a musical scale into the open end of the can. Draw a picture of the reflection.
6. Sing loudly, then softly into the can. Draw the reflection.
7. Make different kinds of sounds. Draw the reflection of each sound.

What did you learn?

1. Compare and contrast the pictures of the reflections produced when you:
   a. sang a musical scale.
   b. sang softly, then loudly.
   c. made different sounds.
2. What kind of sound (a, b, or c) produced the most unusual pattern?

Using what you learned

1. What caused the patterns you saw in the reflections?
2. How did the pictures of your reflections compare with others? Why might they be different?

Properties of Sound

Sounds can be loud or soft. The loudness or softness of a sound is called **volume** (VAHL yum). Loud sounds have more volume and soft sounds have less volume.

What is volume?

Figure 11-4. Sounds can be loud or soft.

Figure 11–5. The musician can make loud or soft sounds with the guitar.

How are loud sounds made?

As you know, sound is a form of energy. Larger amounts of energy produce louder sounds. If a guitar player uses a lot of force to strum a guitar string, it will make a loud sound. You can say

Much energy = Loud sound
Less energy = Soft sound

Vibrations can affect the volume of sounds. Loud volume sounds are made by strong vibrations. Sounds with soft volume are made by weaker vibrations. How can you make a sound very loud or very soft?

Define pitch.

Pitch is the highness or lowness of a sound. High-pitched sounds are made by objects that vibrate or move back and forth very fast. Low-pitched sounds are made by objects that vibrate more slowly.

Musical instruments produce sounds of different pitches. The instruments are made of strings or tubes of various sizes. Look at the saxophones in Figure 11-6. Notice the difference in their sizes. The small saxophone makes sounds with a high pitch. The large saxophones make sounds with a low pitch.

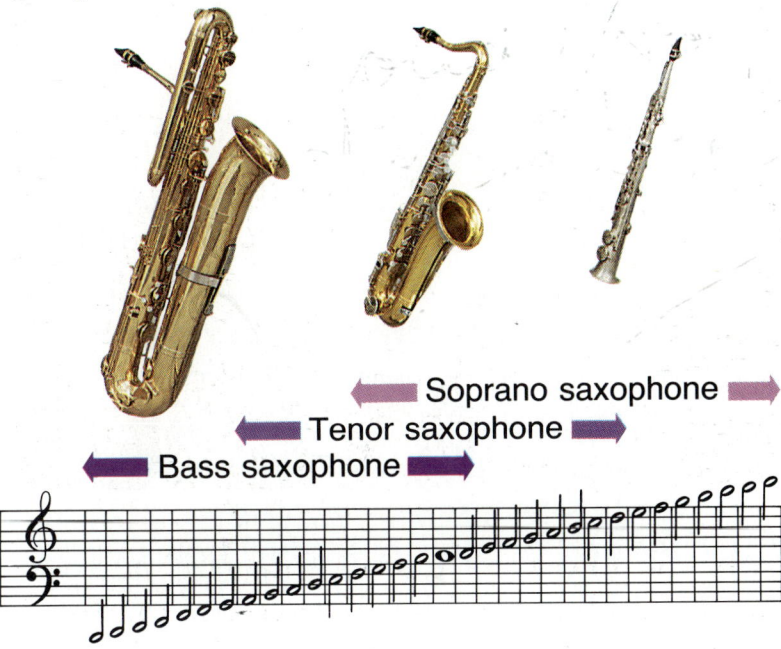

Figure 11-6. Saxophones of different sizes make sounds of different pitches.

Sound is produced by the vibration of a reed on the mouthpiece. A reed is a thin, flat piece of wood that vibrates when air is blown past it. The vibrating reed causes the column of air in the tube part of the saxophone to vibrate. The tube part of the smaller saxophones is shorter than the tube part of the larger saxophones.

When a musician blows into the smaller saxophone, the shorter column of air in the tube vibrates very fast, producing a sound with a higher pitch. When a musician blows into the larger saxophone, the longer column of air vibrates more slowly, producing a sound with a lower pitch.

Activity 11-2 Investigating Pitch

QUESTION How can you make a musical instrument?

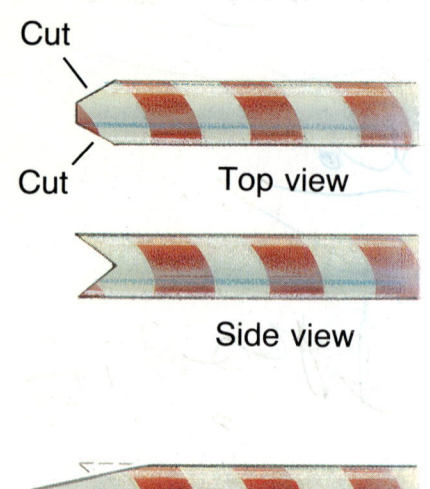
Cut
Cut
Top view

Side view

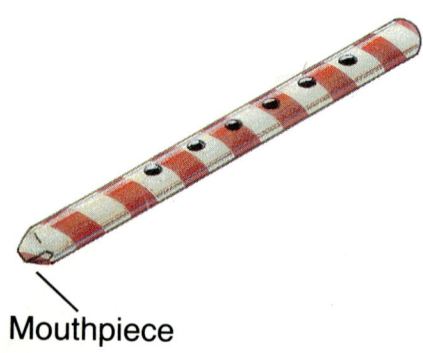
Side view

Mouthpiece

Materials
4 straws
scissors
pencil and paper

What to do
1. Trim one end of a straw with the scissors as shown.
2. Crease this end of the straw as shown. Form your lips tightly over your teeth. Blow on the mouthpiece until you are able to make a sound.
3. Use the pencil point to carefully make 4 to 6 small holes along your straw.
4. Cover and uncover the small holes with your fingers as you play your instrument.
5. Record your observations.

What did you learn?
1. How did you change the volume of the sound?
2. How did you change the pitch of the sound?

Using what you learned
1. What caused the sounds?
2. What kind of sound would be made if you used a shorter straw? A longer straw? Experiment and find out.

The number of times an object vibrates in one second is called its **frequency** (FREE kwun see). An object that vibrates many times in one second has a high frequency. The object will make a higher pitched sound. An object that vibrates fewer times in one second has a lower frequency. It makes a lower pitched sound. The tuba in Figure 11-7 is much longer than the trumpet. When played by a musician, the shorter column of air in the trumpet will vibrate faster and produce a sound with a higher pitch than the sound produced by the tuba.

What is frequency?

Figure 11-7. Tuba and trumpet being played

Lesson Summary

- The sounds around us are caused by vibrations.
- Volume is the loudness or softness of a sound.
- Pitch is the highness or lowness of a sound.
- Frequency is the speed of sound vibrations.

Lesson Review

Review the lesson to answer these questions.

1. What causes sound?
2. What is the volume of a sound?
3. What kind of sound is made by high frequency vibrations?

11:2 Behavior of Sound

LESSON GOALS

In this lesson you will learn
- vibrating objects cause the matter around them to vibrate.
- sound waves travel through gases, liquids, and solids.
- sound waves cannot travel in a vacuum.
- sound waves can be reflected and absorbed.

Figure 11-8. Vibrations inside and outside your classroom cause sounds you can hear.

What sounds can you hear in your classroom right now? Vibrations inside your classroom cause sound waves. Sound waves travel in all directions away from their sources. Some of the sound waves may travel to your ears. You are able to hear your classmates moving, pencils tapping, and papers rustling.

Sound waves travel through different kinds of matter. Sound waves can travel through gases. You know sound travels through air. Air is a gas. Sound can travel through liquids and solids, too. Anyone who lives next door to a person who likes to play music loudly knows that sound can travel through solids. What is one example you know of how sound travels through liquids? We are able to hear sounds all around us because sound can travel through different kinds of matter.

You know that sound waves are caused by the back and forth movements of particles of matter. Sound travels only through matter. Sound waves cannot travel through empty space. Empty space has no matter. A **vacuum** (VAK yewm) is space that contains no matter. Sound cannot travel in a vacuum.

Figure 11-9. Sound waves from the radio can travel through solids, liquids, and gases.

What is a vacuum?

Speed of Sound

Look at Figure 11-10. The first part shows the distance some children can run in one second. The second part shows the distance a speeding car can travel in one second. The third part shows the distance sound can travel in one second in air that is 20°C. Sound waves travel much faster than children or cars. How far can the child run in one second? How far can the car travel? How far can sound travel in one second?

Figure 11-10. Comparing the speeds of a child, car, and sound

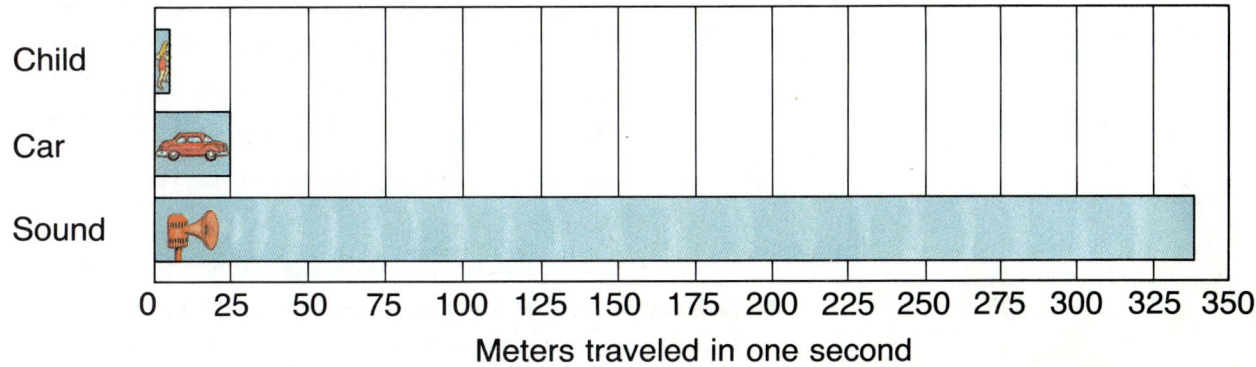

211

There are some things that travel faster than sound. Some airplanes travel about five times faster than sound. Light travels much faster than sound. You would have to travel more than seven times around Earth to equal the distance light travels in one second.

Figure 11-11. Light travels faster than sound.

Recall the example from Lesson 3:1. At a baseball game you may have seen the batter swing and hit the ball before you heard the crack of the bat. Why do you think this happened?

Sound waves travel at different speeds in different kinds of matter. Table 11-1 shows how fast sound waves travel in one second through different kinds of matter. Sound usually travels fastest in solids. Use Table 11-1 to answer the following questions. Through what kind of matter does sound travel slowest? Through what kind of matter does it travel fastest?

Through what state of matter does sound travel fastest?

Table 11-1 Speed of Sound Through Matter

Matter at 20°C	State	Meters per second
Air	Gas	340
Water	Liquid	1,500
Brick	Solid	3,600
Wood	Solid	3,800
Iron	Solid	5,200

212

Activity 11-3   Reflected and Absorbed Sound

QUESTION   How can sound be reflected and absorbed?

Materials
windup clock
shoe box
pieces of wood
aluminum foil
cloth
cotton
carpet scraps
floor tile
pencil and paper

What to do
1. Use a pencil to make a hole in one end of the shoe box.
2. Put the windup clock in the box. Place the clock at the end of the box opposite the hole. Put the lid on the box. Place your ear to the hole and listen for the ticking sound.
3. Cover the inside of the box with each of the materials. Listen for the ticking sound each time.

What did you learn?
1. What material was in the box when you could hear the clock best?
2. What material was in the box when it was hardest to hear the clock?

Using what you learned
1. Which materials reflected sound best?
2. Which materials absorbed sound best?
3. What kinds of materials do you think are used to soundproof rooms?

Figure 11-12. Noise levels in each of these classrooms would be different.

What is an echo?

Reflected and Absorbed Sounds

The path of a sound wave can be changed. Sound waves bounce off or are reflected by some kinds of matter. Smooth, hard surfaces are the best reflectors of sound. The walls and floor of most gyms are smooth and hard. You may have noticed that sounds made in a gym seem loud and have echoes.

An **echo** is a reflected sound. In an echo, sound waves bounce off a surface and are reflected back toward their source. Have you ever heard an echo of your voice? What kind of matter reflected the sound waves?

Not all matter reflects sound waves. Soft or rough surfaces absorb sound waves. Look at Figure 11-12. One classroom has carpet and drapes. The other has a wood floor and no drapes. In which classroom would sound be absorbed better?

Lesson Summary

- Vibrating objects cause matter around them to vibrate.
- Sound waves travel through gases, liquids, and solids.
- Sound waves cannot travel in a vacuum.
- Sound waves can be reflected and absorbed.

Lesson Review

Review the lesson to answer these questions.

1. Through what kinds of matter can sound travel?
2. Name two things that can travel faster than sound.
3. What is an echo?

People and Science

Speaking Clearly

How do you communicate with your friends? Sometimes we use our hands or make a funny face to tell someone what we are thinking. Most of us make ourselves understood by using our voices. We want people to understand us when we talk.

Jim Allen is a speech therapist (THER uh pust) for a school. Teachers send students to Jim when they are concerned about a student's ability to speak clearly.

Jim knows that it is important to have the student feel relaxed with him. He listens carefully to find out what speech problem the student has. He may notice that a student cannot pronounce the letter "l" or the letter "r." If a student stutters, Jim will also talk with the student's family. Jim wants to know when the stuttering occurs.

Learning to speak correctly is like learning to play a musical instrument. Both skills must be practiced every day. Students enjoy using a tape recorder to practice making letter sounds correctly. Jim often uses a video tape recording of each student as well. Jim uses video tape to show the student how the tongue and face help form sounds.

Sometimes Jim has a student who has trouble hearing. He knows that the child cannot repeat a sound that cannot be heard. When this happens, Jim suggests that the child's hearing be tested.

Two afternoons a week Jim also works with adults at a hospital speech clinic. Some adults need to learn how to speak again after an injury, illness, or if they are under stress.

Chapter 11 Review

Summary

1. Sounds are caused by vibrations.   11:1
2. Volume is the loudness or softness of a sound.   11:1
3. Strong vibrations produce loud sounds.   11:1
4. Weak vibrations produce soft sounds.   11:1
5. Pitch is the highness or lowness of a sound.   11:1
6. Frequency is the speed of a vibration.   11:1
7. Sound waves travel through gases, liquids, and solids.   11:2
8. Sound waves cannot travel in a vacuum.   11:2
9. Sound waves travel fastest in solids and slowest in gases.   11:2
10. Sound waves can be reflected and absorbed.   11:2

Science Words

vibration   **pitch**   **vacuum**
volume   **frequency**   **echo**

Understanding Science Words

Complete each of the following sentences with a word or words from the Science Words that will make the sentence correct.

1. A reflected sound is called an _____.
2. The loudness or softness of a sound is called _____.
3. The number of times an object vibrates in one second is called _____.
4. A space that contains no matter is called a _____.
5. The back and forth movement of particles of matter is called _____.
6. The highness or lowness of a sound is called _____.

Questions

A. Recalling Facts

Choose the word or phrase that correctly completes each of the following sentences.

1. High pitched sounds are made by objects that vibrate
   - (a) slowly.
   - (b) in a vacuum.
   - (c) very fast.
   - (d) gently.
2. Sound travels fastest in
   - (a) solids.
   - (b) gases.
   - (c) liquids.
   - (d) vacuums.
3. Surfaces that absorb sound are usually
   - (a) smooth, soft.
   - (b) rough, soft.
   - (c) rough, hard.
   - (d) smooth, hard.
4. An echo is a sound that is
   - (a) reflected.
   - (b) absorbed.
   - (c) refracted.
   - (d) faster than light.
5. Sound travels slower than
   - (a) a speeding car.
   - (b) thunder.
   - (c) a child.
   - (d) light.

B. Understanding Concepts

Answer each of the following questions using complete sentences.

1. How are sounds produced?
2. What are the properties of sound?
3. What causes an echo? Why might a person sometimes hear more than one echo?
4. Give an example of sound traveling through a solid, a liquid, and a gas.

C. Applying Concepts

Think about what you have learned in this chapter. Answer each of the following questions using complete sentences.

1. How can sounds be harmful and helpful?
2. Why is there no sound in a vacuum?

Chapter 12
How We Hear Sound

Look at the ears of the different animals on this page. The ears of all these animals are the same in one important way. They all gather sound waves. Compare them to human ears.

A variety of ears—all for hearing sound

All About Ears   12:1

LESSON GOALS

In this lesson you will learn
- the outer ear catches sound waves.
- your ear has three parts the outer ear, middle ear, and inner ear.
- the middle ear contains small bones called the hammer, anvil, and stirrup.
- the eustachian tube keeps the pressure on the eardrum balanced.

Hearing is a very important sense. Your ears and brain help you understand the sound waves you hear. Your sense of hearing helps you use sound in many ways. You probably learned to talk because you heard other people talking to you. You can also use your sense of hearing to tell where or how far away an object might be. In what other ways do you use your sense of hearing?

How do people use their sense of hearing?

Figure 12-1. Dancers use their sense of hearing in order to dance in time with the music.

219

How We Hear

How does the outer ear help you hear?

The ear is divided into three sections: outer, middle, and inner ear. The cup-shaped outer ear gathers sound waves. They move through the ear canal to the eardrum. The eardrum is a thin, tightly stretched layer of skin between the outer ear and middle ear. Sound waves cause the eardrum to vibrate. The vibrating of the eardrum transfers sound waves into the middle ear.

In the middle ear are the hammer, anvil, and stirrup. The **hammer, anvil,** and **stirrup** are small bones connected to each other and to the eardrum. As the eardrum vibrates, these bones begin to vibrate. Find each bone in Figure 12-3. Notice how the bone called the hammer is shaped like a hammer. How do you think the other bones got their names?

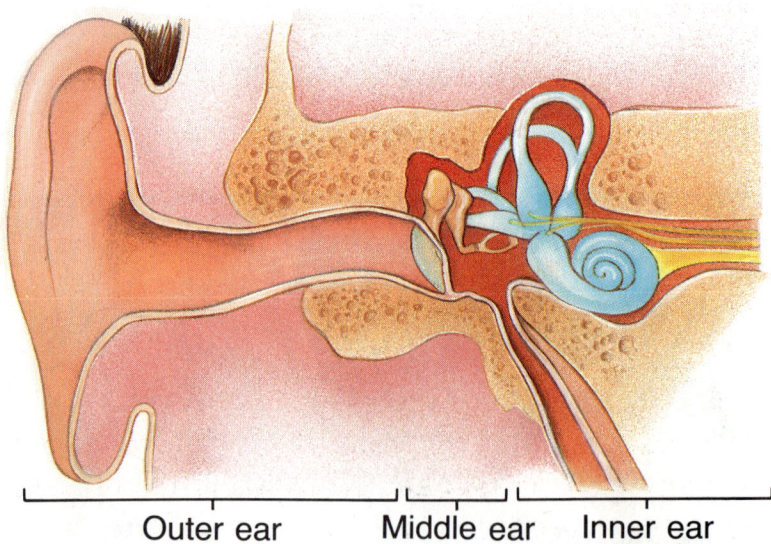

Figure 12-2. The three main parts of the ear are the outer ear, middle ear, and inner ear.

The hammer, anvil, and stirrup transfer the sound waves to the inner ear when they vibrate. The inner ear is shaped like a snail's shell. Find the inner ear in Figure 12-2. The inner ear is filled with liquid.

There are also many very tiny hair-like cells in the inner ear. The sound waves cause the liquid in the inner ear to vibrate. This vibration causes the hair-like cells to vibrate, too. The cells send signals to the auditory (AWD uh tor ee) nerve. The **auditory nerve** is the main nerve that leads from the ear directly to the brain. The auditory nerve sends the signals from the tiny cells to the brain. The brain helps you understand the sounds you hear.

What is the auditory nerve?

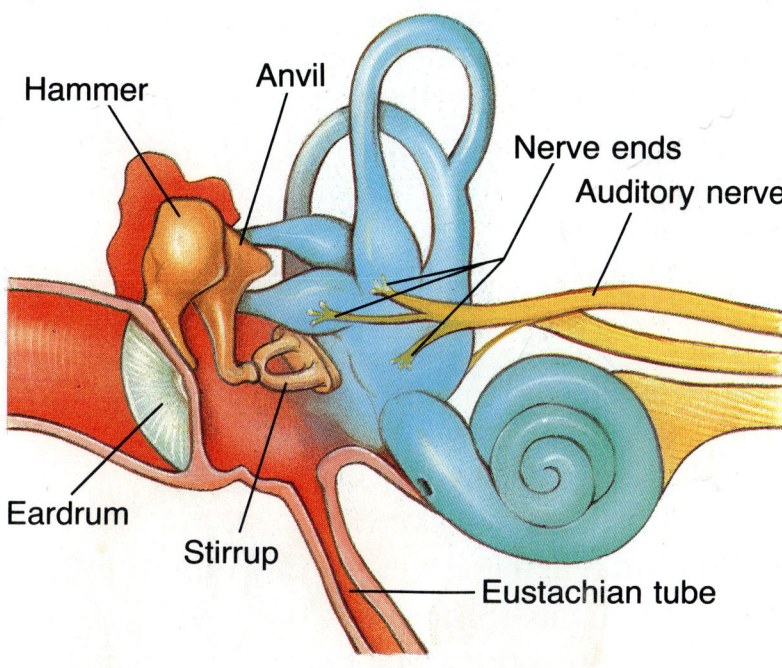

Figure 12-3. The parts of the middle and inner ear in detail

The middle ear also contains the **eustachian** (yoo STAY shun) **tube.** The eustachian tube connects the middle ear and the back of the throat. The eustachian tube keeps the pressure on both sides of the eardrum the same. Without the eustachian tube, differences in air pressure could cause the eardrum to become stretched very tightly. Then the eardrum would not be able to vibrate as well and it would be more difficult to hear sounds.

221

Figure 12–4. Traveling by airplane

Why do your ears sometimes "pop"?

You may have felt your eustachian tubes working while you were riding in an elevator or an airplane. When you go up or down rapidly, your ears sometimes "pop." This is caused by air passing through your eustachian tubes in order to make the pressure on both sides of the eardrum the same.

It is possible for germs from a cold or sore throat to enter the middle ear through the eustachian tube. The result is often an ear infection. The "blocked" feeling in your ears when you have a cold and an ear infection can affect your sense of hearing.

Disease or injuries can affect your sense of hearing. Loud sounds can damage the eardrum. Disease or injury can damage the hammer, anvil, and stirrup. If any part of your ear is damaged, you may suffer some loss of hearing.

Lesson Summary

- The outer ear gathers sound waves.
- Your ear has three parts the outer ear, middle ear, and inner ear.
- The middle ear contains the hammer, anvil, and stirrup.
- The eustachian tube keeps the pressure on the eardrum balanced.

Lesson Review

Review the lesson to answer these questions.
1. Why are most ears cup-shaped?
2. What is the eardrum?
3. How can your ears be damaged?

Science and Technology

Fly the Noisy Skies

The human ear can be damaged by sounds that are too loud. Other noises may not be damaging but can still cause discomfort. The noise made by an airplane propeller, for example, is often very annoying to passengers in the plane. Scientists are trying to find ways to reduce that noise.

As more propeller blades are used to increase speed, noise increases. The blades create one frequency, or tone, whereas jet engines create sound over different frequencies. The steady tone is more comfortable for passengers.

As the propeller spins, it causes vibrations in the wing or the engine mount. The vibrations travel along the wing to the body of the plane. These vibrations in the form of sound waves travel through the body into the aircraft cabin.

Scientists are experimenting with different-shaped propeller blades to reduce noise. Another idea is to build a sound absorbing layer around the body of the plane.

Although jet planes are faster and can fly higher and farther, propeller planes are better suited for some shorter distance flying. The propeller planes use less fuel and require shorter runways for takeoff and landing. In 1986, a large propeller plane was tested at a speed of 968 kilometers per hour. If fuel-efficient, fast propeller planes are to be used in place of jets, scientists must learn how to control cabin noise.

12:2 Hearing Sounds

LESSON GOALS

In this lesson you will learn
- sounds with low volume are hard to hear.
- the pitch of a sound affects whether a sound can be heard.
- most people can hear sounds with frequencies between 20 and 20,000 vibrations in one second.
- about proper ear care.

Figure 12-5. The ear toward a sound hears it louder than the ear that is away from the sound.

Having two ears is better than having one. Two ears allow you to receive more sound vibrations. For this reason, you are able to hear softer sounds. Two ears allow you to tell from what direction a sound is coming. The ear toward the sound hears it louder than the ear that is away from the sound.

Activity 12-1 Finding Direction Using Sound

QUESTION How are two ears better than one?

Materials

noisemakers   cotton pad
blindfold   pencil and paper

What to do

1. Work with nine other students. Have each of the nine students choose a noisemaker.
2. Make a large circle with one person in the center wearing a blindfold.

3. Have the person in the center cover one ear with a cotton pad.
4. Have someone in the circle make a sound with a noisemaker. Have the person in the center point to the direction from which the sound seems to be coming.

5. Do this three times with different people around the circle making the sound.
6. Repeat the activity. This time the center person should listen with both ears.
7. Change the center person and repeat steps 2 to 6.

What did you learn?
1. How many times did you find the right direction using one ear?
2. How many times did you find the right direction using both ears?

Using what you learned
1. Which sound was easiest to find? What direction was it coming from?
2. Which sound was hardest to find? What direction was it coming from?

You Cannot Hear All Sounds

Sound waves with little energy have low volume. Sounds with low volume are hard to hear. Some sounds have such little energy that they cannot be heard at all.

The pitch of a sound also affects whether a sound can be heard. Most people can hear the sound produced by an object that vibrates between about 20 and 20,000 times in one second. People's ears are best able to hear sounds that vibrate between 500 and 5,000 times a second. Most musical instruments make sounds between 30 and 4,000 vibrations a second. Most people's voices make sounds between 100 and 800 vibrations a second.

Why can you not hear some sounds?

Figure 12-6. Sounds most people can hear

Dogs are able to hear higher-pitched sounds than humans. Dogs can hear sounds with vibrations of more than 20,000 times a second. Special whistles can be used to call dogs. These dog whistles vibrate with a frequency of more than 20,000 times a second. People cannot hear this sound. Why can people not hear this sound?

Figure 12-7. Special whistles can be used to call a dog.

Why do dogs hear some sounds that people do not?

Figure 12-8. The bat is able to avoid bumping into objects by using sound waves as a guide.

Many bats are also able to make and hear very high-pitched sounds. This ability explains why many bats are able to fly so well in the dark. Bats send out a very high-pitched sound. This sound forms an echo and bounces back to the bat. In this way, the bat knows where it is flying and keeps from bumping into objects.

Activity 12-2 Measuring Sounds

QUESTION How can you measure the noise level?

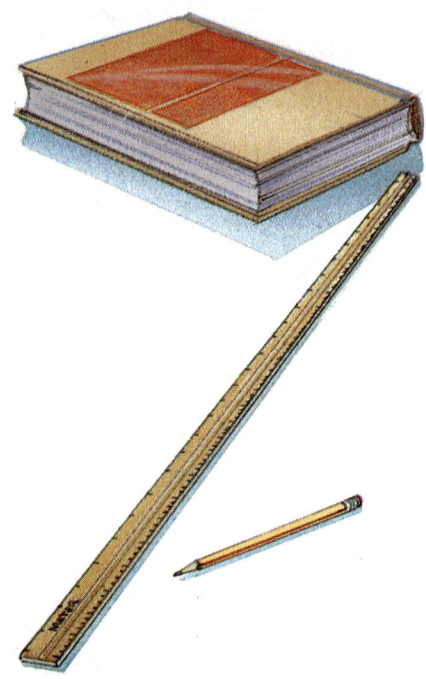

Materials
book
meter stick
pencil and paper

What to do
1. Find two places in or near your school. One should be noisier than the other.
2. Stand facing away from your partner.
3. Have your partner begin reading aloud in a normal voice. Slowly move away from your partner. Stop when you cannot understand what your partner is reading.
4. Measure and record the distance.
5. Repeat steps 2 to 4 at the second place.

What did you learn?
1. At which place did you hear your partner at a greater distance?
2. Which place had a higher noise level?

Using what you learned
1. What areas of your school are noisy?
2. What could be done to lower the noise level around your school?

Ear Care

Taking care of your ears is usually a very simple task. As you know, loud sounds can damage your ears. It is important to avoid very loud sounds. If you must be around loud sounds, you should wear some kind of ear protection. Special ear plugs are one kind of ear protection.

How can you protect your ears from loud sounds?

Figure 12-9. Ear protection should be worn around sources of loud sounds.

Sometimes wax may form in your ears. This wax can usually be removed by gently cleaning with a washcloth. You should not try to clean your ears by putting anything into them. Even a cotton swab can damage your eardrum. Sometimes, too much wax may build up in the outer ear. If this happens, you should see a doctor. The doctor can remove the wax without damaging your eardrum.

Figure 12-10. Child being examined for a possible ear infection

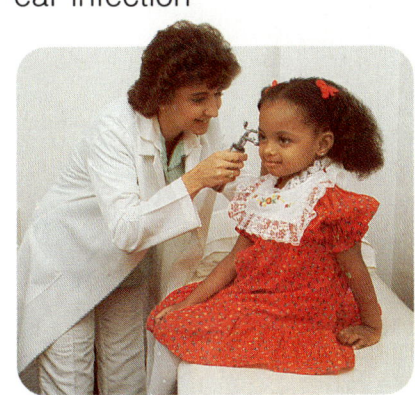

What usually causes an earache?

When you have a cold, you may get an earache. This is usually caused by an infection in the middle ear. It is quite common for children to have ear infections. A doctor can prescribe medicine to help stop the infections. To avoid problems, follow the rules for ear care listed in Table 12–1.

Table 12–1   Ear Care

1. Never insert any object into your ears.
2. Avoid loud sounds; protect your ears around loud sounds.
3. Have a doctor remove ear wax whenever necessary.
4. Wash your ears every day.
5. Blow your nose gently; keep your nostrils open when you sneeze.

Lesson Summary

- Sounds with low volume are hard to hear.
- The pitch of a sound affects whether a sound can be heard.
- Most people can hear sounds with frequencies between 20 and 20,000 vibrations in one second.
- Proper ear care is important.

Lesson Review

Review the lesson to answer these questions.
1. What affects whether a sound can be heard?
2. Why are two ears better than one?
3. What range of frequencies can be heard by most people?
4. Why should you never put anything into your ears?

Language Arts Skills

Inferring

Most people know that a button is pushed to make a doorbell ring. They also know that ringing a doorbell is a way of telling someone that a visitor is at the door. When doorbells ring, people automatically think that someone is at the door. They have made an inference, or reached a conclusion. Read the following. Make an inference.

- What animal is nearby if you hear meowing?

Scientists often make tests to gather facts. They examine the facts. Then they reach a conclusion.

In the middle 1600s, Robert Boyle studied facts about air. He worked with an air pump that was made in Germany. He did a test with a watch. He put the watch inside a glass globe. Then he used the air pump to take all of the air out of the globe. As air was taken out of the globe, it became harder and harder to hear the ticking of the watch. When no air was left inside the globe, the ticking could not be heard at all. Boyle then let air back into the globe. The ticking sound became louder and louder. Boyle examined these facts and reached a conclusion about sound waves.

- What did Boyle decide carried the waves, or vibrations, that his ears picked up as sounds?

Suppose that Boyle had not carefully noticed all the important facts. Suppose that in the middle 1600s Boyle could not possibly have had all the tools, such as the air pump, that made this test possible. His conclusion might have been very different. It would probably have been incorrect. However, it might have been the only conclusion he could have reached based on the facts he was able to collect. Inferences that people make are only as correct or complete as the facts that are used to make them.

Chapter 12 Review

Summary

1. The outer ear gathers sound waves. 12:1
2. Sound waves cause the eardrum to vibrate. 12:1
3. Your ear has three parts: the outer ear, middle ear, and inner ear. 12:1
4. The middle ear contains the hammer, anvil, and stirrup. 12:1
5. The eustachian tube keeps the pressure on the eardrum balanced. 12:1
6. Sounds with low volume are hard to hear. 12:2
7. The pitch of a sound affects whether a sound can be heard. 12:2
8. Most people can hear sounds with frequencies between 20 and 20,000 vibrations in one second. 12:2
9. Proper ear care is important to protect the sense of hearing. 12:2

Science Words

hammer **stirrup** **eustachian tube**
anvil **auditory nerve**

Understanding Science Words

Complete each of the following sentences with a word or words from the Science Words that will make the sentence correct.

1. A small bone in the middle ear shaped like a carpenter's tool is called the _____.
2. The main nerve that leads from the ear directly to the brain is the _____.
3. A small U-shaped bone in the middle ear is called the _____.
4. The tube that connects the middle ear and back of the throat is called the _____.
5. The small block-shaped bone in the middle ear is called the _____.

Questions

A. Recalling Facts
Choose the word or phrase that correctly completes each of the following sentences.
1. The thin, tightly stretched layer of skin between the outer and middle ear is the
   (a) hammer.   (b) eardrum.   (c) anvil.   (d) stirrup.
2. Most people are able to hear sounds that vibrate between
   (a) 30 and 4,000 per second.   (c) 100 and 1,000 per second.
   (b) 20 and 20,000 per second.   (d) 100 and 800 per second.
3. Bats send out
   (a) low pitched sounds.   (c) medium pitched sounds.
   (b) high pitched sounds.   (d) no sounds.
4. Which organ helps you understand the sounds you hear?
   (a) brain   (c) auditory nerve
   (b) eardrum   (d) inner ear
5. The part of the ear that keeps the pressure on both sides of the eardrum the same is the
   (a) hammer.   (c) eardrum.
   (b) auditory nerve.   (d) eustachian tube.

B. Understanding Concepts
Answer each of the following questions using complete sentences.
1. Why are two ears better than one?
2. Why are you not able to hear special whistles used to call dogs?
3. What are some problems that can affect your hearing?
4. What causes your ears to "pop"?

C. Applying Concepts
Think about what you have learned in this chapter. Answer each of the following questions using complete sentences.
1. What are three ways you use sound?
2. Write a short paragraph explaining how you hear.
3. How should you take care of your hearing?

UNIT 6 REVIEW

CHECKING YOURSELF

Answer these questions on a sheet of paper.
1. Make a list of sounds that are helpful and warn of danger.
2. What is an echo?
3. How do you hear sound?
4. What are some ways sound can affect you?
5. What are some ways you could lower the noise level in a room?
6. What kinds of surfaces reflect sound? What kinds absorb sound?
7. What two things affect whether or not you can hear a sound?
8. Through what kind of matter does sound travel fastest?
9. Why can sound not travel in a vacuum?
10. What is volume?
11. What is pitch?
12. What is frequency?

RECALLING ACTIVITIES

Think about the activities you did in this unit. Answer the questions about these activities.
1. What do sound vibrations look like? 11–1
2. How can you make a musical instrument? 11–2
3. How can sound be reflected and absorbed? 11–3
4. How are two ears better than one? 12–1
5. How can you measure the noise level? 12–2

IDEAS TO EXPLORE

1. Make your own list of sounds that are pleasant to you. Make a second list of unpleasant sounds. Describe how you feel when you hear each sound.
2. If you have a cassette recorder, record a variety of sounds. Play the recording for your classmates. See whether your classmates can identify each sound.
3. Investigate what kinds of materials are used for soundproofing in buildings. Prepare a report describing the kinds of materials used for soundproofing. Also include in your report a list of the kinds of places where soundproofing materials are used and the reasons why these materials are needed.

CHALLENGING PROJECT

Make a ripple tank with your teacher's help. Watch waves travel through the water. Explore how waves travel and are reflected. Compare the movement of the waves in the ripple tank to the movement of sound waves through air.

BOOKS TO READ

All About Sound by David Knight, Troll Associates: Mahwah, NJ, © 1983.
    A book of activities and questions about sound.

Sound and Music by Neil Ardley, Franklin Watts: Danbury, CT, © 1984.
    Learn how sound waves create beautiful music.

Sound Experiments by Ray Broekel, Childrens Press: Chicago, © 1983.
    Fun experiments to help you learn about sound.

UNIT 7
Oceans of Earth

Since ancient times, people have been drawn to the oceans of Earth. Their interests include everything from scientific study to simple enjoyment of the ocean's special beauty. Some people traveled over the oceans in search of the unknown. Others developed devices to provide ways for people to explore the fascinating world at the bottom of the ocean. From simple diving suits to complex diving machines, we have come a long way in our efforts to learn about the oceans of Earth.

Jacques Costeau

Modern diving equipment

Chapter 13
The Ocean Around Us

Pretend you are a visitor to Earth from another planet. Suppose you cannot control the direction of your spacecraft. You will be able to land safely but you cannot control where you land. You know that over 70 percent of Earth's surface is covered by water. Where do you think you would be most likely to land, in the ocean or on solid ground?

Earth: the "water" planet

Oceans and Seas   13:1

LESSON GOALS

In this lesson you will learn
- the difference between oceans and seas.
- the importance of oceans and seas.

On Earth's surface there are three very large open bodies of salt water called oceans. They are the Atlantic, Pacific, and Indian Oceans. The Arctic Ocean around the North Pole is also a very large body of water. Smaller bodies of salt water are called seas. Seas may be nearly surrounded by land with only one opening to an ocean. All Earth's oceans are connected.

Figure 13-1. The oceans of the world

239

Figure 13-2. Food from the ocean

What are some natural resources from oceans and seas?

The oceans and seas of the world supply us with many natural resources. These include food, oil, natural gas, and many valuable minerals. The world's oceans also affect the climates of places on Earth.

We must protect our oceans and seas. They are part of the world's water cycle. Earth's water is used over and over again. It moves from place to place by evaporation, condensation, and precipitation. No other resource on Earth is more valuable than water.

Lesson Summary

- Large open bodies of salt water are oceans.
- Seas are smaller bodies of salt water nearly surrounded by land.
- Oceans and seas are important as sources of natural resources and because of their part in the water cycle.

Lesson Review

Review the lesson to answer these questions.
1. What are oceans?
2. What are seas?
3. Name two natural resources found in oceans.

Activity 13-1 Using a Globe

QUESTION Where are oceans and seas located?

Materials
globe
world map
pencil and paper

What to do

1. Find dry land and water areas on the globe.
2. Locate these bodies of water.
   a. Pacific Ocean
   b. Atlantic Ocean
   c. Indian Ocean
   d. Arctic Ocean
   e. Mediterranean Sea
   f. Caribbean Sea
   g. Red Sea
   h. North Sea
3. Label these bodies of water on your world map.

What did you learn?

1. Which body of water is the largest?
2. Which body of water is the smallest?
3. How many ways could you sail into or out of the Pacific Ocean? The Atlantic Ocean?

Using what you learned

1. Name one way seas and oceans are different.
2. Some people say there is just one large world ocean. Why do they say this?

13:2 Properties of Ocean Water

LESSON GOALS

In this lesson you will learn
- ocean water contains dissolved materials.
- the presence of ocean water affects the climate of nearby land.
- the ocean provides many natural resources.

What makes ocean water different from tap water?

Ocean water is very different from water you drink. Ocean water is salty. It contains many different kinds of materials that have been dissolved or broken down into very small particles. The rocks of the land and the gases of the air are some of the materials dissolved in the ocean.

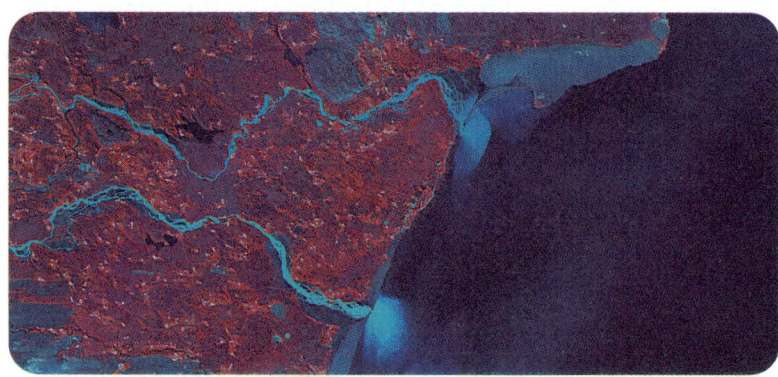

Figure 13-3. The rocks of the land and the gases of the air are dissolved in ocean water.

Why is the ocean salty?

The salty taste of ocean water comes from the dissolved rocks that are found in large amounts in the ocean. Every raindrop that falls and every snowflake that melts runs back into the ocean with a tiny bit of dissolved rock in it. The amount of dissolved materials carried to the ocean is very small. But over a long time, they have collected in large amounts in the ocean and have made the water salty.

The ocean is salty because water is evaporated from the ocean to return to the land as part of the water cycle. Since only the pure water evaporates, the salt is left behind to make the oceans salty. The kinds of salts dissolved in the ocean are the same everywhere. The salts are the same in the Atlantic Ocean and the Pacific Ocean. However, the amount of dissolved salts does vary from place to place. Although there are many different kinds of material dissolved in the ocean, the most abundant material is the same as plain table salt. In fact, the salt you may have used at home this morning was probably once dissolved in the ocean.

Figure 13-4. The sun heats ocean water (a), water evaporates from the ocean (b), clouds form from evaporated water (c), water returns to Earth as precipitation (d).

Figure 13-5. Table salt

Air is also dissolved in ocean water. Oxygen and carbon dioxide are two gases important to life in the ocean as well as life on land. Both of these gases are dissolved in ocean water. These dissolved gases allow fish and plants to live in the ocean. In places where pollution or other conditions have taken the gases from the ocean, there are no fish.

Figure 13-6. The temperature of ocean water varies around the world.

The temperature of ocean water varies around the world. The surface ocean water near the equator gets as warm as 28°C. The surface water at the North and South Poles may be as cold as −1°C. At both poles, the deeper water is about the same temperature as the surface. But in most of the ocean, deeper water is colder. The water at the bottom of the oceans of the world is colder than −1°C.

Because water heats slower and cools slower than the land, climates near the ocean are always cooler in the summer and warmer in the winter than inland climates.

Activity 13-2 A Property of Ocean Water

QUESTION Why is it easier to swim in the ocean?

Materials

tall narrow jar
pencil with eraser
metric ruler
"fresh water"
thumbtack
ball point pen
paper towel
"ocean water"
pencil and paper

What to do

1. Fill the jar with "fresh water" to within 1 cm of the top.
2. Place the pencil with a thumbtack in the eraser, eraser down, into the water. Use the ball point pen to mark the pencil to show the water level.
3. Remove the pencil and dry it with a paper towel. Measure the length, in millimeters, of the pencil above the water level mark. Record the length.
4. Repeat steps 1 to 3 using "ocean water."

What did you learn?

1. In which water did the pencil float higher?
2. Predict how the pencil will float if you add a spoonful of salt to the ocean water. Try it and record your results.
3. Explain what caused the results.

Using what you learned

1. Why is it easier to swim in the ocean than in fresh water?
2. Can a boat carry a heavier load in fresh water or salt water? Why?

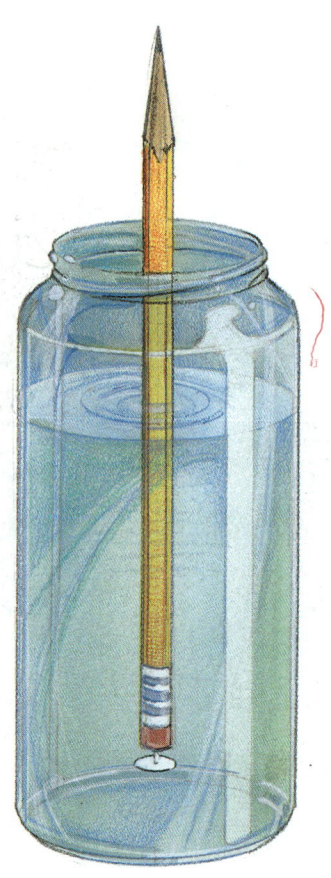

In some places the temperature difference between land and ocean can be noticed on a daily basis. On hot summer days the land is quickly heated while the ocean remains cool. Cool air from over the ocean blows onto the land in the afternoons, in the form of cool breezes. Early in the morning just before daylight, the land may cool down so much that it is actually cooler than the ocean. When this happens the flow of air changes and the cool night air from the land blows out over the ocean.

Fresh Water from Ocean Water

Even though over 70 percent of Earth is covered by water, many parts of the world do not have enough fresh water. The oceans could be a source of fresh water.

Dissolved salts can be removed from ocean water. To remove the salts, ocean water is evaporated. It is then condensed back to liquid water. The salts are left behind. Evaporation is one way to change ocean water to fresh water. Several countries have large factories to change ocean water to fresh water.

What is one way to get fresh water from ocean water?

Figure 13-7. Ocean water can be changed to fresh water at a desalination plant.

For now, this idea for getting fresh water is very expensive. Perhaps you will be one of the scientists who finds an inexpensive way to change ocean water to fresh water!

Ocean Resources

Valuable minerals are found in ocean water or deposited on the ocean floor. Dissolved minerals are removed from ocean water by evaporation. Ocean water is placed in large ponds on land. The water evaporates leaving the salts and minerals behind. The minerals are collected and changed to useful products.

Figure 13-8. Evaporation pond

Some ocean animals remove certain minerals from ocean water. Calcium carbonate (KAL see um • KAR buh nayt) and silica (SIHL ih kuh) are two minerals that make up the skeletons and shells of some animals. When these animals die, their skeletons and shells remain. More animals build on the skeletons, and over many years, thick layers of these skeletons are built up. In some places, rocks formed from these skeletons are used for building materials.

Figure 13-9. The shells of some ocean animals contain calcium carbonate and silica.

Figure 13-10. Manganese nodules

What are nodules?

Some minerals are found on the ocean floor in ball-like lumps. These lumps are called **nodules** (NAHJ ewlz). Manganese (MANG guh neez), cobalt, and nickel are valuable metals found in nodules. These nodules can be collected from the ocean floor.

Manganese is an important metal. It is used in the steel industry. Manganese removes impurities from steel to make a clean metal. Manganese is also used in some paints, dyes, and fertilizers.

People get oil and natural gas by drilling wells on land. They also get oil and natural gas from drilling into the ocean floor. Oil and natural gas are sometimes found in the rocks of the ocean floor in shallow water. From large platforms, wells are drilled into the rocks. The oil and natural gas are brought to shore by ships or pipelines. What are some ways we use gas and oil?

Figure 13-11. Offshore drilling for oil and natural gas

Besides minerals and oil products, there are many important gases found dissolved in ocean water. Two of the most important gases are oxygen and carbon dioxide. Oxygen and carbon dioxide from the air dissolve in water at the surface. Living things in the ocean use oxygen and carbon dioxide to live in their environment.

Figure 13-12. Living things in the ocean use oxygen and carbon dioxide.

Lesson Summary

- Ocean water contains dissolved minerals and salts.
- The presence of ocean water affects the climate of nearby land.
- The ocean provides many natural resources.

Lesson Review

Review the lesson to answer these questions.

1. What are two ways dissolved salts enter the ocean?
2. What is one way to change ocean water to fresh water?
3. Name three metals found in nodules on the ocean floor.
4. Where are oil and natural gas drilled for in the ocean?

13:3   Ocean Movements

LESSON GOALS
In this lesson you will learn
- ocean water is always in motion.
- ocean water movements include waves, tides, and currents.

Ocean water is always in motion. An **ocean wave** is energy that makes the surface of the ocean move up and down. Energy is transmitted through the water by waves. Ocean waves can be caused by wind or Earth movements. Ocean waves caused by wind begin as small ripples. As the wind blows harder energy is gained, and the ocean waves increase in size. Big waves are caused by strong winds.

What causes ocean waves?

Waves have a high point and a low point. See Figure 13-13. The high point of a wave is the **crest.** The low point of a wave is the **trough.**

Ocean waves slow down as they move into shallow water. As they slow down, the crests get closer together. This causes the waves to get steeper until they fall over. We say the wave "breaks" onto the shore. The area where waves break onto the shore is called the surf.

Figure 13-13. Waves have a crest and a trough.

The same Earth movements that cause earthquakes can set huge waves in motion. An ocean wave caused by such Earth movements is called a **tsunami** (soo NAHM ee). Tsunamis travel unnoticed in the open ocean. They become dangerous when they come near the shore. In shallow water the waves stack up and become very high. They may reach as high as 30 meters. They can travel as fast as 700 kilometers per hour. Tsunamis may cause much damage when they reach the shore. Entire towns and villages have been destroyed by tsunamis.

Figure 13-14. Tsunami damage

Tides

The rise and fall of ocean water levels is called a **tide.** Ocean tides are caused by the pull of the force of gravity between Earth and moon. The closer objects are together, the stronger the pull of gravity is between them. Thus, the moon pulls harder on the side of Earth closer to it than on the opposite side. Since water can move more easily than rock, the oceans show the effects of the moon's pull of gravity more than the continents. This action causes ocean water to bulge outward on the side of Earth facing the moon. On the opposite side, the moon's pull is greater on the solid Earth than on the ocean water. This action causes water on the opposite side to bulge away from the moon. Therefore, two bulges form in the oceans, one facing the moon and one opposite the moon. These bulges stay in the same relative positions as Earth rotates underneath them.

What is a tsunami?

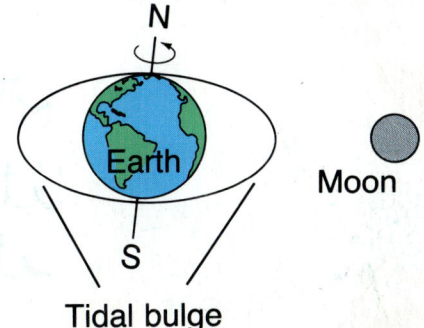

Figure 13-15. Ocean tides are caused by the moon's pull of gravity on Earth.

251

Figure 13-16. High and low tide at Los Angeles, California

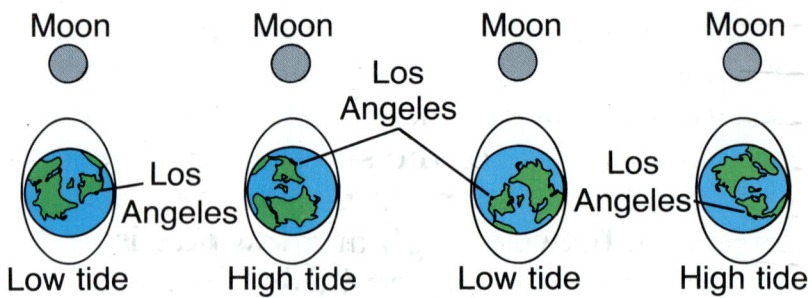

A certain place on Earth moves through these bulges as Earth rotates. This causes the water level to rise at this place. This is called high tide. As the place moves out of the bulge, the water level goes down. This is called low tide. The tidal bulge is like the crest of a very large wave that would seem to travel around the world as Earth rotates.

a

b

Figure 13-17. High tide (a), low tide (b) at Eagle Harbor, Washington

Tides are also affected by the shape and size of the ocean basin. Most places on Earth have two high tides and two low tides each day. But, because of the shape of the ocean basin, some places have only one high tide and one low tide each day. In some places, it is hard to see the difference between high and low tide. In other places, there can be a 15 meter difference.

The height of the tides also depends on the position of the sun, moon, and Earth. During the full and new moon phases the gravitational pull of the sun and moon are in the same direction. At these times the difference between high and low tide is large. During the first and third quarter phases the sun and moon do not pull in the same direction. At these times the difference between high and low tide is small. Although the sun's pull of gravity on Earth affects the ocean tides, the sun is much farther away from Earth than the moon. Therefore, the sun has less effect on tides than the moon.

Energy from the Ocean

Scientists are looking for ways to use the energy from ocean water movements. One way uses the moving water of tides to turn electric generators. By using the energy from ocean water movements we would be able to burn less gas, coal, and oil as fuel for making electricity. As you know, Earth's supply of coal and oil will not last forever. Making electricity from the moving water of tides is called **tidal power.**

The first tidal power plant was built on the coast of France in 1966. There are only a few such plants in the world. To use tidal power, the difference between high and low tide must be very large. Also, the water must flow through narrow channels into a bay. At high tide, water is stored behind the plant in the bay. As the tide moves out, water flows through the generator of the tidal power plant to make electricity.

Where and when was the first tidal power plant built?

Figure 13-18. Tidal power plant

Activity 13-3 Ocean Currents

QUESTION What causes deep ocean currents?

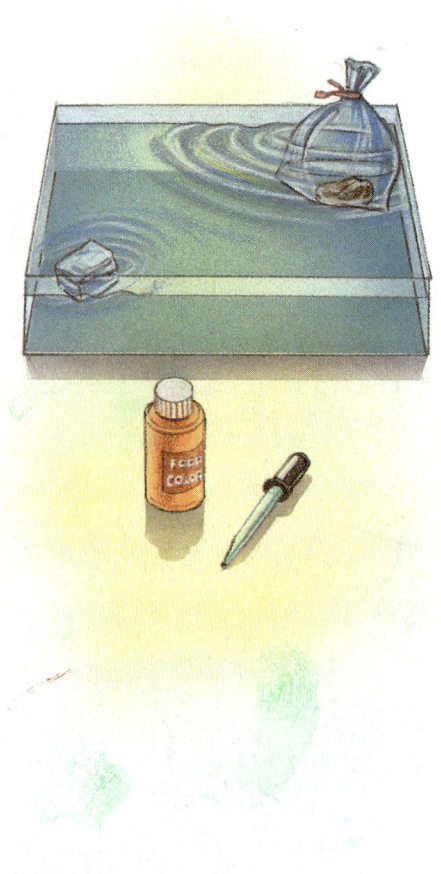

Materials
plastic storage box
tap water
small plastic bag
food coloring
hot tap water
dropper
rock
ice cube
twist tie
pencil and paper

What to do

1. Fill the plastic box ¾ full of tap water. Place it on a table.
2. Place the rock in the plastic bag. Fill the bag ½ full of hot water. Tie the bag closed.
3. Place the bag of hot water in one corner on the bottom of the plastic box.
4. Float the ice cube in the opposite corner from the bag.
5. Use the dropper to add 4 drops of food coloring to the water next to the ice cube.
6. Observe the food coloring carefully for several minutes.
7. Make a drawing of what you observed.

254

What did you learn?

1. Where was the water colder? Warmer?
2. Describe the movement of the food coloring.

Using what you learned

1. How is your container of water like the ocean?
2. The oceans are coldest at the North and South Poles. They are warmest at the equator. How might ocean water move between the poles and the equator?
3. Why does cold water sink?
4. Why does warm water rise?

Currents

Ocean water moves from place to place. The horizontal flow of ocean water is called a **current.** Wind blowing across the surface of water can cause a current. General wind patterns in the atmosphere produce a number of large ocean currents. Certain surface currents move water from near the equator toward the poles. They carry warm water to the poles. The Gulf Stream carries warm water from the Caribbean Sea northward along the eastern coast of the United States. Other surface currents flow toward the equator. They carry cold water to the equator from areas nearer the poles.

There are also deep water currents. These currents help balance the flow of water caused by the surface currents. Deep water currents move cold water from the poles toward the equator.

What are ocean currents?

Figure 13-19. Wind blowing across the surface of water can cause a current.

255

Figure 13-20. World ocean currents

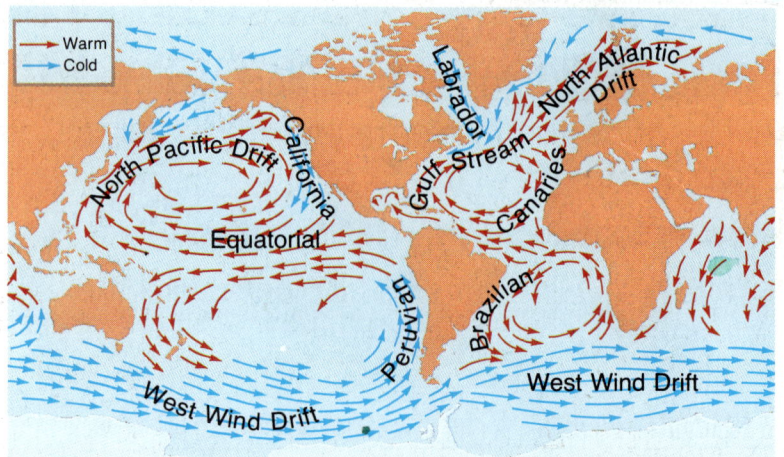

Ocean currents are important. They can affect climate. The Gulf Stream helps keep coastal areas of the eastern United States warmer than might be expected. Deep currents rising toward the surface bring nutrients up into the surface waters. A **nutrient** (NEW tree unt) is a food substance needed by living things in order to survive. These nutrients are used by fish and other ocean life. Look at Figure 13-20. Why do you think the ocean along the Atlantic coast is warmer than along the Pacific coast of the United States?

Lesson Summary

- Ocean water is always in motion.
- Ocean water movements include waves, tides, and currents.

Lesson Review

Review the lesson to answer these questions.
1. When does a tsunami become dangerous?
2. What causes tides?
3. Name two reasons currents are important.

Science and Technology

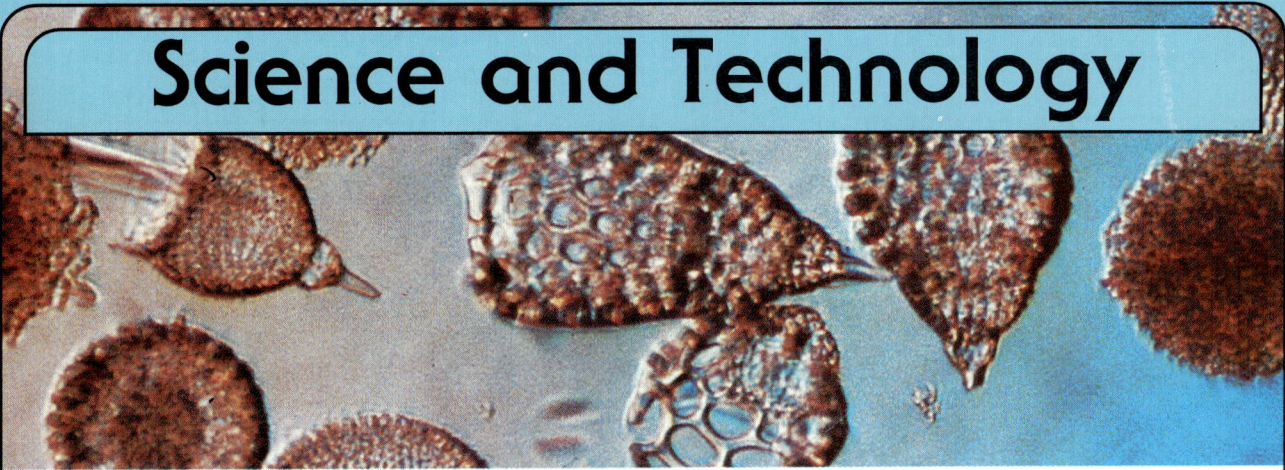

The Golden Gift

What is the busiest energy producer in the ocean? If you were to look at an ocean you would not see this tiny plant, but it would be all around you.

Diatoms (DI uh tahmz), tiny one-celled golden algae, are found in the ocean and some fresh waters. There are hundreds of thousands of diatoms in a bucket of ocean water. Each cell is covered by a hard glittering shell made of silica. Diatoms are the most important plants in the ocean. Tossed and churned by the constant movement of ocean currents, diatoms are kept exposed to sunlight. They use the sunlight as energy to produce large amounts of oxygen and food for other sea life. A large humpback whale may feed on several hundred billion diatoms every few hours.

When diatoms die, their tiny silica shells drop to the ocean floor in layers called ooze. Millions of years of build-up of these layers have made the oceans a good source for silica. Some of these layers are also found on land where the oceans once flowed. The largest deposit is in California, where layers are 420 meters thick. These deposits are called diatomite mines.

Diatomite is ground into powder and used to polish and clean metals. It is also used to make dynamite. Another use for diatomite is to filter liquids. For example, dry-cleaning fluids are reused because they are expensive. The fluids are filtered through diatomite to remove dirt. Raw sugar is filtered through diatomite in the process of making table sugar. Diatomite is also used to filter fruit juices, liquid soap, and vegetable oils.

Diatoms have many important uses. Both the living plants and the shells are needed by many other plants and animals.

Chapter 13 Review

Summary

1. Much of Earth's surface is covered by water. 13:1
2. Oceans and seas are important for their natural resources. 13:1
3. Certain minerals are dissolved in ocean water. 13:2
4. Fresh water can be made from ocean water. 13:2
5. The temperature of ocean water varies around the world. 13:2
6. The presence of oceans affects the climate of nearby land. 13:2
7. Ocean water is always in motion. 13:3
8. Waves, tides, and currents are examples of ocean water movements. 13:3

Science Words

nodules   trough   tidal power
ocean wave   tsunami   current
crest   tide   nutrient

Understanding Science Words

Complete each of the following sentences with a word or words from the Science Words that will make the sentence correct.

1. The rise and fall of ocean water levels is called a _____.
2. Mineral lumps found on the ocean floor are called _____.
3. The high point of an ocean wave is the _____.
4. The up and down motion of surface water is called an _____.
5. Making electricity from moving water of tides is called _____.
6. Earthquakes can cause a large destructive ocean wave called a _____.
7. The low point of a wave is the _____.
8. The horizontal movement of ocean water is called a _____.
9. A food substance needed by living things to survive is a _____.

Questions

A. Recalling Facts

Choose the word or phrase that correctly completes each of the following sentences.

1. What percent of Earth's surface is covered by oceans and seas?
   - (a) less than 29
   - (b) about 50
   - (c) less than 65
   - (d) over 70
2. The most abundant dissolved substance in ocean water is like
   - (a) table salt.
   - (b) nitrogen.
   - (c) manganese.
   - (d) sulfur.
3. Dissolved salts can be removed from ocean water to produce fresh water by
   - (a) tidal power.
   - (b) warm currents.
   - (c) evaporation.
   - (d) waves.
4. Tides are caused by
   - (a) wind.
   - (b) gravity.
   - (c) currents.
   - (d) high temperatures.
5. The two most important gases dissolved in ocean water are
   - (a) hydrogen and oxygen.
   - (b) hydrogen and helium.
   - (c) oxygen and carbon dioxide.
   - (d) oxygen and silica.

B. Understanding Concepts

Answer each of the following questions using complete sentences.

1. How do minerals get into ocean water?
2. Describe what happens to the surface temperature of ocean water as you go from the poles toward the equator.
3. How does wind speed affect the size of waves?
4. Describe the motion of deep water currents.

C. Applying Concepts

Think about what you have learned in this chapter. Answer each of the following questions using complete sentences.

1. Why is the ocean an important resource?
2. How do oceans affect climates?

Chapter 14
Probing the Ocean

Ocean water is a habitat for many kinds of living things. Some ocean life is too small to be seen without a microscope. Other ocean life, such as a whale, may be larger than a school bus. What are the names of some living things found in the ocean? In what parts of the ocean do they live? How do scientists study ocean life?

Ocean life

Ocean Life 14:1

LESSON GOALS

In this lesson you will learn
- where different kinds of ocean life can be found.
- names of some kinds of ocean life.
- characteristics of different forms of ocean life.

Ocean life can be found anywhere in the world's oceans. Plants are food for many kinds of ocean life. Plants need sunlight and other nutrients to live. Rivers and ocean currents carry nutrients to coastal areas. These waters are warmed by sunlight and the nutrients are mixed throughout the water. Therefore, most of the ocean life is found in shallow, warm waters along the edges of continents. Plants and animals that drift and move by surface currents are called **plankton** (PLANG tun). Most plankton are so small they can only be seen with a microscope. Many animals feed on plankton.

Larger organisms like sea turtles and fish are nekton (NEK tun). They swim and float near the surface. Squid, dolphins, and whales are also nekton. **Nekton** are free-swimming animals.

Benthos (BEN thahs) are plants and animals that live on the ocean bottom. Some, like barnacles and oysters, attach themselves to the ocean bottom. Others move along the ocean bottom. Clams and other shelled animals burrow into the mud and sand on the ocean bottom.

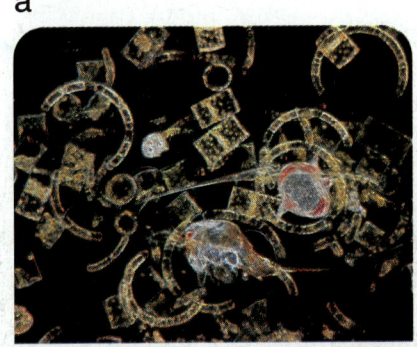

Figure 14-1. Plankton (a), squid (b), and a clam (c)

Figure 14-2.

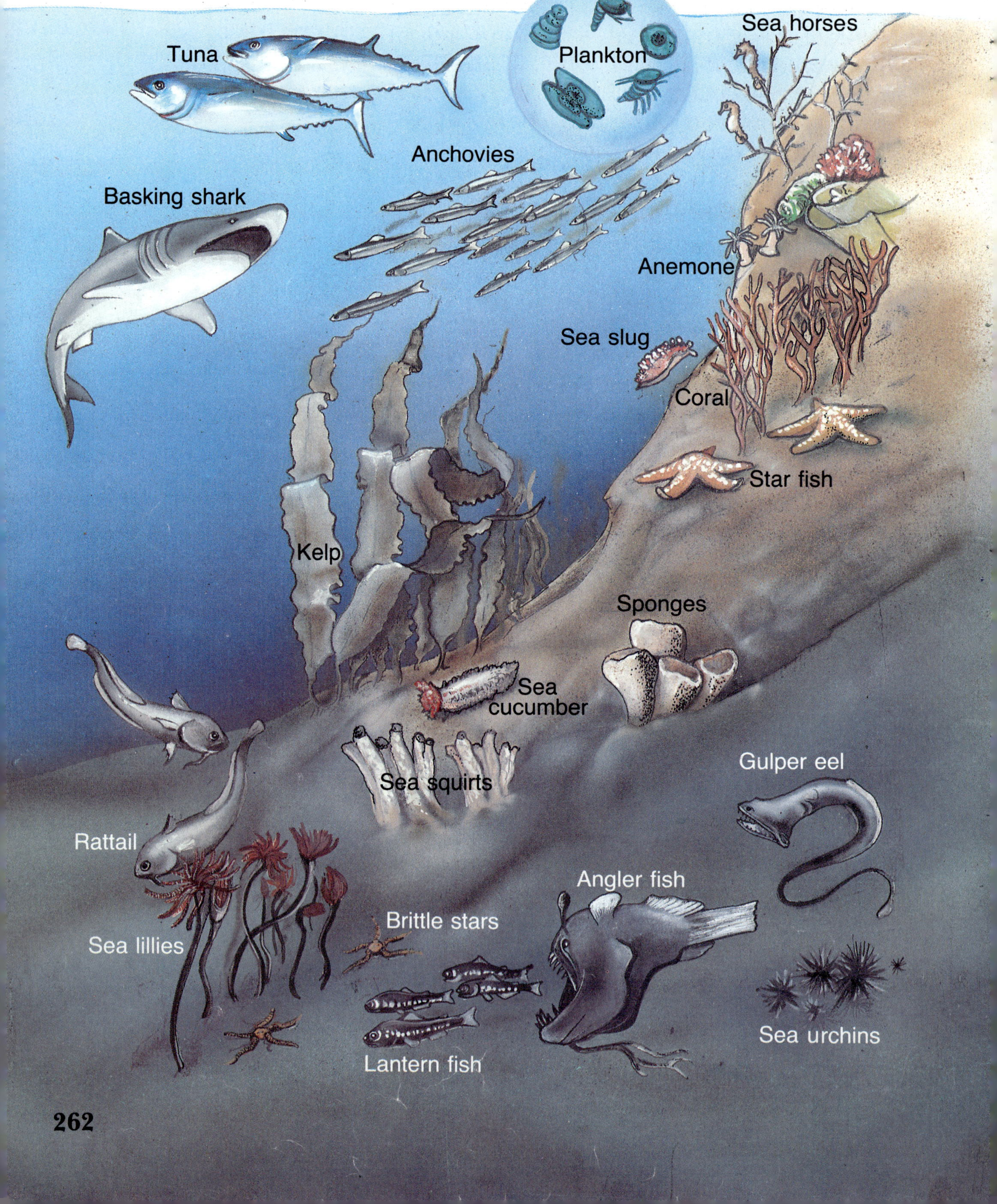

Scientists have been able to photograph some of the animals that live on the bottom of the deep, open ocean. They are strange looking creatures with shapes different from shallow-water fish. Some have body parts that glow in the dark. Since there is no sunlight in the deep ocean, these lights help these animals communicate with or attract other animals.

One example is the angler fish. The angler fish has an unusual adaptation. The angler fish has an antenna-like organ on the top of its head. The angler fish can make the tip of this organ glow. Other deep sea creatures are attracted by the light. When a curious animal comes too close, it becomes dinner for the angler fish.

Deep ocean animals prey on each other or feed on the remains of dead plants and animals that drift down from the waters above them. Figure 14-2 shows some examples of ocean life.

Lesson Summary

- Most ocean life is found in shallow, warm waters along the edges of continents.
- Some organisms in the ocean are plankton, nekton, and benthos.
- Fish found on the deep, open ocean bottom are different in appearance from shallow-water fish.

Lesson Review

Review the lesson to answer these questions.
1. What are plankton?
2. What are nekton?
3. What are benthos?

14:2 Mapping the Ocean

LESSON GOALS

In this lesson you will learn
- ocean floor mapping is done from ships.
- the features of the continental shelf, slope, and ocean floor.

Few people have ever seen the ocean floor. Most of the ocean is too deep. Light does not reach the bottom. Suppose you could see the basins of the oceans and seas. A basin is the land that holds the water. It is impossible to drain the ocean. However, scientists have "seen" much of the ocean floor. Scientists use sound waves and their echoes to map the ocean floor.

Figure 14-3. Sonar instruments are used to map the ocean floor.

How do scientists map the ocean floor?

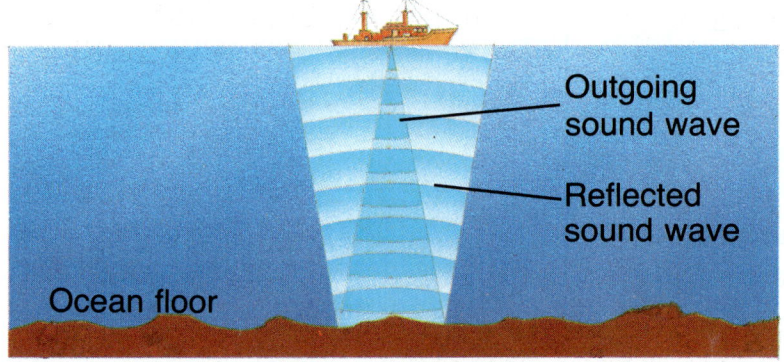

Ocean floor mapping is done from ships. The ships use sonar as a method of mapping the ocean floor. **Sonar** is an instrument that uses sound waves to locate objects in the water. The sonar wave travels through the water. It bounces off the ocean bottom back to the ship. The deeper the ocean bottom, the longer time it takes the sonar wave to come back. Sonar waves return quickly when the water is shallow.

264

Scientists use the length of time it takes the sonar wave to return to the ship to make maps of the ocean floor. They have located broad flat plains, long mountain chains, deep trenches, and volcanoes. Ocean floor features are just as varied as features on land.

Continental Shelf

The **continental shelf** is the gently sloping part of the continent covered by shallow ocean water. The shelf slopes downward like a theater aisle, but not quite as steep. The width of the shelf varies from a few meters to about 1,300 kilometers. The average width is 70 kilometers.

The continental shelf is very important to industry. The world's best fishing is done along the continental shelf. Many countries have large fleets of fishing boats and ships. Fishers catch haddock, herring, cod, halibut, and tuna. They also gather the shellfish such as lobsters, oysters, and clams that live on the floor of the shelf. The fish and shellfish are caught and taken to markets and canneries.

Where is the world's best fishing done?

Figure 14-4. Fishing is done along the continental shelf.

Figure 14-5. Kelp

What is kelp?

Fish are not the only source of food in the oceans. **Kelp** is brown seaweed. Kelp grows very fast. Kelp and other seaweeds are rich in minerals. Matter in seaweed is used in some ice cream, candy, jellies, and salad dressings. Seaweed is used in some medicines and cosmetics too. Seaweed is also used to make fertilizers that help crops grow.

Figure 14-6. A view of the ocean bottom

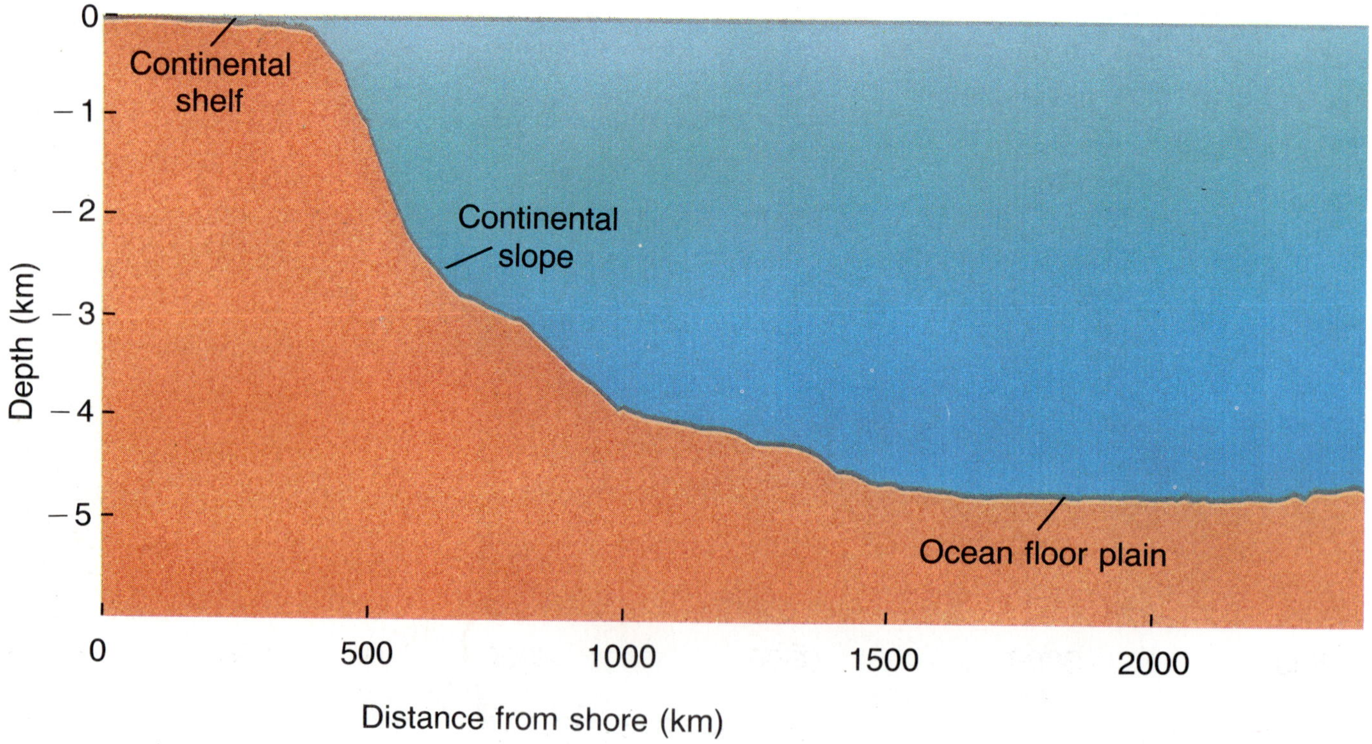

Oil and natural gas can be found on the continental shelf. Oil and natural gas form in certain rocks of the shelf. Wells are drilled from large platforms in the water. The oil is brought to shore by ships or pipelines.

Continental Slope

The **continental slope** is the area that begins where the continental shelf suddenly drops. Beyond the continental shelf the water is very deep. Many steep-sided canyons are found in the slope. Some of the deep canyons in the slope begin on the continental shelf. Some scientists think the canyons are cut by sand, mud, and water moving to the ocean bottom. Some ocean canyons that occur on the continental slope are deeper than the Grand Canyon.

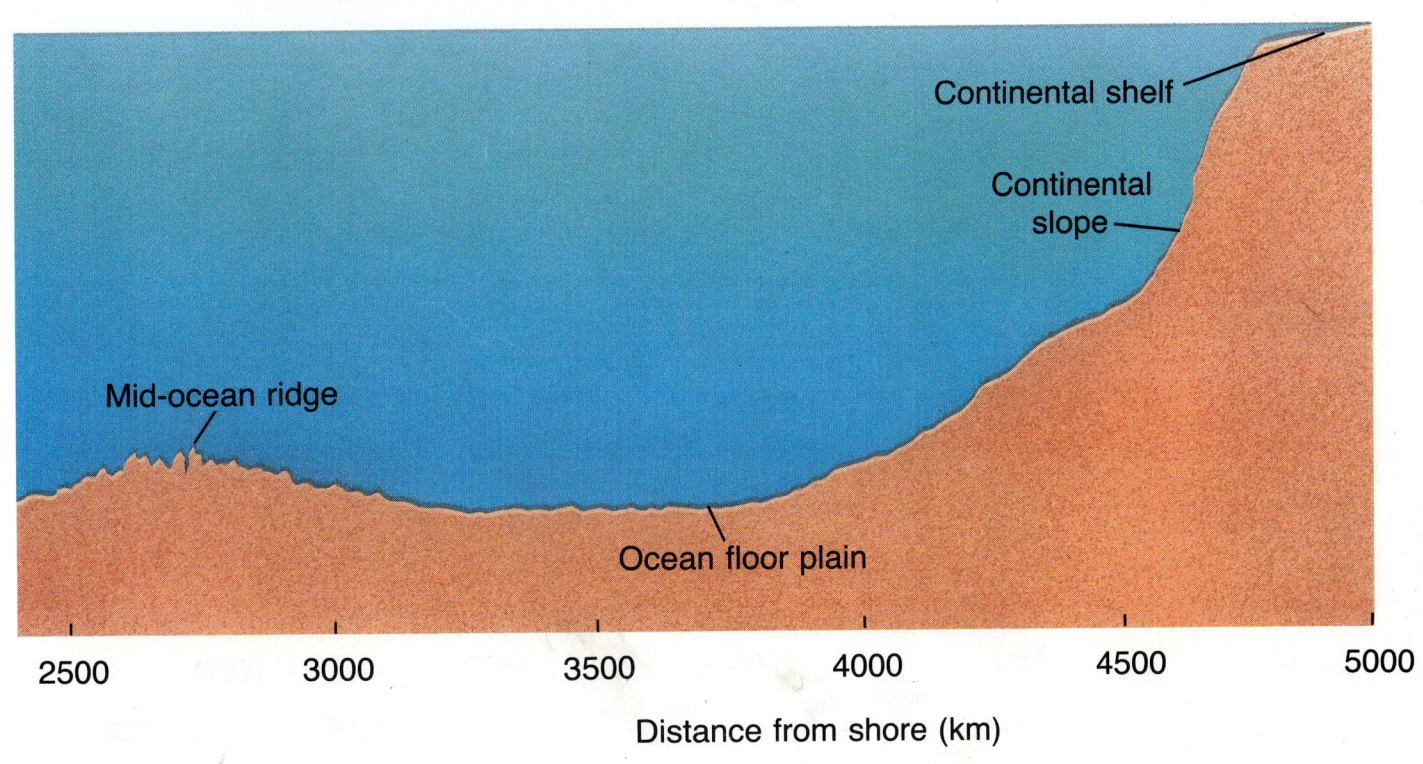

Figure 14-7. Exploring the deep, open ocean

Why are so few living things found along the ocean plain?

Water over the slope is deep and cold. It is also dark. Sunlight cannot reach the bottom. Few animals live in the deep water of the slope. Most of the animals that live here feed on the living things that die and are washed down from the shelf area.

Ocean Floor Plain

The bottom of the deep, open ocean is called the **plain.** The plain is very flat and level. In some places there are volcanoes. The plain is covered with mud. This mud contains dead microscopic plants and animals. The water here is very deep, and the pressure is very great. Also, the temperature is very cold, and there is no light. Because of the water depth, pressure, and temperature, few living things can be found along the plain.

Lesson Summary

- Ocean floor mapping is done from ships using a sonar device.
- The continental shelf is the gently sloping part of the continent covered by shallow ocean water. It is important to world industry.
- The continental slope is the area that begins where the shelf suddenly drops.
- The plain is the bottom of the deep, open ocean. It is covered with mud.

Lesson Review

Review the lesson to answer these questions.
1. How do scientists map the ocean floor?
2. Why is the continental shelf important to industry?

People and Science

Underwater Photography

Many people enjoy walking in the woods in the fall as trees change their colors. Pictures may be taken to remind everyone of a particularly beautiful spot.

Color isn't limited to land, however. Using special cameras, underwater photographers capture on film colorful plants and animals in the ocean. Their pictures bring a lively, bright world of anemones, starfish, and sea biscuits to the surface for us to learn about and enjoy.

Just as you might choose a favorite spot for fall colors, underwater photographers choose places where varieties of sea life will be found. Colorful creatures are found in cold as well as warm, tropical waters. Most fish are found along the continental shelf and where food and shelter are available in coral reefs.

Daylight does not shine very far below the surface of the water. The photographer has to take light to the subject. Strong lights called strobe lights are used. Without this light, everything would appear blue.

Cameras used for underwater photography must be waterproof or be protected by a special waterproof covering.

Besides protecting the equipment, the photographer may also need to be protected. In cold water, especially, a photographer may wear a dry suit to keep warm when underwater for a long time.

Many people use underwater photography. Some are professional divers. However, anyone who works in the ocean, such as a marine biologist, may combine work with the pleasure of capturing sea life on film.

14:3 Deep Ocean Features

LESSON GOALS

In this lesson you will learn
- underwater mountain chains are found in areas called rift zones.
- special kinds of living things are found along the rift zones.
- a trench is a deep, narrow valley in the ocean floor.

Some of the largest mountain chains in the world are found on the ocean bottom. These mountains are found in areas called rift zones. Earthquakes and volcanoes are common along the rift zones. **Rift zones** are systems of cracks in the ocean floor through which magma rises. Magma rises through the cracks and cools to form new ocean floor.

What are rift zones?

Figure 14-8. Rift zones are systems of cracks in the ocean floor.

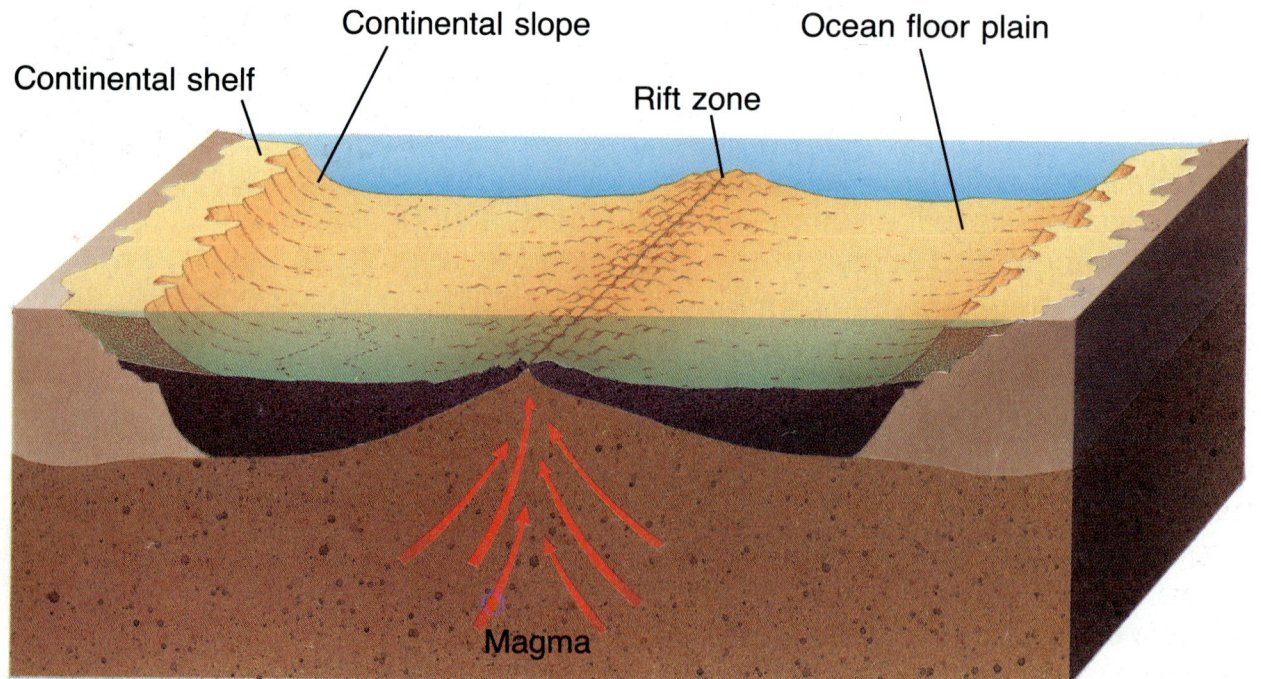

Over time, mountain chains called mid-ocean ridges form along the rift zones. Such a rift system in the Atlantic Ocean formed the Mid-Atlantic Ridge. The Mid-Atlantic Ridge runs from near Greenland to below the tip of Africa. It reaches Earth's surface in Iceland. Some of the mountains in this ridge extend nearly 3,000 meters above the plain. A few of these peaks stick out of the water to form islands. The Azore Islands are mountain peaks in one part of the Mid-Atlantic Ridge.

Figure 14–9. Tube worms live in the warm water surrounding vents.

Special types of living things are found in spots along the rift zones. They live around openings along the rift zones called vents. Water that comes from the vents is very hot. This hot water warms the water surrounding the vents. It also carries nutrients into the water. Unusual forms of large worms, crabs, and clams live in the warm water around the vents. They eat microscopic life-forms that feed on the nutrients in the hot water.

What are some animals that live around vents in the ocean floor?

Trenches

The Pacific Ocean has some of the deepest trenches in the ocean floor. A **trench** is a deep narrow valley in the ocean floor. Trenches form where ocean floor crust is forced down under the continents. Ocean trenches are longer and deeper than any land trenches or canyons.

Figure 14-10. The world's main oceanic trenches

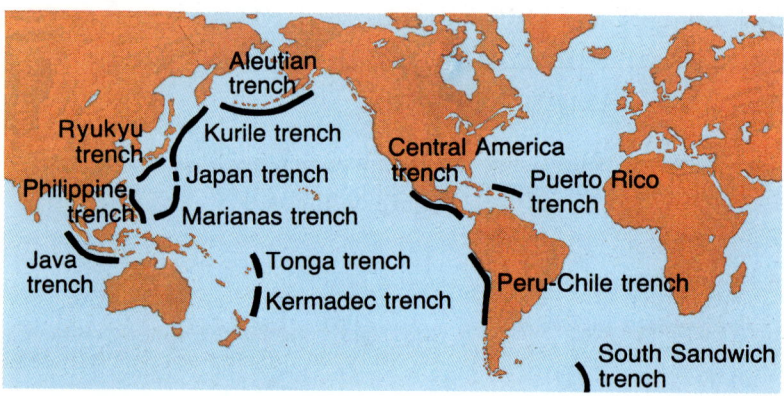

Lesson Summary

- Underwater mountain chains are found in areas called rift zones.
- Unusual forms of large worms, clams, and crabs are found near vents along the rift zones.
- A trench is a deep, narrow valley in the ocean floor.

Lesson Review

Review the lesson to answer these questions.
1. Where is one of Earth's largest mountain chains found?
2. Where can living things be found along the rift system?
3. Compare ocean trenches and land trenches.

Activity 14-1 Mapping the Ocean Bottom

QUESTION How does the ocean bottom look?

Materials
drawing paper
crayons
pencil and paper

What to do
1. Draw a picture of the ocean bottom. Use your textbook to help you.

2. Draw and label the following:
   (a) continental shelf   (d) trench
   (b) continental slope   (e) volcano
   (c) mid-ocean ridge   (f) plain
3. Add some drawings of living things. Be sure to put them in their proper environment.

What did you learn?
1. Where were most living things found?
2. Which was flatter, the shelf or the slope?

Using what you learned
1. Where would the best fishing be done? Explain your answer.
2. Where might an oil field be found? Put an oil rig in your drawing in a proper place.

273

14:4 Protecting the Ocean

LESSON GOALS

In this lesson you will learn
- the importance of ocean resources.
- examples of pollution problems.
- our responsibility to protect ocean resources.

The oceans are very important resources. People need the food sources and minerals found in the oceans. Oil and gas are also valuable resources from the ocean floor. Oceans may be a source of fresh water in the future. Also, ships are used on the oceans to transport people and other cargo. Some people vacation at the ocean. In what other ways do we depend on the oceans?

The oceans must be protected for the future. People must not take too many fish from the oceans. Some fish are becoming hard to find. Some people think that certain sea animals will become extinct. Once these animals are gone, they will be gone forever. Why might they become extinct?

Figure 14-11. An endangered species: sea otter

Oceans have pollution problems. Oil wells in the ocean can cause pollution. Sometimes shipwrecks cause oil spills. Often these oil spills drift to the shore. They kill living things on or near the surface of the ocean. They can also kill living things that live on the shore. Oil spills are very hard to clean up. Clean-up is also very expensive.

Many cities empty sewage wastewater into the oceans as well as wastewater from factories. There may be harmful chemicals in wastewater. These chemicals can kill many living things. Therefore, people must be careful to keep some kinds of wastewater out of the oceans.

Everyone must help conserve the resources of the ocean. Laws are needed to control some types of fishing. Pollution must be controlled and stopped. Factories and cities must process wastewater to remove harmful chemicals. What will happen to our need for the oceans as the world population increases? What will happen if we do not protect the oceans?

Figure 14-12. Pollution must be controlled and stopped.

Lesson Summary

- People need ocean resources for food, minerals, and fresh water.
- Oil spills and dumping waste materials are two examples of pollution.
- Everyone must help conserve ocean resources.

Lesson Review

Review the lesson to answer these questions.
1. How are oceans important?
2. Give two examples of ocean pollution.

Time Travel Television

Welcome, class, to *Archeology Today,* the school's first class to use the 23rd century's greatest invention—Time Travel Television! The TV fixed to each desk is your own personal viewer. Today we are using the system to look back in time to see how people were able to recover objects lost in the oceans.

Our first look at the past shows the oldest way of bringing back items—simple diving. If the shipwreck was in fairly shallow water, people could swim down and pick up what they wanted. However, the only air they had to breathe was what they could get by holding their breath. Most things had to be close to the shore for people to be able to recover them. About 30 meters is as deep as a person can dive without diving gear. Therefore, only cargo from shipwrecks near the shore could be saved.

A ship carrying valuable Japanese vases once sank in water too deep for simple dives. Someone thought of a new way to bring back the cargo. Octopi were used as divers! You may not have known it, but the octopus is a shy animal. It is not at all mean as shown in stories and legends. Octopi hide in cracks and holes in rocks and will run away from an enemy.

Several octopi were caught. Strings were tied to each one. Then they were lowered into the water where the ship had sunk. The frightened animals hid in the first dark places they could find—the vases. All the people had to do was pull in the octopi and tow in the vases at the same time.

The next scene on your screen is of 16th century divers using a diving bell to bring back cannons from a shipwreck near Europe. People knew that taking an air supply on dives would make the work easier. They could also explore deeper areas of the ocean. Diving bells were invented. A diving bell is a hollow metal

Now your screen is showing you a scene from 1986. Scientists from the Woods Hole laboratory used a submarine-like camera to find the wreck of the ocean liner, *Titanic*. It sank near Newfoundland in 1912 on its first voyage. Scientists found the wreck in 1985. The wreck was in water too deep for people to dive, even with scuba gear.

In 1986, a camera called Jason Junior photographed the *Titanic*. The robot camera was designed to work far below the water's surface. During the 1986 trip, computers ran the camera to make it swim in and around the shipwreck taking motion pictures for scientists to study.

box with no floor. When the box is lowered by chains into the water, air is trapped inside. People could walk along the ocean floor and breathe inside the pocket of air. Work was slow. The people could only look down through the box and around their feet. If the spot of a shipwreck was known, they could recover items in fairly deep water.

Like windows in a submarine or the lens of the swimming camera, our Time Travel Television has helped us get a look at the bottom of the oceans!

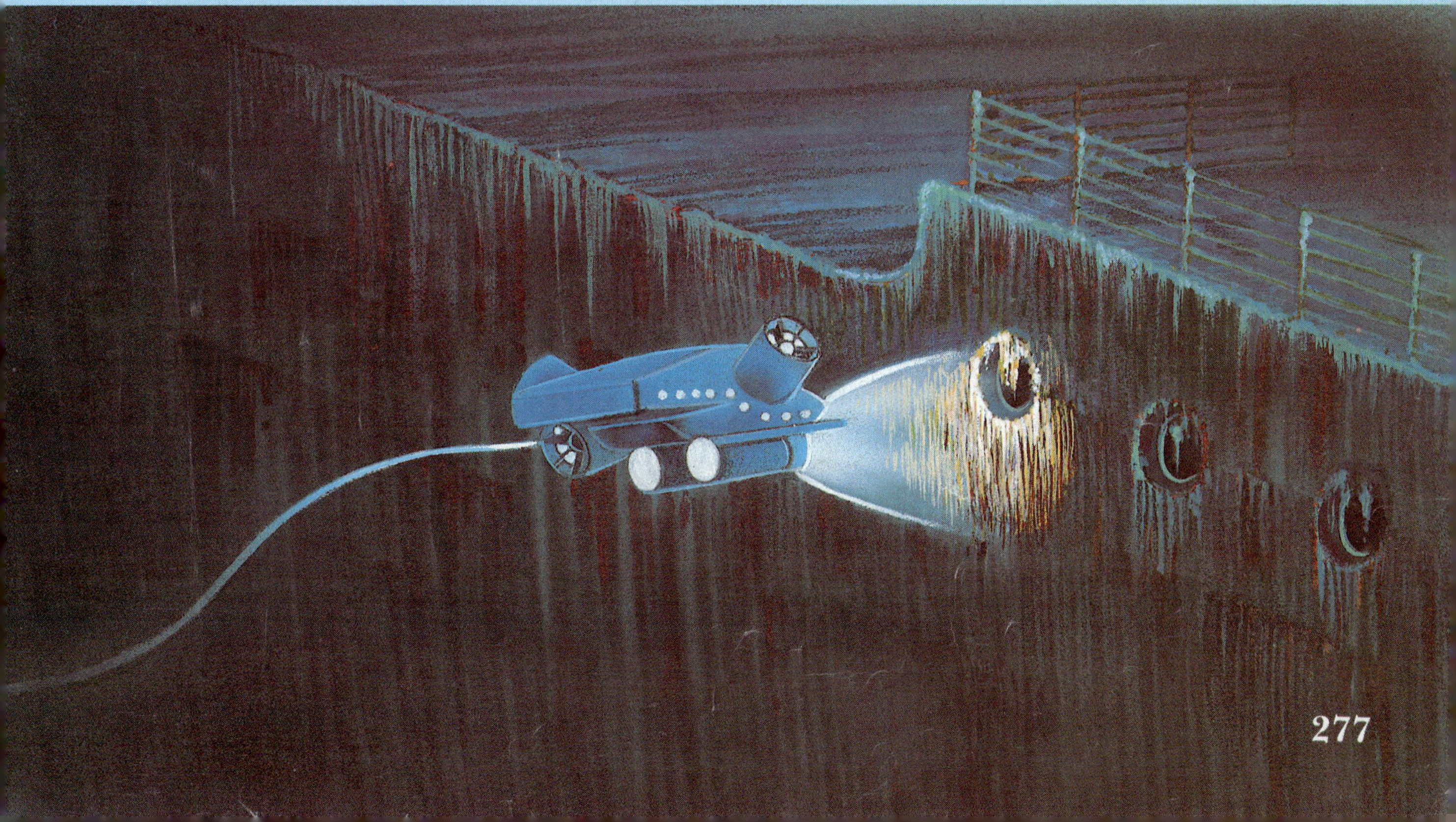

Chapter 14 Review

Summary

1. Most ocean life is found in shallow, warm waters along the edges of the continents. 14:1
2. The continental shelf is the gently sloping part of the continent covered by shallow ocean water. 14:2
3. The continental slope is steep with deeply-carved underwater canyons. 14:2
4. The ocean floor plain is the bottom of the deepest part of the ocean. 14:2
5. Rift zones, mid-ocean ridges, and trenches are special features on the ocean floor. 14:3
6. Oceans are very important resources on Earth and must be protected. 14:4

Science Words

plankton **continental shelf** **plain**
nekton **kelp** **rift zones**
benthos **continental slope** **trench**
sonar

Understanding Science Words

Complete each of the following sentences with a word or words from the Science Words that will make the sentence correct.

1. Free-swimming ocean animals are called _____.
2. Most of the living things found in the ocean are found on the _____.
3. A deep, narrow valley on the ocean floor is called a _____.
4. Maps of the ocean floor are made by using _____.
5. The nearly flat level area on the bottom of the deepest oceans is called the _____.
6. Underwater canyons have been formed in the _____.
7. The Mid-Atlantic Ridge was formed along a _____.
8. Plants and animals that live on the ocean bottom are _____.

9. Plants and animals that move and drift by surface currents are called _____.
10. The name for brown seaweed is _____.

Questions

A. Recalling Facts

Choose the word or phrase that correctly completes each of the following sentences.

1. The world's best fishing is done
   (a) on the ocean bottom.
   (b) in underwater canyons.
   (c) along the continental shelf.
   (d) in the open ocean.
2. Thick layers of mud are found
   (a) on the continental shelf.
   (b) in the surf area.
   (c) in rift zones.
   (d) on the ocean floor plain.
3. The greatest ocean depths are found in
   (a) ocean trenches.
   (b) underwater canyons.
   (c) shelf areas.
   (d) rift zones.
4. Ocean animals found near vents along rift zones include
   (a) plankton and fish.
   (b) worms and clams.
   (c) fish and kelp.
   (d) tuna and haddock.

B. Understanding Concepts

Answer each of the following questions using complete sentences.

1. What part of the ocean supports the most life? Why?
2. Give two examples of ocean life found near ocean vents.
3. Why are few living things found on the plain?
4. Describe the features of the ocean floor.
5. How are people harming the oceans?

C. Applying Concepts

Think about what you have learned in this chapter. Answer each of the following questions using complete sentences.

1. Why is it hard to study the ocean floor?
2. Why are ocean resources important to people?
3. How can every person help to protect our oceans?

UNIT 7 REVIEW

CHECKING YOURSELF

Answer these questions on a sheet of paper.
1. How do oceans affect climate?
2. Describe three kinds of ocean life and give an example of each.
3. Explain what causes tides.
4. How are waves produced?
5. Where are oil and natural gas found in the ocean?
6. What makes ocean water salty?
7. How does the temperature of ocean water vary with location? With depth?
8. Why are manganese nodules important ocean resources?
9. What is tidal power?
10. How can people conserve the resources of the oceans?

RECALLING ACTIVITIES

Think about the activities you did in this unit. Answer the questions about these activities.
1. Where are oceans and seas located? 13-1
2. Why is it easier to swim in the ocean? 13-2
3. What causes deep ocean currents? 13-3
4. How does the ocean bottom look? 14-1

IDEAS TO EXPLORE

1. Make a list of products from the ocean. Collect examples whenever possible.

2. Send a letter to students in a school near the ocean. Ask them to send you a plastic bottle of ocean water. Send them something from your area in return. Evaporate a small amount of the ocean water. Observe the salt crystals left behind. Draw a picture of the crystals.
3. Visit an ocean water aquarium. Select your favorite plant or animal. Find out where and how it lives. Share your information with your class by giving a report.

PROBLEM SOLVING

Pretend you are an engineer or architect who has been asked to design an underwater city. When you prepare your proposal to submit to the planning commission, tell how you will solve the problems of air, food, water, pressure, and salt water-resistant materials. Draw a picture or construct a model to show what your city will look like. Use reference materials to help you solve this problem. Has anyone ever tried to build an underwater city before? What problems were mentioned in your reading about this? Include your solutions for these in your report. Present your plans to your classmates.

BOOKS TO READ

The First Travel Guide to the Bottom of the Sea by Rhoda Blumberg, Lothrop, Lee, and Shepard: New York, © 1983.

Journey through the sea and learn many things.

Mysterious Seas by Mary Elting, Grosset and Dunlap: New York, © 1983.

Explore the mysteries of life in the underwater world.

Night Dive by Ann McGovern, Macmillan Publishing: New York, © 1984.

Take a diving adventure in the Caribbean.

UNIT 8
Electricity and Magnets

Thomas Edison opened his lighting plant in 1882. At that time, the total number of customers was 59. Today, power plants all over the world supply many millions of people with electricity. Think of the many ways electricity plays a part in your daily life. How do you use electricity?

Edison's lighting plant—1882

Electricity for many people

Chapter 15
Electricity

Electricity supplies energy. Electricity can be used to make light and heat. It can also be used to operate machines. You use electricity many times each day. How might your life be different without electricity?

Using electricity

Static Electricity 15:1

LESSON GOALS

In this lesson you will learn
- the parts of an atom.
- the cause of static electricity.
- what causes a static discharge.

Carlos walks across a carpeted room and receives a shock when he touches a doorknob. In another room, his little sister is interested in knowing why the laundry is making a crackling sound while her mother tries to separate the socks from the sweaters.

Carlos and his mother and sister are observing a form of electricity called static electricity (STAT ihk • ih lek TRIHS ut ee). To understand why Carlos received a shock and why the laundry items cling to each other, you must learn some new facts about atoms.

Figure 15-1. An example of static electricity

285

What is the smallest part of matter?

You have learned that the smallest part of matter is an atom. The only things smaller than an atom itself are its parts. Figure 15-2 shows a model of an atom. The core, or center, of an atom is the **nucleus** (NEW klee us). Two kinds of particles stay in the nucleus of an atom. One kind of particle is called a **proton** (PROH tahn). Another kind is called a **neutron** (NEW trahn). A third kind of particle, called an **electron** (ih LEK trahn), can be found outside the nucleus. Electrons form a cloud outside the nucleus. An electron is a very tiny particle of matter. A proton is 2,000 times larger than an electron!

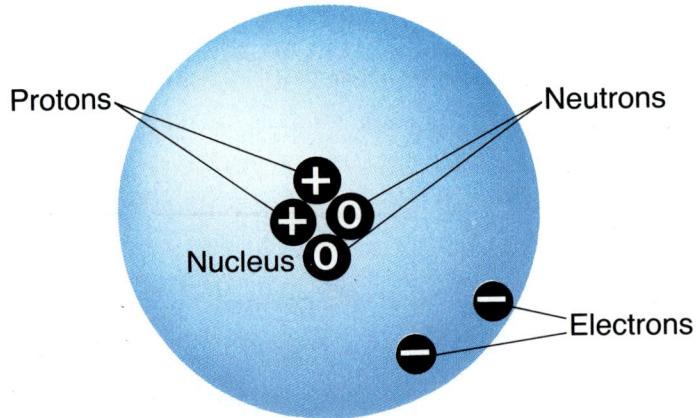

Figure 15-2. Model of an atom

Two of the three particles, protons and electrons, have an **electric charge.** This means that protons and electrons contain a small amount of electricity. There are two kinds of electric charges: positive and negative. Protons have a positive charge. Electrons have a negative charge. Usually, the number of protons and electrons in an atom is the same. Therefore, the atom has the same number of positive and negative charges. Because the charges balance each other, the atom as a whole has no electric charge.

What is the charge on most atoms?

In many materials, electrons are free to move from atom to atom. The result of this movement of electrons is electricity. Rubbing two objects together can cause some of the electrons, or negative charges, to move from one object to the other.

Figure 15-3. Balanced and unbalanced charges

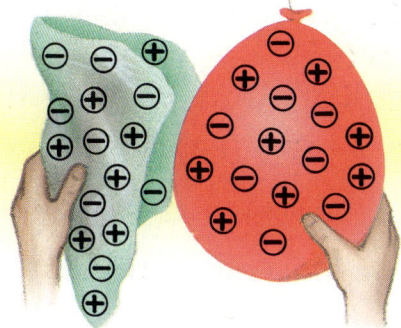
Charges balanced

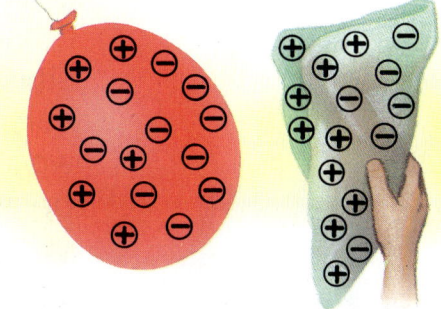
Charges unbalanced

Think about rubbing a rubber balloon with a wool cloth. When the balloon and wool are rubbed together, some of the electrons (negative charges) move from the atoms of one object to the atoms of the other object. In this example the balloon gains electrons and the wool loses electrons.

The atoms of the balloon now have more electrons (negative charges) than protons. Since the number of electrons is greater than the number of protons, the atoms as a whole have an electric charge. Because of this gain in electrons, the atoms of the balloon now have a negative charge. The atoms of the wool have more protons than electrons. Therefore, the atoms of the wool cloth have a positive charge. The number of protons and electrons in the atoms of each object is now unequal. The result is static electricity. **Static electricity** is the charge on an object that has an unequal number of protons and electrons.

What is static electricity?

Activity 15-1 Static Electricity

QUESTION What is static electricity?

Materials
2 balloons
masking tape
string
scissors
wool cloth
pencil and paper

What to do
1. Blow up 2 balloons and tie the ends. Tie a piece of string to each balloon.
2. Tape the strings to your desk as shown in the picture.
3. Rub each balloon with a piece of wool. Observe what happens.
4. Draw a picture of the position of the balloons before and after you rubbed them with wool.

What did you learn?
1. What happened to the balloons when you rubbed them with wool?
2. Where else have you seen this effect of static electricity?

Using what you learned
1. How can you explain what happened to the balloons?
2. What do you think would happen if you touched each balloon after you rubbed it? Try it.

You may have noticed an effect of static electricity while combing your hair! Electrons from your hair can be rubbed off onto the comb. This causes the comb to gain more electrons. The comb now has more negative than positive charges. This is because it now has more electrons than protons. The comb has a negative electric charge. What about your hair? Since it lost electrons, your hair now has more protons than electrons. For this reason, your hair now has a positive electric charge.

Objects with static charges may attract or repel other objects. Objects with opposite charges attract, or pull toward, each other. Objects with the same charge repel, or push away from, each other. Your hair and the comb are attracted to each other because they have opposite charges.

What kind of electric charges attract? Repel?

Figure 15-4. The girl's hair loses electrons as it is combed.

Figure 15-4 shows an example of how objects with like charges repel each other. The girl's hair lost electrons when it was combed. The atoms of her hair have more protons than electrons. Therefore, her hair has a positive charge. Since each hair has a positive charge, the hairs repel each other.

Think of the example of clothes clinging together when taken out of a dryer. While being tumbled together in a dryer, clothes rub against each other. Electrons move from one kind of clothing to another. The clothing that lost electrons has a positive charge. The clothing that gained electrons has a negative charge. Remember: opposite charges attract. As a result, the clothes cling together!

Sometimes electrons (negative charges) will "jump" to an object that has a positive charge. The "jumping" of electrons to an object with a positive charge is a spark. You may see the spark. You may hear a crackling sound. You can feel an electric shock when charges jump to or from your body. This is what happened to Carlos after he walked across the rug and then touched the doorknob. The movement of electrons from one object to another is called **static discharge.**

What is a static discharge?

Figure 15–5. Electrons "jumping" to an object with a positive charge

Lightning is another example of a static discharge. Electrons can build up on clouds under certain weather conditions. When the charge builds up enough, the electrons (negative charges) jump to an object with a positive charge such as another cloud or to Earth. A giant spark can be seen. We call it lightning.

Figure 15–6. Lightning is an example of static discharge.

Lesson Summary

- The parts of an atom are protons, neutrons, and electrons.
- Static electricity is the charge on an object that has atoms with an unequal number of protons and electrons.
- The movement of electrons from one object to another is a static discharge.

Lesson Review

Review the lesson to answer these questions.
1. What part of an atom has
   a. a positive charge?
   b. a negative charge?
   c. no charge?
2. What causes static electricity?

15:2 Current Electricity

LESSON GOALS

In this lesson you will learn
- current is the movement of electrons along a circuit.
- the difference between insulators and conductors.
- a switch can be used to open and close a circuit.
- electricity is used to do work.

What is an electric current?

The movement of electrons along a path is called a **current**. An electric current is made only of flowing electrons. The protons in an atom do not move. Negatively charged electrons flow toward positively charged protons. You can say electric current flows from negative to positive.

You can compare an electric current to a stream. The water in a stream follows a path. Electric current follows a path. The path through which a current flows is called a **circuit** (SUR kut).

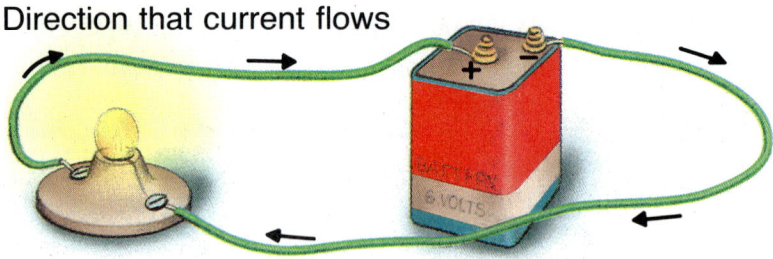

Direction that current flows

Figure 15-7. A complete circuit

A battery can be used to produce an electric current. The path from the battery through the wire and light bulb and back to the battery is a circuit. Look at Figure 15-7. Trace the circuit with your finger.

292

Activity 15-2 Making a Circuit

QUESTION How can you make the bulb light?

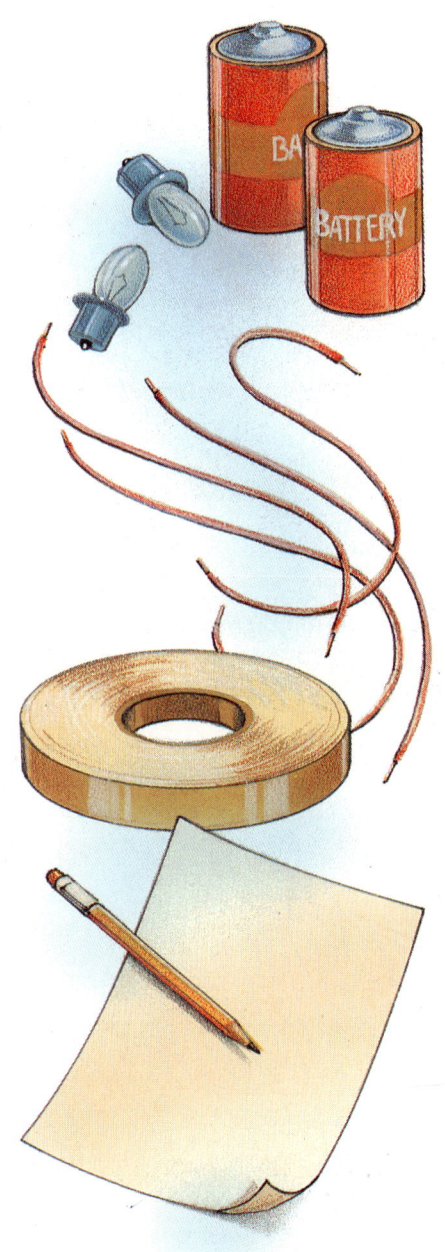

Materials
2 flashlight batteries
2 flashlight bulbs
4 pieces of bell wire
masking tape
pencil and paper

What to do

1. Using one battery and two wires, make the bulb light. Use the masking tape to hold the wires in place.
2. Draw a picture to show the circuit you made.
3. Light the bulb using two batteries. Draw the circuit you made.
4. Try to light both bulbs at once. Draw the circuit you made.

What did you learn?
1. How did you make the bulb light each time?
2. What supplied electric current to light the bulbs?
3. What difference was there when you used two batteries?

Using what you learned
1. Why was there a difference when two batteries were used to light the bulb?
2. What would the difference be if one battery and two bulbs were used? Why?

Figure 15-8. Plastic insulator on wire, and glass insulators on power lines

Electrons can flow through some matter more easily than through other matter. Matter through which electrons do not flow easily is called an **insulator** (IHN suh layt ur). Air, glass, plastic, and rubber are four examples of insulators. Matter through which electrons can flow easily is called a **conductor** (kun DUK tur). Most metals are conductors of electrons. For this reason, most electric wires are made of metal. Copper and aluminum are the two most common metals used to make wire. The covering around the wire is often made of plastic or rubber. Why do you think insulators are used to make the covering around electric wires?

How are conductors and insulators different?

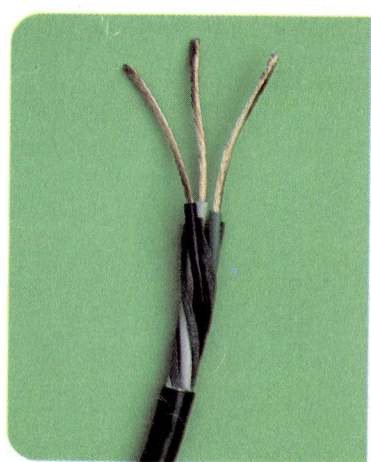
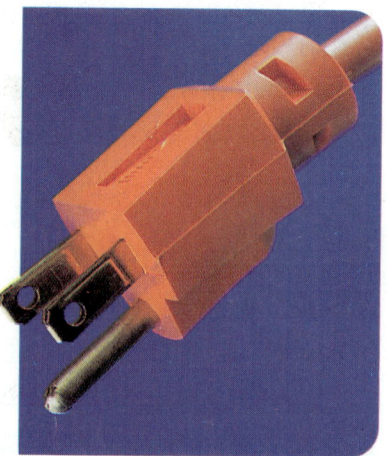

Figure 15-9. Metals used as conductors of electricity

Activity 15-3 Finding the Conductors

QUESTION Which materials are conductors?

Materials

flashlight battery
flashlight bulb
bulb holder
bell wire
masking tape
nail
coins
eraser
water glass

key
aluminum foil
foil gum wrapper
cardboard
plastic spoon
rubber comb
rock
pencil and paper

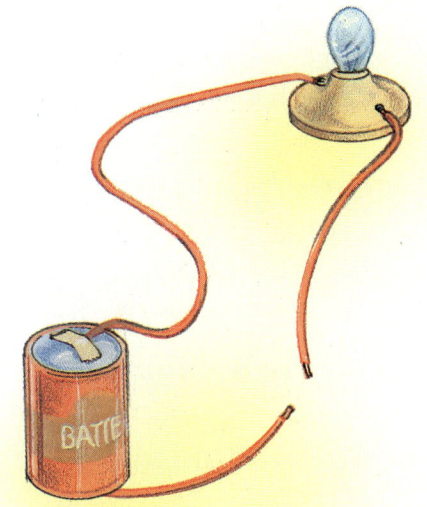

What to do

1. Connect the battery, wire, bulb, and bulb holder as shown.
2. Touch the two loose wire ends together. Observe what happens.
3. Touch the ends of each wire to the nail. Observe what happens.
4. Sort the other objects into two piles. Place those you think are conductors in one pile. Place those you think are insulators in the other pile.
5. Test each object as you tested the nail.

What did you learn?

1. Which objects were conductors?
2. Which objects were insulators?

Using what you learned

1. What kinds of materials made the best conductors?
2. What kinds of materials were insulators?

295

Figures 15-10a and b show two electric circuits. In Figure 15-10a current can flow from the battery through the wire to the bulb and back to the battery. The circuit is complete, or closed. The bulb will light.

Figure 15-10. Closed circuit (a), open circuit (b)

a
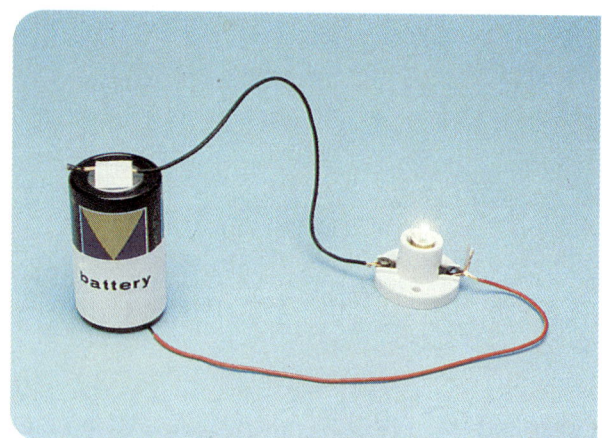

b
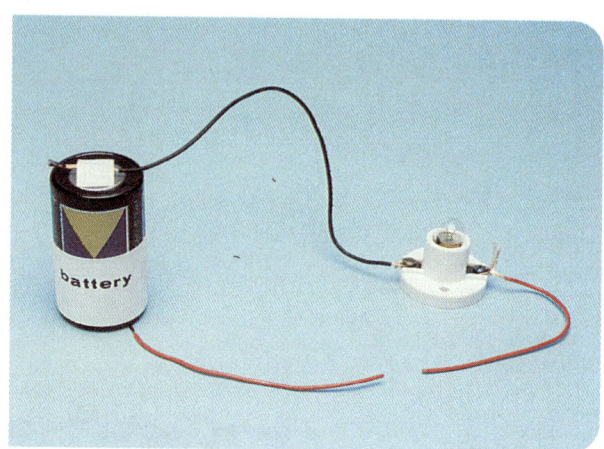

In Figure 15-10b there is a gap in the wire. The circuit is incomplete, or open. Therefore, the bulb will not light.

You close a circuit every time you turn a light on. You open a circuit when you turn a light off. A **switch** is a device that is used to open or close a circuit. A switch is made of material that is a conductor. However, the handle of the switch is an insulator.

Figure 15-11. Closed circuit (a), open circuit (b)

a
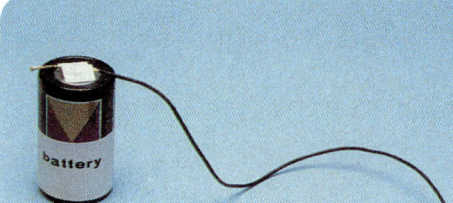

b
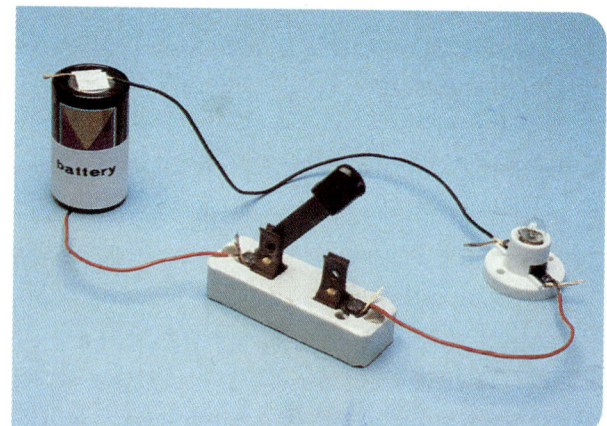

Look at Figure 15–11 of closed and open circuits with switches. The switch is the conductor. When the handle of the switch is down, there is a complete circuit. When the switch is down, the circuit is closed. What happens to the circuit when the handle of the switch is up?

The light switches in your home or school work the same way. When the switch is on, a conductor in the switch connects two wires. Current can flow through the lights. When the switch is off, the circuit is open. What happens to the current when the handle of the switch is off?

How does a switch work?

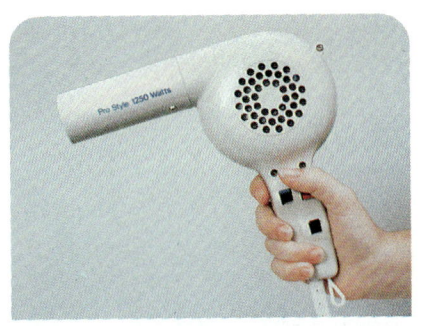

Electricity is very useful to people. Electric current is used to produce light and heat. How is light produced in your classroom? Most artificial light is produced by means of an electric current. Also, electric current is sometimes used to produce heat. Figure 15–12 shows devices that use electric current to produce heat. How are these devices used? Make a list of other devices that use electric current to produce heat.

Figure 15–12. Electric current can produce heat.

297

Electric current can also be used to cause motion. A current can be used to make a motor turn. When a motor turns, work can be done. Remember, work is done when a force causes an object to move. Think about a record player. The electric motor causes the record to turn. Work is done when the record turns. Look at the pictures. How are these electric motors doing work?

Figure 15–13. Electric current can be used to do work.

Lesson Summary

- Current is the movement of electrons along a conductor in a path called a circuit.
- Electrons flow easily through conductors. Electrons do not flow easily through insulators.
- A switch can be used to open and close a circuit.
- Electricity is used to do work.

Lesson Review

Review the lesson to answer these questions.
1. What is electric current?
2. How are conductors and insulators different?
3. What is the purpose of a switch?

Science and Technology

Thirsty Watches

We water our houseplants and our gardens. We give fresh water to our pets and fill bird baths. But did you ever water your watch? Usually we must keep our watches out of the water. If you have ever worn a watch in the shower or pool, you know what happens. Unless your watch is waterproof, it is ruined. Waterproof watches must have special cases that keep water and other liquids away from the inside parts of the watch. But if your waterproof watch leaks, even it will be ruined.

Soon you will be able to buy a new type of watch that must be watered every few days. The watch will work on a simple type of battery. The battery is called a voltaic (vohl TAY ihk) cell. Dry cells and car batteries are voltaic cells. Technologists have found a surprising use for voltaic cells in these new watches.

The cell in the watch consists of layers of copper and zinc metals separated by a liquid. Electrons flow automatically from zinc to copper in a liquid. No additional power source is needed. In the watch, electrons flow from the zinc through wires to the copper. The flow of electrons through the watch makes a current. The current makes the watch work.

A certain amount of liquid must be kept in the watch at all times. The zinc and copper must be in a liquid in order for the electrons to move between the metal plates. Most liquids can be used to "water" this watch. Water will work, of course, but so will soda pop, tea, and fruit juice. The watch "drinks" through tiny holes in its case.

This new watch could last up to ten years if cared for properly. There is nothing to wind and no batteries to buy. Watch owners will need to take their watches for a swim or bath. Someday you may be sharing a soda with your watch!

Chapter 15 Review

Summary

1. The parts of an atom are protons, neutrons, and electrons.   15:1
2. Static electricity is the charge on an object that has atoms with an unequal number of protons and electrons.   15:1
3. The movement of electrons from one object to another is a static discharge.   15:1
4. The path through which a current flows is called a circuit.   15:2
5. A switch can be used to open and close a circuit.   15:2

Science Words

nucleus	**electric charge**	**circuit**
proton	**static electricity**	**insulator**
neutron	**static discharge**	**conductor**
electron	**current**	**switch**

Understanding Science Words

Complete each of the following sentences with a word or words from the Science Words that will make the sentence correct.

1. Protons and electrons that contain a small amount of electricity have an _____.
2. The movement of electrons from one object to another is called _____.
3. The core of an atom is called the _____.
4. The charge on an object that has an unequal number of protons and electrons is called _____.
5. The movement of electrons along a path is called a _____.
6. A device that is made to open or close a circuit is called a _____.
7. A positive charged particle found in the nucleus is called a _____.

300

8. Matter through which electrons do not flow easily is called an _____.
9. A particle found in the nucleus that has no electric charge is called a _____.
10. The path that a current follows is called a _____.
11. Matter through which electrons can flow easily is called a _____.
12. A negative charged particle found outside the nucleus of an atom is called an _____.

Questions

A. Recalling Facts

Choose the word or phrase that correctly completes each of the following sentences.

1. When the charges of an atom balance each other, the atom as a whole has
    (a) a positive charge.
    (b) a small charge.
    (c) a negative charge.
    (d) no charge.
2. The basic parts of an atom found inside of the nucleus are
    (a) neutrons and a charge.
    (b) protons and neutrons.
    (c) nucleus and electrons.
    (d) electron cloud and nucleus.

B. Understanding Concepts

Answer each of the following questions using complete sentences.

1. What is the job of a switch?
2. Name some examples of static electricity.

C. Applying Concepts

Think about what you have learned in this chapter. Answer each of the following questions using complete sentences.

1. What causes static electricity?
2. What is an electric current?

Chapter 16
Magnetism and Electricity

A long time ago in a place called Magnesia, a mineral was found that had a special property. When it came in contact with certain metals, the mineral and the metals would stick together. Some people thought this property was a kind of magic. What do you think?

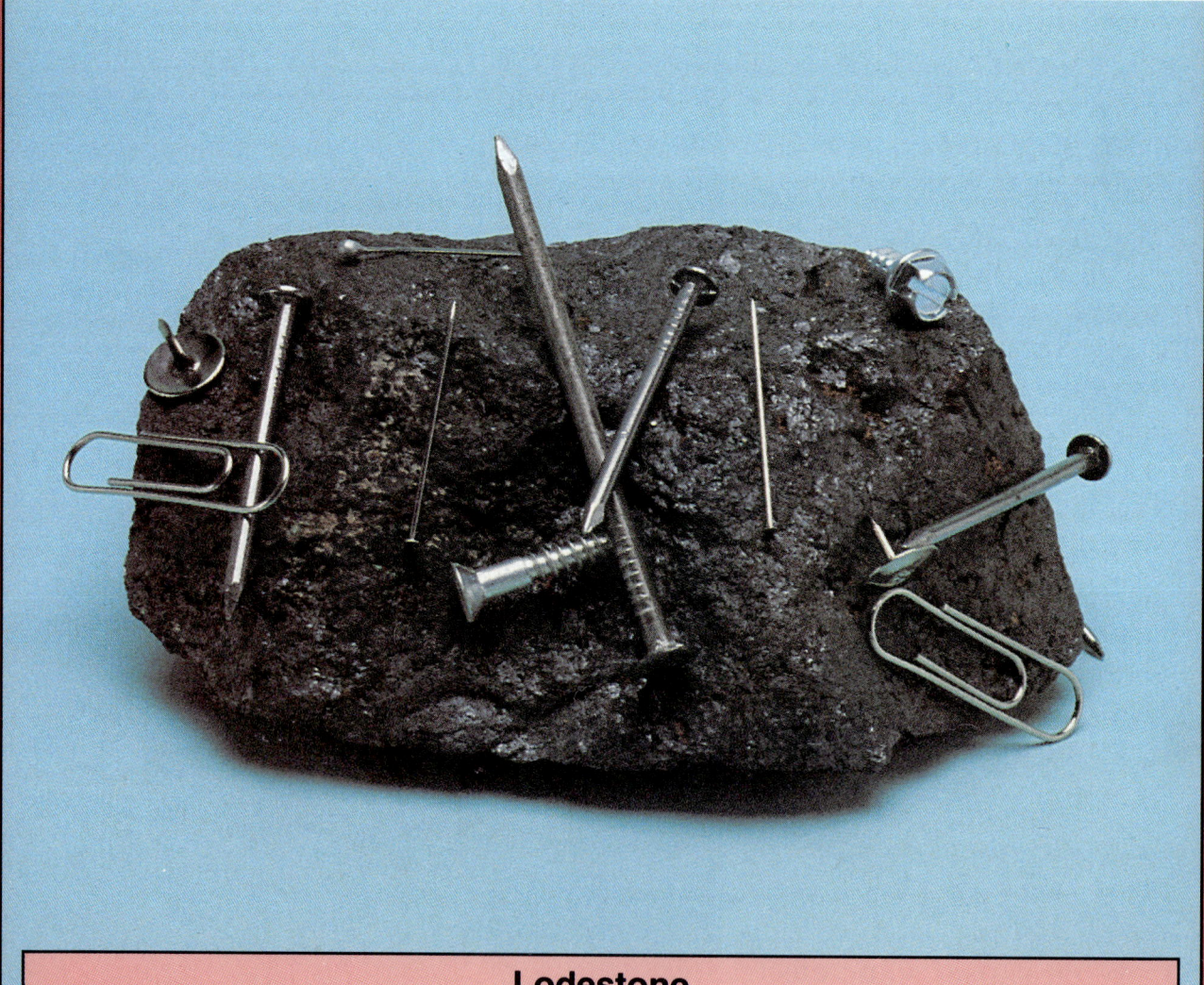

Lodestone

Magnets 16:1

LESSON GOALS

In this lesson you will learn
- a magnet attracts some materials.
- magnetic forces control the behavior of magnets.
- the area around a magnet is the magnetic field.

The people in Magnesia thought the mineral was a magic stone. It was really what we call a natural magnet. By "natural" magnet we mean one found in nature, not made by people. A natural magnet is called a **lodestone**. Lodestones were the first magnets known to people.

A lodestone is not the only kind of magnet. A **magnet** is an object that is able to attract some materials. Certain metals can be magnetized, or made into magnets. Iron, nickel, and cobalt can be magnetized. Most magnets are made of these metals or a mixture of them.

What is a magnet?

You can use a magnet to make another magnet. Suppose you want to magnetize an iron nail. One way is to place the nail in contact with a magnet. The nail will become magnetized.

a

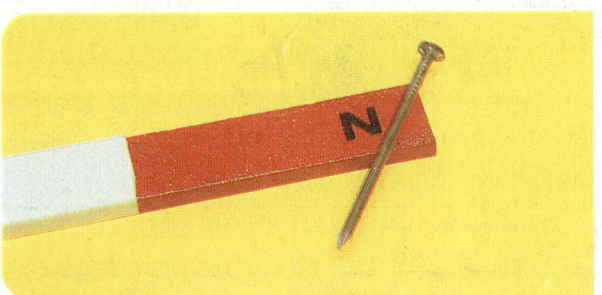

b

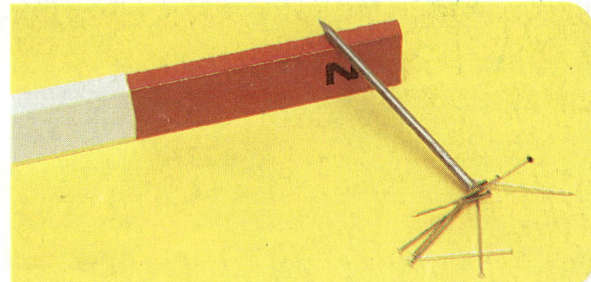

Figure 16-1. An iron nail placed in contact with a magnet (a) will become magnetized (b).

303

Another way to magnetize the nail is to stroke the nail with the magnet. Each stroke must be made slowly in one direction only. Be sure to use the same end of the magnet each time. As you stroke, the nail will become magnetized.

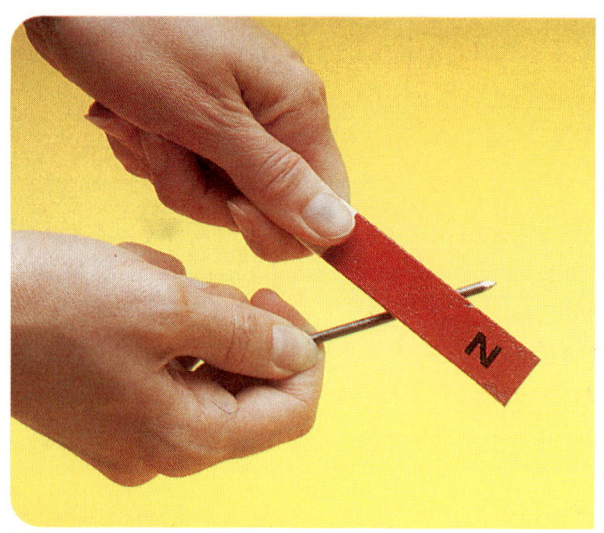
a

b

Figure 16-2. Stroking an iron nail with a magnet (a) will magnetize the nail (b).

Suppose you use a magnet to magnetize a nail. You stroke the nail many times with the magnet. Then you test the nail by moving it close to some paper clips. It picks up some paper clips. The nail is now a magnet. However, its appearance has not changed.

Figure 16-3. Bar magnets

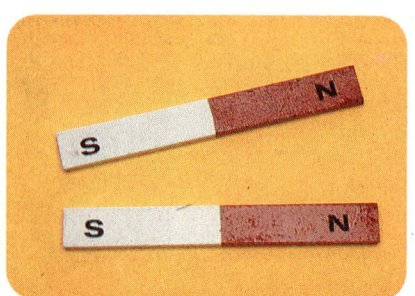

Figure 16-3 shows two bar magnets that are permanent magnets. Each magnet has two ends. The ends of a magnet are called **poles.** All magnets have two poles. On many bar magnets the poles are marked. One pole is marked with an N and the other with an S. The pole marked with an N is called the north-seeking pole. What do you think the pole marked with an S is called?

Suppose you hang a bar magnet from a string so it is free to swing. Then suppose you bring another bar magnet near the one hanging from the string. The north pole of one magnet will attract or pull toward the south pole of the other magnet. Two north poles repel or push away from each other. What do you think happens when two south poles come together? This behavior of magnets is always the same. Like poles of a magnet repel each other. Unlike poles attract each other.

Magnets can be different sizes and shapes. They can be made of different materials. However, all magnets behave in the same way. Magnetic forces cause magnets to attract or repel other magnets. Magnets can also attract certain other objects. Objects that are attracted by a magnet are called magnetic objects. What magnetic objects can you name?

The forces of attraction or repulsion are not the same all around a magnet. Magnetic forces are greatest at the poles of a magnet.

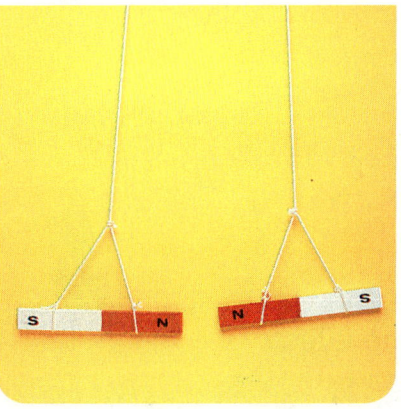

Figure 16-4. Opposite poles attract (a). Like poles repel (b).

What is a magnetic field?

The area around a magnet where the magnetic force acts is called the **magnetic field.** A magnetic field cannot be seen.

Although it cannot be seen, you can feel the effects of a magnetic field. You can feel the push or pull when you bring two magnets together. You feel the magnetic field when you bring an object, such as a paper clip, close to a magnet. As you move the paper clip closer to the magnet, you reach a point where you can feel the magnet pulling the clip.

Although you cannot see a magnetic field, you can see its effect. When iron filings are placed near a magnet, they form a pattern. This pattern shows the shape of the magnetic field. The pattern seems to end at the surface of the magnet. You cannot see it, but the magnetic field goes through the magnet also.

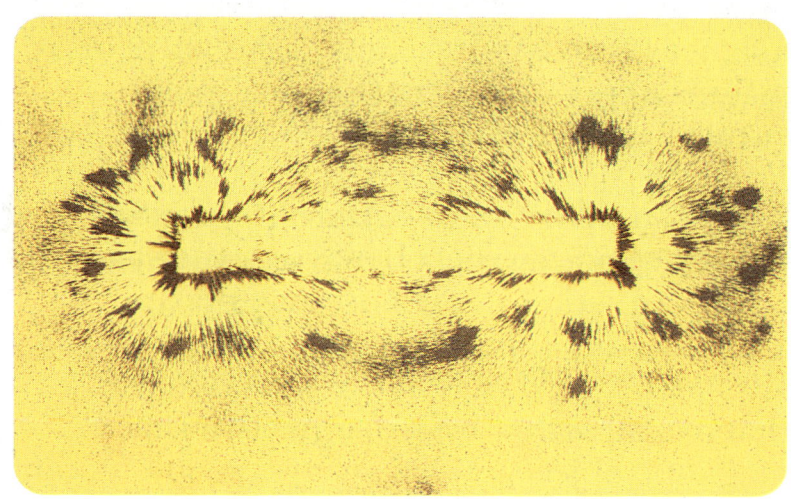

Figure 16-5. You can see the effects of a magnetic field.

Lesson Summary

- A magnet is an object that attracts some materials.
- Magnetic forces control the behavior of magnets.
- The area around a magnet where the magnetic force acts is called the magnetic field.

Lesson Review

Review the lesson to answer these questions.
1. Of what are most magnets made?
2. How do the poles of magnets affect one another?
3. What is a magnetic field?

People and Science

Speaking of Energy

Phyllis Miranda works for an electric company. She speaks to school children and other groups about energy. Sometimes she talks about how energy can be conserved or how energy should be used safely. Geothermal (jee oh THUR mul) energy is her newest topic.

Geothermal energy comes from inside Earth. One way to get geothermal energy is to drill a hole into hot, dry rocks deep inside Earth. Water is pumped into the hole. The rocks heat the water and change it to steam. The steam is pumped out of the hole. The steam is used to drive turbines at power plants. The turbines power generators that produce electricity for many people.

As part of her speech, Phyllis describes the research her company does. She explains that a hole about four kilometers deep was drilled at the test power plant. The geothermal energy at the test site can produce enough electricity for a town of 4,000 people.

Phyllis Miranda hopes that people will learn from her speeches. She hopes they will learn the importance of conserving energy resources and the need for finding new energy sources. The natural resources of our world cannot last forever. Phyllis Miranda wants us all not only to take care of our needs today, but provide for the needs of people who will live in the future.

16:2　Magnets and Electricity

LESSON GOALS

In this lesson you will learn
- an electromagnet is a temporary magnet made using an electric current.
- power plants are sources of large amounts of electricity.

How can you make an electromagnet?

A temporary magnet can be made by using electric current. In Figure 16-6a you can see that a wire has been wrapped around a bolt. The free ends of the wire have been attached to a battery. An electric circuit has been made. As electric current flows through the coil a magnetic field is produced. We know this because we can observe the effects of the magnetic field. The bolt has become a magnet and has attracted the paper clips.

When the circuit is broken, the current stops. The bolt is no longer a magnet. It does not attract any paper clips. See Figure 16-6b. The bolt in this example became a temporary magnet. A temporary magnet made using electric current is an **electromagnet** (ih lek troh MAG nut).

Figure 16-6. A complete circuit (a) and a broken circuit (b)

a

b

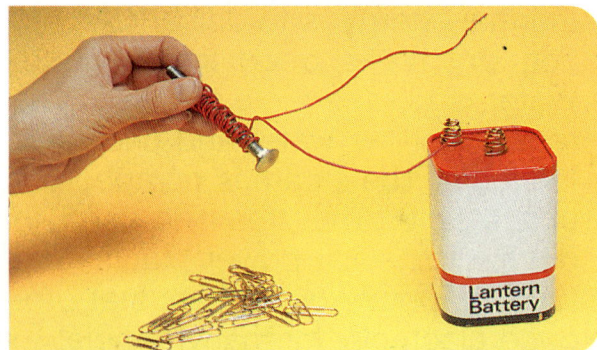

Activity 16-1 An Electromagnet

QUESTION How can you make an electromagnet?

Materials
2 batteries
bell wire (1 meter) (15 cm)
paper clips
switch
nail
pencil and paper

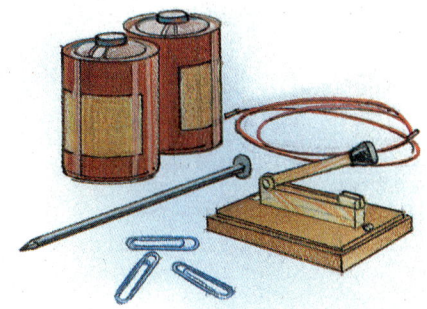

What to do

1. Wrap the 1-meter wire around the nail 15 turns.
2. Connect the battery, switch, and the nail as shown.
3. See how many paper clips you can pick up with the electromagnet. Record all results.
4. Repeat steps 2 and 3 using 2 batteries.
5. Repeat using 30 turns of the wire.

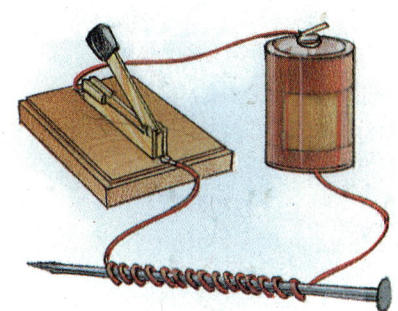

What did you learn?

1. How many paper clips did you pick up each time?
2. When was your electromagnet strongest?

Using what you learned

1. When does the nail lose its magnetism?
2. How is an electromagnet different from a permanent magnet?

How are electromagnets used?

The scrapyard crane in Figure 16-7 uses an electromagnet. When an electric current flows through a coil of wire inside the plate on the crane, the plate becomes magnetized. The crane with its magnetized plate is then used to lift scraps of metal. Electromagnets also are used in doorbells, televisions, stereo speakers, washers and dryers, and other appliances with electric motors. Where might you find electric motors in use in your school?

Figure 16-7. The plate on the scrapyard crane is an electromagnet.

Much electricity is used every day. Batteries alone cannot make enough electricity to run homes, schools, factories, and hospitals.

Power plants are the sources of large amounts of electricity. Power plants use generators to make electricity. A **generator** (JEN uh rayt ur) is a machine that produces an electric current. A generator uses magnets and loops of wire to make electricity.

How does a generator produce an electric current?

Figure 16-8. A generator

A generator can produce electric current because of the relationship between electricity and magnetism. You know that an electric current flowing through a wire produces a magnetic field. In the same way, if a coil of wire is moved through a magnetic field, an electric current will flow through the wire. As long as the coil of wire moves through the magnetic field, a current is made. The more loops of wire, the stronger the electric current.

Generators have many loops of wire. The loops pass through the magnetic fields of large magnets. The loops of wire are spun very fast within a magnetic field. The amount of current depends on the number of turns, the speed of the motion, and the strength of the magnetic field.

The power needed to run generators in a power plant comes from turbines. A **turbine** is a device that has blades attached to an axle. The power to turn the turbine blades comes from sources such as the pressure of steam. In most cases, the steam needed to run a steam turbine is produced by burning such fuels as coal, oil, or natural gas. In nuclear power plants, the energy from atoms is used to heat water and produce steam.

What is a turbine?

Figure 16-9. Generators and turbines in a power plant

311

After the steam is produced, it rushes through the turbine, causing the blades to turn rapidly. The circular motion of the blades and axle causes huge coils of wire to spin. The coils spin in a strong magnetic field produced by powerful electromagnets. Power lines connected to the generator carry current electricity from the power plant to towns and cities. Where is the power plant nearest you? Look for the power lines leading into your school and home.

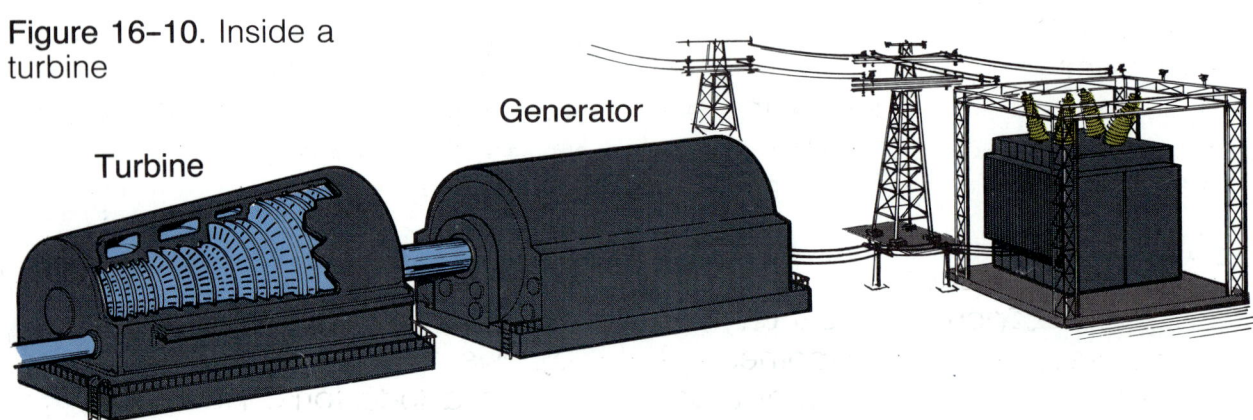

Figure 16-10. Inside a turbine

Lesson Summary
- An electromagnet is a temporary magnet made using an electric current.
- Power plants are sources of large amounts of electricity.

Lesson Review
Review the lesson to answer these questions.
1. What is an electromagnet?
2. How is magnetism related to electric current?
3. What fuels are used to produce electricity?

Language Arts Skills

Hypotheses About Magnets

Do you think one magnet can be divided into two separate magnets? Write your answer on a sheet of paper. Your teacher will show you a long, thin nail. It has been filed down in the middle. Your teacher will stroke the nail with a magnet until it also is a magnet. Next, the nail will be broken into two pieces. You will notice that both pieces of the nail are now magnets. Both pieces have north and south poles. Was your guess correct?

A scientist makes a guess about what will happen in an experiment. This guess is called a hypothesis. A hypothesis is based on what a scientist has learned in the past. A scientist writes down what he or she thinks will happen in an experiment. After the experiment, the scientist checks the hypothesis. It is either true or not true. If it is not true, the scientist may write a new hypothesis.

There were many hypotheses about magnets in ancient times. Sailors used natural magnets called lodestones to guide them at sea. The lodestones floated on pieces of cork. They always moved into a north-south line. The sailors didn't understand why the lodestones moved. They thought it was a mysterious "force" at work.

In the 1500s, an Englishman named William Gilbert studied magnets. Gilbert made an important hypothesis. He guessed that Earth itself is a lodestone. He tested his idea over and over. He found that a swinging needle pointed toward the North Pole. Gilbert's "dipping needle" showed that Earth has magnetic poles. Gilbert had proved that his hypothesis was correct.

Chapter 16 Review

Summary

1. A magnet is an object that is able to attract some materials.   16:1
2. Magnetic forces control the behavior of magnets.   16:1
3. The area of force around a magnet is called the magnetic field.   16:1
4. An electromagnet is a temporary magnet made using electric current.   16:2
5. Power plants are sources of large amounts of electricity.   16:2
6. Power plants use generators to make electricity.   16:2

Science Words

lodestone   **magnetic field**   **generator**
magnet   **electromagnet**   **turbine**
poles

Understanding Science Words

Complete each of the following sentences with a word or words from the Science Words that will make the sentence correct.

1. An object that is able to attract some materials is called a _____.
2. A device that has blades attached to an axle is called a _____.
3. The area around a magnet where the magnetic force acts is called a _____.
4. The ends of a magnet are called _____.
5. A temporary magnet made using electric current is called an _____.
6. A machine that produces an electric current is called a _____.
7. A natural magnet is called a _____.

314

Questions

A. Recalling Facts

Choose the word or phrase that correctly completes each of the following sentences.

1. Magnetic forces are greatest
   - (a) in between the poles.
   - (b) outside the poles.
   - (c) at the poles.
   - (d) at the north pole.
2. Sources of large amounts of electricity are
   - (a) wire.
   - (b) coal mines.
   - (c) electromagnets.
   - (d) power plants.
3. You can feel the effect of a magnetic field with
   - (a) a compass.
   - (b) a generator.
   - (c) a turbine.
   - (d) two magnets.
4. More loops of wire in a generator produce
   - (a) less electricity.
   - (b) a stronger current.
   - (c) a magnetic field.
   - (d) a weaker current.
5. The behavior of a magnet is controlled by
   - (a) magnetic forces.
   - (b) light.
   - (c) pressure.
   - (d) generators.

B. Understanding Concepts

Answer each of the following questions using complete sentences.

1. What behavior of magnetic poles is always the same?
2. Describe two ways an object can be magnetized.
3. Where might you find electric motors at home and school?
4. What is the purpose of a generator?

C. Applying Concepts

Think about what you have learned in this chapter. Answer each of the following questions using complete sentences.

1. How can an electromagnet be made using a wire, a bolt, and a dry cell battery?
2. How can you see the effects of a magnetic field?

UNIT 8 REVIEW

CHECKING YOURSELF

Answer these questions on a sheet of paper.
1. What causes lightning?
2. What are the three basic parts of an atom?
3. What causes static electricity? Give two examples.
4. What kind of charge does an electron have?
5. What is a switch?
6. How is electricity carried from a power plant to your school or home?
7. What is a magnetic field?
8. What is a current?
9. How can a magnet lose its magnetic properties?
10. What poles of a magnet attract each other? What poles repel each other?
11. How does a generator produce electricity?
12. What are electromagnets? How are they used?
13. What kind of electric charge does a proton have?
14. What kinds of particles make up the nucleus of an atom?

RECALLING ACTIVITIES

Think about the activities you did in this unit. Answer the questions about these activities.
1. What is static electricity? 15–1
2. How can you make the bulb light? 15–2
3. Which materials are conductors? 15–3
4. How can you make an electromagnet? 16–1

IDEAS TO EXPLORE

1. Place signs saying "Light," "Heat," and "Magnet" on the bulletin board. Collect pictures of objects that use electricity to produce heat and light and objects that make electromagnets. Post them under the proper signs.
2. Draw a picture of a flashlight. Show the path of electricity using arrows.
3. Learn how to use a compass. Plot a course in the schoolyard using compass directions. Challenge other students to follow it.

PROBLEM SOLVING

How can you make a compass? Magnetize a steel sewing needle by stroking it with one pole of a strong bar magnet. Cut a groove across the center of a large cork. Put the needle into the groove. Place the cork and needle into a glass pan filled with water. Add one spoonful of dish detergent to the water. This will keep the cork from moving around too much. The needle will soon behave like a compass, and point in a north-south direction. Why does this happen? Check the position of the needle with a compass.

BOOKS TO READ

Amazing Magnets by David Adler, Troll Associates: Mahwah, NJ, © 1983.
   Your questions about magnets are answered.

Discovering Electricity by Neil Ardley, Franklin Watts: Danbury, CT, © 1984.
   This book describes investigations in electricity.

Electricity by Mark Bailey, Raintree Publishers: Milwaukee, © 1983.
   An interesting introduction to electricity.

UNIT 9
Growing Up Healthy

Two of the world's best athletes, Jim Thorpe and Evelyn Ashford, probably never met, but they have at least two important things in common: healthy body care and good eating habits. Imitate these two great athletes. Learn how to develop healthful habits. Do the very best you can for yourself. Be the very best person you can be!

Jim Thorpe—1912

Evelyn Ashford—1984

Chapter 17
Taking Care of Yourself

Keeping your body healthy is a lifetime task. You can learn about what you can do to keep your body healthy. You can form good body care habits while you are young. By taking care of your body now, you may be able to avoid some health problems as an adult. What are some body care habits you have formed?

Body care—get the habit!

Exercise and Sleep 17:1

LESSON GOALS

In this lesson you will learn
- how exercise affects your health.
- why sleep is necessary for a healthy mind and body.

Rosa is a member of a soccer team at school. The team practices three days a week. Each practice lasts one and a half hours. Matthew rides his bicycle to and from school every day. A round trip takes 40 minutes. Seth and Ann take dancing lessons twice a week. Each lesson is two hours long. Erik walks his dog every day. He uses a jogging trail near his home. The trail is two kilometers long. Which of these children is exercising regularly? What kinds of exercise do you do regularly?

Figure 17-1. Regular exercise is a good body-care habit.

321

What is exercise?

Exercise is any activity that uses the muscles of the body. Exercising can improve and keep up your overall physical health in several ways.

Circulation

Exercise improves your circulation. Circulation, as you know, is the flow of blood through your body. Exercise improves circulation to your skin, arms, legs, brain, and other body parts. People who do not exercise may have difficulty falling asleep. They may awaken feeling tired. A person with good circulation will often sleep better. He or she will feel rested when awakened. Students who exercise regularly may notice that they feel better about school work and about themselves.

How might exercise benefit you as a student?

Muscles

Exercise makes the muscles of the body stronger and firmer. As you exercise, you may notice that you are able to work and play for longer periods of time without getting tired. You have many different muscles in your body. These muscles need to be exercised to keep them strong.

How does exercise affect muscles?

There are many ways to exercise the different muscles in the body. Pushing, tensing, lifting, and pulling types of exercises will strengthen your skeletal muscles. Running, swimming, walking, dancing, and bicycling are exercises that make the heart and lungs stronger. Figure 17-2 shows some different exercises for strengthening the whole body.

Figure 17-2. Exercise makes the muscles of the body stronger.

Table 17-1 Calories in Food	
Food	Calories
1 fresh apple	80
1 slice cake	180
3 pancakes with syrup	350
3 slices pizza and 1 cola drink	580
1 glass milk	165
1 pork chop	260
1 sweet potato	155
1 tomato	30

What is a Calorie?

Table 17-2 Calories Used Per Hour	
Activity	Calories used
eating	84
reading	72
watching TV	80
swimming	300
walking	216
dancing	330
sleeping	60
bicycling (fast)	250

Weight Control

Exercise is an aid to weight control. People who exercise regularly usually eat foods in the correct amounts, which means they do not overeat. When you exercise, you use energy. This energy comes from the food you eat. A **Calorie** (KAL uh ree) is a measure of the amount of energy in foods. Some foods, such as cakes, pies, and other desserts, are high in Calories. Other foods, such as vegetables, are low in Calories. How many Calories you use depends upon how active you are. Table 17-1 shows a few foods and their Calorie amounts. Table 17-2 shows how many Calories you use when you do different exercises.

Suppose you ate all of the foods listed in Table 17-1 in one day. What would be the total number of Calories you ate? Suppose during the same day you used energy to eat three meals, watch TV for three hours, and sleep for eight hours. How many Calories would your body use for all of these activities? Remember that it is important to balance the Calories your body needs for daily activities with the Calories you eat. By doing this, you will develop good eating habits that will help control your body weight.

Exercise is important for overall physical health. Keep your exercise plan from becoming boring. Choose activities you enjoy doing that are also a form of exercise. Choose what interests you! Your exercise plan will change as you grow older, but you should form this body care habit now. Exercise should be a lifetime habit!

Activity 17-1 Planning for Exercise

QUESTION   How can you exercise your body?

Materials
exercise chart   pencil and paper

What to do
1. Use a chart like the one shown. List 5 activities you enjoy that are types of exercise. Eating and watching TV have been included as nonexercise activities.
2. Write how much time you spend doing an activity each day for a week.

Activity	Time spent per day							Total time for 1 week
	Sun.	Mon.	Tues.	Wed.	Thurs.	Fri.	Sat.	
a. eating								
b. watching TV								
c.								

3. Add the time you spend each day and record the total.

What did you learn?
1. How much time per week do you spend exercising?
2. How much time per week do you spend eating? Watching TV?

Using what you learned
1. Do you spend more of your time involved in exercise or nonexercise activities?
2. How can you improve your activity schedule so you have a better balance between exercise and nonexercise activities?

Sleep

Sleep is a state of restfulness. When you sleep, your muscles relax. The number of times your heart beats per minute decreases. You also take fewer breaths per minute as you sleep. Everyone needs sleep, but in different amounts. Babies in the first few weeks after birth may sleep as many as 16 hours a day. The average adult needs about 7 or 8 hours of sleep a day.

Most children your age need 10 to 12 hours of sleep each night. There are two important reasons for getting enough sleep at your age. First, most children take part in many activities and get a lot of exercise. Therefore, you need sleep in order for your body to rest. Second, most children your age are growing rapidly. During times of growth, the body needs more rest. While you sleep, special chemicals called growth hormones are released into the circulatory system. You could say you are growing as you rest and sleep!

Getting Enough Sleep

If you feel rested and refreshed within an hour after awakening, you have had enough rest. Being rested and refreshed means you should be able to think clearly and have the energy to do your daily schedule.

Sometimes you may have trouble getting to sleep. Worry about problems and events can keep you from sleeping. Some suggestions for getting a good night's sleep are
- be sure to have a firm mattress for your bed.

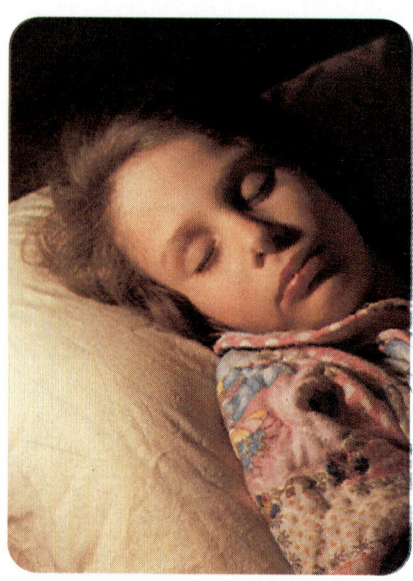

Figure 17-3. Sleep is a state of restfulness.

What happens to the body during sleep?

What are some suggestions for getting a good night's sleep?

- be sure the place where you sleep is quiet or play soft, restful music.
- discuss problems with a responsible adult so that worry will not disturb your sleep.

If you still have trouble sleeping, do some relaxation exercises or drink a glass of warm milk. Milk contains substances that relax the body.

People who do not get enough sleep usually feel tired all the time. Some people have headaches, loss of memory, or find out that they cannot concentrate on their work. Scientists think the effects of lost sleep are not permanent. Once a person is able to get enough sleep, the tired feeling, headaches, and lack of concentration stop. How many hours of sleep do you get each night?

Figure 17-4. People who do not sleep well feel tired and cannot concentrate.

Lesson Summary

- Exercise affects your health.
- Exercise improves circulation, makes muscles firmer and stronger, and helps control body weight.
- Sleep is necessary for a healthy mind and body.

Lesson Review

Review the lesson to answer these questions.
1. How does exercise improve the muscles of the body?
2. How can exercise help you control your weight?
3. What happens to muscles of the body while you sleep?
4. What are some causes of sleeplessness?

17:2 Personal Cleanliness

LESSON GOALS
In this lesson you will learn
- the importance of cleanliness.
- personal cleanliness is a body care habit that promotes physical health.
- a well-groomed person has a neat and clean appearance.

What is cleanliness?

Body care habits that promote personal cleanliness also promote physical health. **Cleanliness** is the state of neatness a person maintains by being well-groomed. A well-groomed person has a neat and clean appearance. Being well-groomed requires attention to the following areas.
a. bathing regularly
b. caring for skin, nails, hair, and teeth
c. wearing clean clothes
d. eating a variety of foods
e. exercising regularly
f. getting enough sleep

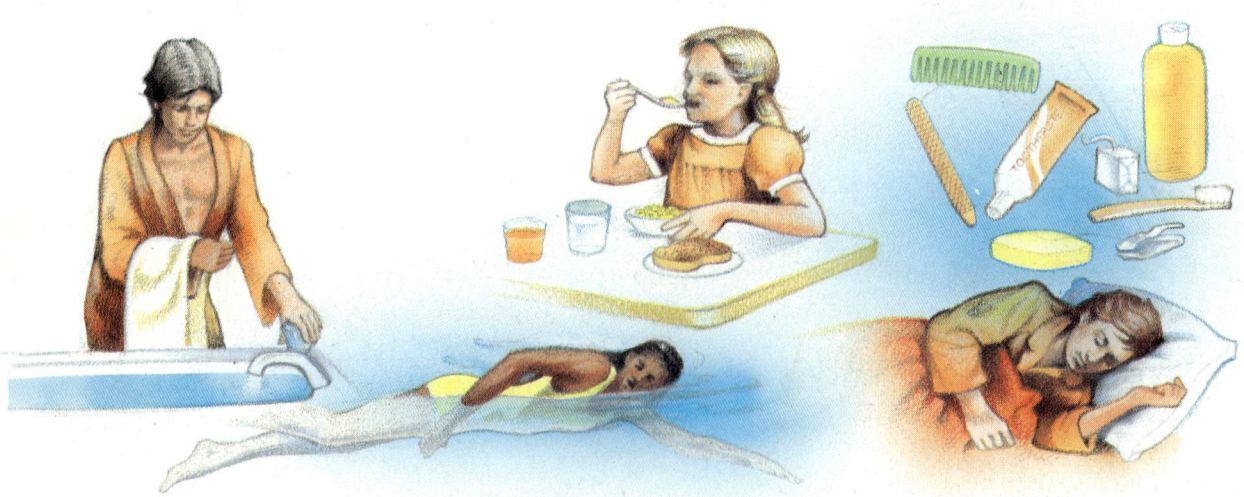

Figure 17-5. Personal cleanliness promotes personal health.

Skin Care

Skin is the organ that covers your body. Skin has two layers. There is an outer and inner layer. The outer layer of skin is made of dead cells that are constantly being replaced by new cells. Dead cells fall off or are rubbed off. The outer layer of skin is also a place where body oils, dirt, and perspiration collect. Bathing or showering regularly with soap breaks down the oils on your skin and washes away extra oil, dirt, germs, perspiration, and dead skin cells. This is why it is always important to wash after exercising.

The skin on your face and hands requires special attention. Wash your face at least two times a day with soap and water. Wash your hands more often. Always wash your hands after using the bathroom. Wash your hands before eating or preparing food. Wash your hands when you are ill and after visiting a person who is ill. Scientists have found that hands spread more cold germs than coughing or sneezing. Washing your hands with soap and water helps to remove germs.

Nail Care

Fingernails and toenails need to be cleaned daily. A nailbrush or nail file should be used to clean under the nails. Keep fingernails and toenails trimmed. Some people prefer their fingernails trimmed straight across, others prefer their fingernails to have rounded edges. Toenails should be trimmed straight across. After trimming, use a nail file to smooth away rough edges.

Figure 17-6. Wash your face at least twice a day.

When should you wash your hands?

Figure 17-7. Clean your nails every day.

Why is nail biting unhealthy?

Never bite your fingernails. Nail biting can be unhealthy. While you are biting your nails, germs from under the nails may enter your mouth. Biting often breaks open the skin around the nail. Germs can enter your body through broken skin. Well-groomed nails are an important part of overall appearance.

Hair Care

Use shampoo to wash your hair at least two times a week. If you have oily hair or exercise regularly, you may need to wash your hair more often. When you shampoo, wet your hair and apply the shampoo. Then, rub it into your scalp with your fingertips. Rinse well. Apply more shampoo, rub it in, and rinse well again. Be sure to rinse out all the shampoo. If you do, your scalp will not itch from leftover shampoo and your hair will shine.

Figure 17-8. Shampoo your hair at least twice a week.

Clothing

What you wear affects your overall appearance. Learn to take care of your own clothes. Keep them clean. Keep them repaired by mending them or asking an adult to mend them for you. Some of your clothes can be stored neatly in drawers or on shelves. Put other clothes on hangers. Well cared for clothes look better and last longer. Well cared for clothes make you look well-groomed.

Teeth

When you eat, particles of food may stick to your teeth or may be caught between your teeth. These particles may form plaque. **Plaque** is a sticky material that forms on teeth and is harmful to dental health. Brushing and flossing are two ways to remove and prevent plaque from forming on your teeth. Brush your teeth at least two times a day. Always brush after eating foods that contain sugar if you can. How many times a day do you brush your teeth?

What is plaque?

Figure 17-9. Regular dental checkups are a good body-care habit.

Dental checkups and fluoride treatments are extra steps you can take to avoid teeth and gum problems. Well cared for teeth are important for a well-groomed appearance.

Food, Exercise, and Rest

To complete your grooming plan, remember to eat a variety of foods and not just your favorites. The food you eat supplies your body with the energy you need to work well and enjoy the time you spend working and playing. Regular exercise will keep your body in its best possible shape. After a day spent working, playing, and practicing good grooming habits, you will be ready for a good night's rest. What is your personal grooming plan? How might you improve your plan?

Figure 17-10. Eat a variety of foods.

Lesson Summary

- Body care habits promote personal cleanliness.
- Personal cleanliness promotes physical health.
- A well-groomed person has a neat and clean appearance.

Lesson Review

Review the lesson to answer these questions.
1. Why is skin care important?
2. Why are clean hands important?
3. Why are clean clothes an important part of being well-groomed?

People and Science

Dancing For Good Health

Donna Lopez knows that exercise can be fun. She is an exercise teacher at a health club. Donna helps people plan exercise programs for themselves and teaches active exercise classes.

Aerobic (er ROH bikh) exercise is a kind of exercise that makes the body use a lot of oxygen. Aerobic exercise makes the heart work better. It also makes the muscles stronger, bend easier, and able to work longer. Aerobic dance classes usually meet for about an hour three or four times a week. Donna's students dance to the music she selects, copying her movements. The dance movements are aerobic exercises done to all types of music.

Donna thinks two things make aerobic dancing more fun than other forms of exercise. People keep going to aerobic dancing because they love music and like to exercise with a group. Her students encourage each other to work hard. They make new friends exercising in a group.

Donna's students know that she plans their dance programs carefully. She always starts with 10 to 15 minutes of warm-up stretches. Then at least 20 minutes of dance exercise for the large muscle groups of the arms, legs, and trunk. Class ends with 15 minutes of cool-down before resting. Donna always reminds her students that each person must do his or her best at each class. She likes helping students learn to take care of their health. Her students know that what they do makes a difference in their health and lives. Almost before they know it, her students feel better, look healthier, and are bursting with energy.

Chapter 17 Review

Summary

1. Exercise affects your health by improving circulation, making muscles firmer and stronger, and helping control body weight. 17:1
2. Sleep is necessary for a healthy mind and body. 17:1
3. Body care habits promote personal cleanliness. 17:2
4. Personal cleanliness leads to physical health. 17:2
5. A well-groomed person has a neat and clean appearance. 17:2

Science Words

exercise   Calorie   sleep   cleanliness   plaque

Understanding Science Words

Complete each of the following sentences with a word or words from the Science Words that will make the sentence correct.

1. A person stays neat and well-groomed by practicing _____.
2. Any activity that uses the muscles of the body can be called _____.
3. A measure of the amount of energy in foods is a _____.
4. Your muscles relax, you take fewer breaths, and the number of times your heart beats per minute decreases when you _____.
5. A sticky material that forms on teeth is _____.

Questions

A. Recalling Facts

Choose the word or phrase that correctly completes each of the following sentences.

1. Which of the following spreads the most germs?
    (a) hands   (c) sneezing
    (b) coughing   (d) perspiration

2. Which food is the highest in Calories?
   - (a) a tomato
   - (b) cup of milk
   - (c) an apple
   - (d) a sweet potato
3. Pushing, tensing, lifting, and pulling are exercises that help strengthen your
   - (a) skeletal muscles.
   - (b) heart.
   - (c) circulation.
   - (d) lungs.
4. What can be an effect of sleep loss?
   - (a) more growth hormones
   - (b) greater concentration
   - (c) feeling refreshed
   - (d) headaches
5. Particles of food that get stuck between the teeth may form a sticky material called
   - (a) fluoride.
   - (b) cavity.
   - (c) plaque.
   - (d) floss.

B. Understanding Concepts

Answer each of the following questions using complete sentences.
1. Why is personal cleanliness important to your physical health?
2. Why do you need the proper amount of rest?
3. Suppose for dinner you had a pork chop, a sweet potato, two tomatoes, and a cup of milk. How many Calories did you eat?
4. What kind of exercises could you do to use up all the Calories you ate in the dinner described in question 3?

C. Applying Concepts

Think about what you have learned in this chapter. Answer each of the following questions using complete sentences.
1. Why is it important to have your own personal health care plan?
2. How can exercise improve your physical health?
3. How can not getting enough sleep affect how you feel about yourself?

Chapter 18
Healthful Eating

Now is the best time to form healthful eating habits. These habits will help keep you healthy throughout your lifetime. What is a balanced diet? How can you get the nutrients your body needs to stay healthy?

Choose a balanced diet.

Nutrients   18:1

LESSON GOALS

In this lesson you will learn
- what nutrients your body needs.
- food sources for these nutrients.
- how these nutrients affect your body.

All living things need food. People need good food to supply body needs. Food is needed for energy. The body also needs food for growth and repair of body tissue. All the food a person eats is a **diet.** When you eat the right amount of food from each of the food groups every day, you are keeping your diet balanced.

What is diet?

Figure 18-1. All the food a person eats makes up that person's diet.

Foods contain nutrients. As you know, nutrients are substances in food that the body uses for growth, energy, and repair. Growth, energy, and repair are processes the body must carry on so that you can live. Your body needs more than 50 nutrients to stay healthy. You will learn about six main kinds of nutrients your body needs in balanced amounts every day. These six important nutrients are protein, carbohydrates, fats, vitamins, minerals, and water.

What are six important nutrients?

337

Proteins

Proteins (PROH teenz) are nutrients that are needed for growth and repair of your body cells. After water, protein is the most plentiful material in your body. It is used as building material for muscles, blood, skin, hair, nails, and internal organs such as your heart and liver. Protein helps keep the right amount of water in your body. It helps form substances that regulate your body activities such as growth and repair of body cells. Proteins form substances that fight disease and infection. Protein is also a source of energy for the body.

Good sources of protein are meat, fish, poultry, eggs, milk and dairy products, whole grains, and soybean products. Some foods contain all the essential protein nutrients. They are called complete protein foods. Incomplete protein foods do not contain all the essential protein nutrients. Most meat and dairy products are complete protein foods. Most fruits and vegetables are incomplete protein foods.

What foods are good sources of protein?

Figure 18-2. Foods that are sources of protein

Carbohydrates

Carbohydrates (kar boh HI drayts) are nutrients that provide the main source of energy for your body. They supply energy for all your body functions and for use by your muscles. You need carbohydrates to help digest and use the food you eat. Carbohydrates are the main source of energy for the brain and nervous system. They provide the body with energy.

The main carbohydrates in food are sugars, starches, and cellulose. Sugars such as those in honey and fruits are easy to digest. Starches have to be broken down into sugars for digestion. Cellulose, or fiber, is mostly indigestible by humans. Therefore, cellulose is not an energy source. It is, however, important for intestinal regularity.

Carbohydrates can be made in the body from food you eat. The best food sources of carbohydrates are whole grains, sugar, syrup, honey, fruits, and vegetables. Carbohydrates in processed foods are low in vitamins, minerals, and cellulose. For example, white flour, white sugar, and polished rice are lacking in the B vitamins and other nutrients. Some vitamins and nutrients are added to white flour. When this is done, it is called enriched flour. But even the enriched flour contains fewer vitamins and minerals than whole wheat flour.

If you eat too many starchy and sweet foods, you may neglect the fruits and vegetables that are important for good health. Eating too many foods containing sugar could lead to weight gain and tooth decay.

Figure 18-3. Some foods that are sources of carbohydrates

What are the best food sources of carbohydrates?

Figure 18-4. Foods that are sources of fats

Why are fats needed by the body?

Fats

Fats are nutrients that provide your body with the most concentrated form of energy. Fats are needed by the body to transport, store, and absorb some vitamins. Fat deposits protect and hold your organs in place. Fat insulates and shapes your body. Foods that contain fats are butter, oils, margarine, nuts, seeds, meat, whole milk, eggs, and cheese.

Too much fat in the diet can lead to unwanted weight gain. It can also cause very slow digestion and absorption of nutrients. If you lack carbohydrates and water in your diet, fats cannot be completely digested. Fats may become toxic, or poisonous, to your body. Nutritionists suggest that you limit the fat in your diet.

Vitamins

Vitamins (VITE uh munz) are nutrients that help your body use protein, fat, and carbohydrates. Vitamins help change fat and carbohydrates into energy. They help form bone and other body tissue. They aid in building all your body parts and help regulate your digestion. Vitamins are necessary for proper growth and health.

Table 18-1 shows the foods that contain different vitamins. Each vitamin is needed by your body. A variety of food must be eaten to be sure you get all the vitamins you need.

Minerals

Minerals are nutrients that are needed in every part of your body. They are necessary for your mental and physical health. Minerals are important for strengthening

Why are minerals important?

Table 18–1 Vitamins: Sources and Functions

Vitamin	Food Source	Function
A	milk, butter, margarine, liver, leafy green and yellow vegetables	growth: health of eyes and skin
B_1 (thiamine)	cereals, bread, fish, lean meat, liver, milk, green vegetables	growth: working of the heart, nerves, and muscles
B_2 (riboflavin)	meat, soybeans, milk, green vegetables, eggs, poultry	healthy skin, prevents sensitivity of eyes to light, builds and repairs tissue
B_{12}	green vegetables, liver	prevents anemia
Niacin	meat, poultry, fish, peanut butter, potatoes, whole grain	healthy nervous system
C (ascorbic acid)	citrus fruits, leafy vegetables, fruits	healthy blood cells, strong body cells
D	fish-liver oil, liver, fortified milk, eggs	aids body's use of calcium and phosphorus
K	leafy vegetables	aids blood clotting

your skeleton, making strong teeth, keeping your heart strong and your brain working as it should. You need about 16 different minerals for proper nutrition. Since minerals make up only a very small amount of your body weight, you only need small amounts of each mineral. Minerals come from the food you eat. See Table 18-2 to find out what foods are sources of minerals your body needs.

What is a source of minerals?

Activity 18-1 Testing for Fats

QUESTION How can you test for fats?

Materials
brown paper bag
peanut butter
margarine
cooking oil
meat
bread
green vegetable
pencil and paper

What to do
1. Rub a small sample of cooking oil on the paper bag.
2. Watch for any changes that happen on the paper bag.
3. Rub the other foods on the paper bag. Record what you observe.

What did you learn?
1. What changes did you observe on the paper bag when fat was present in a food?
2. Which foods contained fats?

Using what you learned
1. Tell how you would test other foods for fats.
2. Why is it important to know what is in the foods you eat?

Table 18-2 Some Minerals Needed by the Human Body		
Mineral	Food Source	Body Function
Calcium	milk, cheese, canned salmon, sardines	blood clotting, formation of bones and teeth
Iron	meat, fish, poultry	part of red blood cells
Phosphorus	meat, fish, milk	formation of bones and teeth
Potassium	milk, fruit, beans, fish, meat, squash, potatoes	fluid levels in cells
Sodium	milk, fish, meat, eggs, processed foods	controls amount of fluids in body
Zinc	soybeans, nuts, seeds, poultry, fish, meat	growth of tissue, helps heal wounds

Water

Water is a liquid needed by all living things. It makes up about two-thirds of your body weight. It is also the nutrient most needed by your body. Water is a necessary part of every cell in your body. Water is part of nearly every body process. It is needed in digestion, circulation, and excretion. Water is part of blood. It moves nutrients through your body. Water helps keep a normal body temperature and carries waste material out of the body.

There are many ways that you get the water your body needs. You may drink water or get water in other beverages. You also get water in soups, fruits, and vegetables. Fruits and vegetables are good sources of water. Your body absorbs the water from food during digestion. How do you obtain water for your body's needs?

What is the nutrient most needed by the body?

Figure 18-5. You may drink water or get water from other sources.

Lesson Summary

- Everyone needs six nutrients: protein, carbohydrates, fats, vitamins, minerals, and water.
- You get the nutrients your body needs from eating a variety of foods.
- The six main nutrients provide materials for growth and repair of your body cells and for the energy you need for work and play.

Lesson Review

Review the lesson to answer these questions.
1. What foods provide protein in your diet?
2. How much fat do nutritionists recommend that you have in your diet?
3. Why is it important to have water in your diet?
4. What nutrient is the main source of energy?

Science and Technology

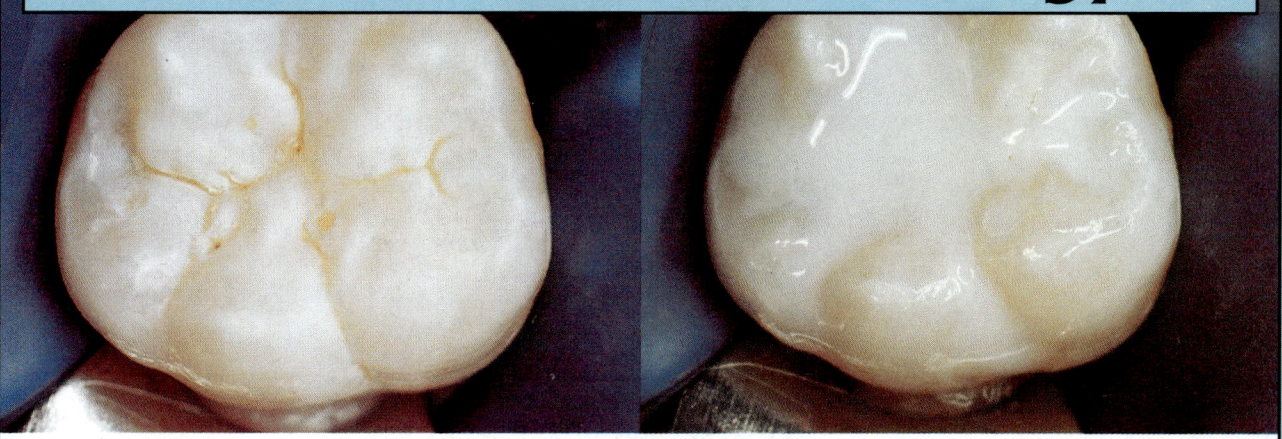

Tooth Paint

There are finger paints, nail polishes, hair dyes, and face paints. But did you know that there is also a tooth paint? Tooth paint is a plastic sealer that prevents tooth decay. It works better than fluoride, especially on back teeth.

Children between 5 and 17 years old get most of their cavities in the top surfaces of their back teeth. The back teeth, or molars, are used for chewing. These teeth have many small grooves that trap food and germs. The sealer is painted on the chewing or top surfaces of back molars. It forms a protective layer on the top surfaces of teeth. This new treatment will prevent many of the cavities that form on these teeth.

To seal teeth, a dentist follows these three steps. First the teeth are cleaned and dried. Next, the teeth are rubbed with a solution of weak acid. After one minute the acid is rinsed off and the teeth are dried again. The sealer holds better on teeth that are treated with the acid. Next the sealer is painted on the teeth with a small brush. In only one half hour all four back molars can be sealed.

The treatment is simple and painless. The only unpleasant part of the treatment is that the material used to seal teeth does not taste very good. However, the bad taste does not last long. The sealer lasts up to five years. The sealed teeth should be checked for cracks or worn spots at regular checkups.

Maybe someday soon you will add a new item to your list of good dental care habits. Besides eating a balanced diet, brushing, flossing, and getting regular checkups, you may also add tooth painting!

18:2 Food Groups and Nutrition

LESSON GOALS

In this lesson you will learn
- about food groups and the kinds of nutrients each group supplies.
- the number of servings you need daily from each food group.
- nutrition needs vary with age.

Another important body care habit concerns eating. If you make a daily effort to eat foods that contain the six main nutrients, you will form the very best eating habit you can. Scientists have divided the foods we eat into five groups according to the main nutrients they contain. The food groups are Milk, Meat, Fruit-Vegetable, Grain, and Combination. You can use the food groups to plan a balanced diet. Remember, the food groups are only a guide.

Food Groups

Foods in the Milk group contain these important nutrients: calcium, vitamin B_2, vitamin D, and protein. These nutrients are needed for strong bones and teeth, healthy skin, and good vision. Examples of foods in this group are milk, yogurt, pudding, cheese, and ice cream.

Foods in the Meat group contain protein, iron, and vitamin B_1. These nutrients are needed for muscle, bone, blood cells, and healthy skin and nerves. This food group includes cooked lean meat, fish and poultry, eggs, and peanut butter.

What are the food groups?

The Fruit-Vegetable group contains vitamins A and C. These vitamins are good for night vision, and they help the body fight infection and heal injuries. This food group includes juices and all fruits and vegetables, either raw or cooked.

Foods in the Grain group contain carbohydrates, vitamin B_1, and iron. The body needs these nutrients for energy and a healthy nervous system. This food group includes bread, cereal, pasta, and rice.

The fifth food group is called the Combination group. It contains materials from more than one food group. Foods in the Combination group supply the same nutrients as the foods they contain. Some examples of Combination foods are soup, stew, chili, and pizza.

Figure 18-6. Example of foods in the combination group

Table 18-3 Other Foods

Sweets	Fats and Oils	Chips	Beverages	Seasonings
brownies	butter	corn	coffee	catsup
cookies	margarine	potato	soft drinks	mustard
candy	cream	pretzels	tea	olives
jelly, jam	gravy	tortilla	fruit-flavored	pickles
sugar	mayonnaise	chips	drinks	sauces
doughnuts	salad dressing			spices

Some foods do not supply the body with needed nutrients. These foods are placed in a separate group. These foods should not be used as replacements for foods in the five food groups. See Table 18-3 for examples of foods in this group.

Table 18-4 shows the four main food groups and the servings of each you need every day.

Table 18-4   Food Groups and

MILK

Supplies these key nutrients:
- calcium
- vitamin B$_2$
- protein

for strong bones and teeth, healthy skin, and good vision

A serving is
- 1 cup (237 mL)   Milk
- 1 cup (237 mL)   Yogurt
- 1½ oz (47 g)   Cheese (1½ slices)
- 1 cup (237 mL)   Pudding
- 2 cups (474 mL)   Cottage cheese
- 1¾ cups (415 mL)   Ice cream

Number of Suggested Servings per Day

3

MEAT

Supplies these key nutrients:
- protein
- iron
- vitamin B$_1$

for muscle, bone, and blood cells, and healthy skin and nerves

A serving is:
- 2 oz (62 g)   Cooked lean meat, fish, or poultry
- 2   Eggs
- 2 oz (62 g)   Cheese
- 1 cup (237 mL)   Dried peas or beans
- 4 tbsp (59 mL)   Peanut butter

Number of Suggested Servings per Day

2

Suggested Servings Per Day

FRUIT-VEGETABLE
Supplies these key nutrients:
- vitamin A
- vitamin C

for night vision and to help resist infections and heal wounds

A serving is:

½ cup (118.5 mL)	Juice
½ cup (118.5 mL)	Cooked fruit or vegetable
1 cup (237 mL)	Raw fruit or vegetable
Medium	Apple, banana, or orange
½	Grapefruit
½	Cantaloupe

Number of Suggested Servings per Day

4

GRAIN
Supplies these key nutrients:
- carbohydrate
- vitamin B_1
- iron

for energy and a healthy nervous system

A serving is:

1 slice	Bread
1 cup (237 mL)	Ready-to-eat-cereal
½ cup (118.5 mL)	Cooked cereal
½ cup (118.5 mL)	Pasta
½ cup (118.5 mL)	Rice
½ cup (118.5 mL)	Grits

Number of Suggested Servings per Day

4

Activity 18-2 Checking Your Diet

QUESTION How balanced is your diet?

Materials
record chart
food groups table
pencil and paper

What to do

1. Keep a record of everything you eat and drink for two days. Be sure to include snacks. Use a chart like the one shown.

Name _____ Diet for _____ and _____							
Food Eaten							
Breakfast		Lunch		Dinner		Snacks	
eggs	2	hot dog	2	chili	5	potato chips	6
milk	1	bun	4				
orange juice	3						

2. Check the food groups in Tables 18–3 and 18–4. Decide in which food group each food or drink belongs.

3. In the spaces provided, label the groups in this way:
   Milk–1   Grain–4
   Meat–2   Combination–5
   Fruit-Vegetable–3   Snacks–6

4. See the chart. One example has been done for you.

5. After two days, total the number of foods from each food group.

What did you learn?
1. Which food group do you eat most often?
2. Which food group do you eat least often?

Using what you learned
1. How many servings from each food group should you eat every day? How many servings did you actually eat?
2. How can you balance your diet?

Different Foods for Different Ages

An infant, two weeks to eighteen months old, grows very rapidly. The growth of the brain and nervous system is very fast. By the time the infant is six months old, the brain has doubled in size. During this period, the infant grows rapidly in length and has a large weight gain. At about six months, the first teeth appear and bones begin to harden. This rapid growth and change in the body requires extra Calories. An infant needs large amounts of protein for cell growth and calcium for bones and teeth.

This growth period continues until about age four, but at a slower rate. It is very important for children to get all the nutrients at this time. It is especially important that they get plenty of protein for cell growth and to fight disease and infection. Calcium is needed for bone development and vitamin A for the eyes. What is a good source for calcium?

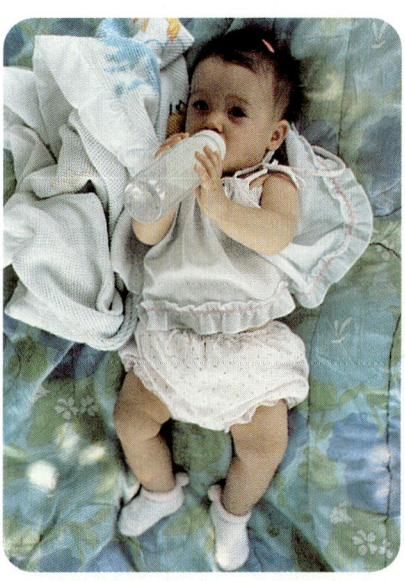

Figure 18-7. Children need a balanced diet during periods of rapid growth.

What does the body need during a rapid growth period?

Figure 18-8. Nutrition needs vary with age.

From about age four to twelve, the average child tends to grow five to seven centimeters a year. Girls have a growth spurt at about age twelve and boys at about age fourteen. The need for protein, calcium, phosphorus, and vitamin D increases at this time. The number of Calories needed per day increases also. Protein is again especially important. As people age and become less active, they need fewer Calories. However, they still need all six nutrients as part of a balanced diet. These six nutrients are:

- proteins
- carbohydrates
- fats
- vitamins
- minerals
- water

Lesson Summary

- You should eat foods from the four main food groups daily.
- You need three servings each day from the Milk group and two from the Meat group.
- You should eat four servings from both the Fruit-Vegetable and Grain groups.
- Nutrition needs vary with age.

Lesson Review

Review the lesson to answer these questions.

1. Which food group is a good source of vitamins A and C?
2. How many servings should you eat each day from the Fruit-Vegetable group?
3. Why should you be careful not to overeat foods such as candy, potato chips, and doughnuts?

Language Arts Skills

Discussing

After you read information in a science book, you often discuss what you read with your teacher and other students. When you discuss, you recall the main points and suggest details that prove those points.

Read the following paragraphs. Pay close attention to the main points and the details that prove them.

All people need a certain amount of fat in their diets every day. However, it is best to be careful about the kinds of fats that you eat. Large amounts of animal fat, coconut oil, and the fat in chocolate can be harmful to your health. The best fats for your health are vegetable oil and oils from seeds and seafood.

Fats of any kind should not be eaten in large amounts for two reasons. They contain more Calories per bite than any other food. This means that fats will make you gain weight. The second reason is that fats affect your blood as soon as they are eaten. When you eat fats, your blood becomes thicker. Many doctors feel that the thickening of blood causes the blood to clot inside the veins. This condition can cause heart attacks.

Use the following questions to select the main points and details that might be included in a discussion.

- What do all people need in their diets?
- What fats are good for your health?
- What fats can be harmful to your health?
- Why should you not eat large amounts of fat?

353

Chapter 18 Review

Summary

1. The six nutrients that everyone needs, proteins, carbohydrates, fats, vitamins, minerals, and water, are found in a variety of foods. 18:1
2. The six main nutrients provide materials for growth and repair of the body cells and for energy. 18:1
3. You need the following daily servings from the four main food groups: three from the Milk group; two from the Meat group; four from both the Fruit-Vegetable and Grain groups. 18:2
4. Nutrition needs vary with different ages. 18:2

Science Words

| diet | carbohydrates | vitamins | water |
| proteins | fats | minerals | |

Understanding Science Words

Complete each of the following sentences with a word or words from the Science Words that will make the sentence correct.

1. A liquid nutrient that your body needs the most is _____.
2. All the food a person eats is called a _____.
3. Nutrients that help your body use protein, fat, and carbohydrates are called _____.
4. Nutrients that give the body energy are found in foods containing _____.
5. Calcium and iron are examples of _____.
6. Nutrients that are building blocks of the body are called _____.
7. Whole grains, sugar, syrups, honey, fruits, and vegetables are the best sources of _____.

Questions

A. Recalling Facts
Choose the word or phrase that correctly completes each of the following sentences.
1. A mineral needed for the formation of bones and teeth is
    (a) sodium.   (c) potassium.
    (b) iron.   (d) phosphorus.
2. Carbohydrates are the main source of energy for the
    (a) heart and circulatory system.   (c) skeletal system.
    (b) brain and nervous system.   (d) digestive system.
3. Vitamin C is important for
    (a) healthy blood cells.   (c) healthy skin.
    (b) growth of muscles.   (d) blood clotting.
4. What an infant of six months needs in large amounts for cell growth is
    (a) calcium.   (c) vitamin A.
    (b) protein.   (d) phosphorus.

B. Understanding Concepts
Answer each of the following questions using complete sentences.
1. How many daily servings of each of the four main food groups is needed by people your age?
2. Name the four main food groups and the nutrients found in each.

C. Applying Concepts
Think about what you have learned in this chapter. Answer each of the following questions using complete sentences.
1. Why are proteins needed to build a healthy body?
2. Why does a twelve-year old girl have different nutritional needs than a fifty-year old woman?

UNIT 9 REVIEW

CHECKING YOURSELF

Answer these questions on a sheet of paper.
1. Why are rest and sleep important to a growing child?
2. What must you do to be well-groomed?
3. Name the main food groups and two examples of food from each group.
4. Why is water necessary for all living things?
5. Why should you wash your hands often?
6. What are the six main nutrients?
7. Explain how the body uses carbohydrates.
8. What nutrients are contained in the Grain group?
9. How does exercise affect the body?
10. Name four foods that are sources of protein.

RECALLING ACTIVITIES

Think about the activities you did in this unit. Answer the questions about these activities.
1. How can you exercise your body? 17–1
2. How can you test for fats? 18–1
3. How balanced is your diet? 18–2

IDEAS TO EXPLORE

1. Choose two classmates to help you role-play a family situation with a sick child. Show how the parent, the sick child, and brother or sister use healthful practices in caring for and treating someone with an illness.

2. Pretend you are doing a radio or TV commercial. Here is what you are trying to sell.
   (a) A Balanced Diet for Good Health
   (b) Exercise and Rest for a New Year
   (c) Body Care Habits for Good Health
3. Interview an orthodontist. Learn about problems that make braces necessary.

CHALLENGING PROJECT

Ask people you know if they are allergic to any foods. What reactions do they have? Record the information on a chart. Some people may be allergic to more than one kind of food. List them separately for each allergy. Try to interview thirty people. Write a summary of the information you gather. What foods caused the most allergic reactions? Are the reactions the same for these foods in different people? What percentage of people you surveyed are not allergic to any foods? Use reference books and interview a doctor who treats food allergies to check the information you gathered and to prepare an oral report about food allergies to give the class.

BOOKS TO READ

The Force Inside You by John Burstein, Coward-McMann, Inc.: New York, © 1983.
   Read about exercises for the body and the mind.

Nutrition by Paul Thompson, Franklin Watts: New York, © 1981.
   Discusses how the body uses nutrients.

What to Eat and Why by Ronald V. Fodor, William Morrow and Co.: New York, © 1979.
   Discusses the relationship between a diet and health.

Glossary

This book has words that you may not have read before. Many of these words are science words. Some science words may be hard for you to read. You will find the science words in **bold print.** These words may appear two ways. The first way shows how the word is spelled. The second way shows how the word sounds. The list below shows the sounds each letter or group of letters makes.

Look at the word **igneous** (IHG nee us). The second spelling shows the letters "ee." Find these letters in the list. The "ee" has the sound of "ea" in the word "leaf." Anytime you see "ee," you know what sound to say. The capitalized syllable is the accented syllable.

a . . . back (BAK)
er . . . care, fair (KER, FER)
ay . . . day (DAY)
ah . . . father (FAHTH ur)
ar . . . car (KAR)
ow . . . flower, loud (Flow ur, LOWD)
e . . . less (LES)
ee . . . leaf (LEEF)
ih . . . trip (TRIHP)
i (i+con+e) . . .
   idea, life (i DEE uh, LIFE)
oh . . . go (GOH)
aw . . . soft (SAWFT)
or . . . orbit (OR but)
oy . . . coin (KOYN)

oo . . . foot (FOOT)
yoo . . . pure (PYOOR)
ew . . . food (FEWD)
yew . . . few (FYEW)
uh (u+con) . . .
   comma, mother (KAHM uh, MUTH ur)
sh . . . shelf (SHELF)
ch . . . nature (NAY chur)
g . . . gift (GIHFT)
j . . . gem, edge (JEM, EJ)
ing . . . sing (SING)
zh . . . vision (VIHZH un)
k . . . cake (KAYK)
s . . . seed, cent (SEED, SENT)
z . . . zone, raise (ZOHN, RAYZ)

A

adaptation (ad ap TAY shun): anything that helps an animal live in its environment

anvil: a small, anvil-shaped bone in the middle ear

asteroid (AS tuh royd): a space object that orbits the sun between Mars and Jupiter

atmosphere (AT muh sfihr): the name for the gases that surround a space object

auditory (AWD uh tor ee) **nerve:** the main nerve that leads from the ear directly to the brain

aurora (uh ROR uh): brightly colored light seen in the night sky

B

behavior: a living thing's response to any stimulus in its environment

benthos (BEN thahs): plants and animals that live on the ocean bottom

Braille: a way of writing that uses letters made of raised dots

bulb: a short underground stem with fleshy leaves; it can grow into a new plant

C

Calorie (KAL uh ree): a measure of the amount of energy in foods

camouflage (KAM uh flahj): an adaptation for blending into the environment

carbohydrates (kar bo HI drayts): nutrients that provide the main source of quick energy for the body

cast: the hardened form or shape of a fossil plant or animal

chlorophyll (KLOR uh fihl): the green matter in plants that traps light energy to produce food

circuit (SUR kut): the path through which a current flows

cleanliness: the state of neatness a person maintains by being well-groomed

comet: a space object made of ice mixed with dust particles

concave lens: a transparent object thinner at its middle and thicker at the edge

conductor (kun DUK tur): matter through which electrons can flow easily

continental shelf: shallow, sloping area beyond the surf

continental slope: area that begins where the continental shelf drops off steeply to the plain

convex lens: a transparent object thick at its middle and thinner at the edges

cork: tough, spongy bark of the cork oak tree

corona (kuh ROH nuh): the main outer part of the sun's atmosphere

countershading: a form of camouflage in which different colors appear on the top and bottom sides of an animal

crest: the high point of a wave

crystal (KRIHS tul): the visible shape of a mineral's atom pattern

current (KUR unt): a strong flow of ocean water; the movement of electrons along a path

cutting: a leaf or stem used to start a new plant

D

diet: all the food a person eats

dye: a substance used for coloring

E

echo: a reflected sound

electric charge: the small amount of electricity that the protons and electrons contain

electromagnet (ih lek troh MAG nut): a temporary magnet made using electric current

electron (ih LEK trahn): a particle found outside the nucleus of an atom

ellipse (ee LIHPS): the egg-shaped pathway of a planet's orbit

erosion (ih ROH zhun): the removal of soil by wind and water

eustachian (yoo STAY shun) **tube:** a tube that connects the middle ear and the back of the throat

exercise: any activity that uses the muscles of the body

extrusive igneous (ihk STREW sihv · IHG nee us) **rock:** rock that forms on the surface from lava

F

fats: nutrients that provide your body with the most concentrated form of energy

fertilization (furt ul uh ZAY shun): the joining of egg cells and sperm cells

fiber: threadlike cells that can be woven into cloth, rope, string, or thread

flower: plant part in which seeds are formed

fossil: any record of ancient life on Earth

frequency (FREE kwun see): the number of times an object vibrates in one second

fruit: an enlarged ovary

fusion (FYEW zhun): the joining together of hydrogen atoms to form helium

G

generator (JEN uh rayt ur): a machine that produces an electric current

geologist (jee AHL uh just): a scientist who studies Earth

germination (jur muh NAY shun): the early growth of a plant from a seed

H

hammer: a small, hammer-shaped bone in the middle ear

hardness: the measure of how easily a mineral can be scratched

I

igneous (IHG nee us) **rock:** rock formed from cooled magma

image: a picture formed when refracted light comes together on the back of the eye

inborn behavior: behavior patterns with which an animal is born

instinct (IHN stingt): a complex inborn behavior that includes more than one action

insulator (IHN suh layt ur): matter through which electrons do not flow easily

intrusive igneous (ihn TREW sihv · IHG nee us) **rock:** rock that forms when magma cools deep in Earth

iris: the colored part of the eye

K

kelp: brown seaweed

L

latex (LAY teks): milky substance from a rubber tree

learned behavior: behavior that is caused by experience; can be changed

lens: a part of the eye behind the pupil; a transparent object with at least one curved surface

lodestone: a natural magnet

luster: the kind of shine a mineral has when light strikes it

M

magma: hot liquid rock

magnet: an object that is able to attract some materials

magnetic field: the area around a magnet where the magnetic force acts

metamorphic (met uh MOR fihk) **rock:** rock formed by heat and pressure

meteor (MEET ee ur): a stray piece of metal or rock from space that enters Earth's atmosphere and glows

meteorite (MEET ee uh rite): a meteor that strikes Earth's surface

meteoroid (MEET ee uh royd): a piece of metal or rock that orbits the sun

mimicry (MIHM ih kree): a protective adaptation in which a harmless animal looks similar to a more dangerous animal

mineral: solid chemical matter formed in nature by Earth processes; nutrient needed in every part of the body for mental and physical health

mold: the hollow space left by a fossil body

mummification (mum ih fuh KAY shun): the process by which animal bodies dry up rather than decay

N

nekton (NEK tun): free-swimming ocean organisms

neutron (NEW trahn): a particle in the nucleus of an atom

nodule (NAHJ ewl): mineral lump found on the ocean bottom

nucleus (NEW klee us): the core of the atom

nutrient (NEW tree unt): material needed by living things for survival

O

ocean wave: the up and down motion of surface water

opaque (oh PAYK) **matter:** matter through which light cannot pass

ophthalmologist (ahf thuh MAHL uh just): a medical doctor who specializes in diseases and disorders of the eye; can perform eye surgery and prescribe medication

optician (ahp TIHSH un): a specially trained person who grinds and shapes the lenses according to a prescription

optic nerve: a path for nerve signals between the eye and the brain

optometrist (ahp TAHM uh trust): a person who examines eyes, prescribes eyeglasses or contact lenses if needed, but cannot prescribe medication

orbit: the path an object follows when it revolves around a larger object

ore: useful metal found in rocks

ovary (OHV ree): flower part that contains egg cells

P

petal: the outer part of a flower that is usually brightly colored

petrified (PEH truh fide) **fossil:** a once-living plant or animal, the parts of which have been replaced by minerals

photosynthesis (foht oh SIHN thuh sus): the process by which plants make food

physical property: a characteristic that can be observed

pistil: the female part of a flower that contains the ovary

pitch: the highness or lowness of a sound

plain: the bottom of the deep, open ocean

planet: a large space object that moves around the sun

plankton (PLANG tun): living plants and animals that drift with the ocean currents

plaque (PLAK): a sticky material that forms on teeth and is harmful to dental health

poles: the ends of a magnet

pollen grain: flower part of a plant that contains sperm cells

pollination (pahl uh NAY shun): the transfer of pollen grains to the sticky part of the pistil

prism (PRIHZ um): a transparent object that refracts light

proteins (PROH teenz): a nutrient needed for growth and repair of body cells

proton (PROH tahn): a particle in the nucleus of an atom

pupil: a clear opening in the center of the iris of the eye

R

raw material: any matter that can be made into useful products

reflex (REE fleks): simple inborn behavior; usually connected with some kind of action

reflection (rih FLEK shun): the bouncing back of light from a surface

refraction (rih FRAK shun): the bending of light

resin (REZ un): a raw material from pine trees used to make turpentine, household cleaners, and other products

respiration (res puh RAY shun): the process that breaks down food and releases energy

retina (RET nuh): the part of the eye where the image forms

rhizome (RI zohm): an underground stem, often of a grass; can produce new plants

rift zone: a system of cracks in the ocean floor through which lava rises

rock: a solid mixture of one or more different minerals

runner: a stem that grows along the ground and forms new plants

S

sedimentary (sed uh MENT uh ree) **rock:** layers of sediment that become cemented together

sepal (SEE pul): outer part of a flower that protects a bud before it opens

skin: the outer covering of an animal's body

sleep: a state of restfulness

social behavior: the behavior of animals living together in an organized way

solar eclipse (ih KLIHPS): an event during which the moon comes directly between Earth and the sun

solar flares: storms that spray gases and small bits of solar particles far out into space

solar system: the name for our sun and all the space objects traveling around it

sonar: an instrument that uses sound waves to locate objects in the water

sphere (SFIHR): an object shaped like a ball

stamen (STAY mun): flower part that produces pollen grains

static (STAT ihk) **discharge:** the movement of electrons from one object to another

static electricity (STAT ihk · ih lek TRIHS ut ee); the charge on an object that has an unequal number of protons and electrons

stimulus (STIHM yuh lus): anything in the environment, such as light, sound, touch, or smell, that causes a living plant or animal to respond

stirrup: a small, stirrup-shaped bone in the middle ear

streak: the color of the powdered mineral

sunspots: dark spots that appear on the surface of the sun

switch: a device that is used to open or close a circuit

T

tannic acid: a chemical from tree bark

territory: the area defended by one or more animals against rivals

tidal power: electricity made from the moving water of tides

tide: the rise and fall of ocean water levels caused by the gravitational pull of the moon

translucent (trans LEWS unt) **matter:** matter that scatters light in many directions

transparent (trans PER unt) **matter:** matter that light can pass straight through

trench: a deep narrow valley in the ocean floor

trough (TRAWF): the low point of a wave

tsunami (soo NAHM ee): a huge sea wave that travels at very fast speeds

tuber: a swollen underground root or stem that can form new plants

turbine: a device that has blades attached to an axle; it provides power to run a generator

V

vacuum (VAK yewm): a space that contains no matter

vibration (vi BRAY shun): the back and forth movement of particles of matter

visible spectrum: the band of colors that make up white light

vitamins (VITE uh munz); nutrients that help the body use protein, fat, and carbohydrates

volume (VAHL yum): the loudness or softness of a sound

W

water: liquid needed by all living organisms

white light: a mixture of many colors; can be separated into a band of colors

wood pulp: a soft, spongy material made by combining wood chips, chemicals, and steam

Index

A

Absorbed sound, 214; *act.*, 213
Adaptation. *See* Animal adaptation
Aerobic exercise instructor, 333; *illus.*, 333
Aluminum, 134
Amber, 142; *illus.*, 142
Amethyst, *illus.*, 121, 125
Animal adaptations, 158-174; camouflage, 170-171; counter shading, 171-172; feathers, 163; feet, 165-166; fur, 164; mimicry, 172-173; mouthparts, 166-167; scales, 161; skin, 160-161; teeth, 167-168; warning coloration, 172; wings, 165; *act.*, 162, 174; *illus.*, 159, 160, 161, 163, 164, 165, 166, 167, 168, 170, 171, 172, 173
Animal behavior, 156, 178-192; inborn, 180; instinct, 183-185; learned, 186-188; reflex, 181; social, 189-190; territorial, 191-192; *act.*, 182, 188; *illus.*, 156, 157, 178, 179, 180, 181, 183, 184, 185, 186, 187, 188, 189, 190, 191, 192
Anvil, 220; *illus.*, 220
Asteroid, 107
Atmosphere, 86
Atom, model of, 286; *illus.*, 286
Auditory nerve, 221
Aurora, 83; *illus.*, 83

B

Basalt, 128
Battery, 292
Behavior. *See* Animal behavior
Benthos, 261
Bill, 166-167; *illus.*, 166, 167
Biometric security system, 55; *illus.*, 55
Bird: behavior of, 180, 181, 183-185; bill of, 166-167; coloring of, 171; countershading of, 172; feathers of, 163; *illus.*, 163, 166, 167, 171, 172, 180, 181, 183, 184, 185
Braille, 64-65; *illus.*, 65
Bulb, 30; *illus.*, 30

C

Calcium carbonate, 247
Calorie, 324; *tables*, 324
Camera, 38
Camouflage, 170-171; *illus.*, 170, 171
Carbohydrates, 339
Carbon dioxide, 249
Cast, 142
Cellulose, 339
Ceres, 107
Chlorophyll, 6
Circuit, 292, 296-298; *act.*, 293; *illus.*, 292, 296
Circulation, 322

Classifying, 151
Clay, 135, 136
Cleanliness, 328-331
Clothing, 331
Coal, 130, 146; *illus.,* 130
Color, 50-54; seeing, 52-53; using, 53-54; *act.,* 51; *illus.,* 50, 52
Coloration, warning, 172
Comet, 107-109; *illus.,* 107, 108
Comet Halley, 95, 109; *illus.,* 108
Concave lens, 66; *illus.,* 66, 67
Conductor, 294; *act.,* 295; *illus.,* 294
Conglomerate, 129
Continental shelf, 265-267
Continental slope, 267-268
Convex lens, 66; *illus.,* 66, 67
Cork, 14
Corona, 86; *illus.,* 86
Cotton fiber, 14; *illus.,* 14
Countershading, 171-172; *illus.,* 171, 172
Cousteau, Jacques, 236
Crest, 250; *illus.,* 250
Crystal, 124-125; *illus.,* 125
Current: electric, 292-298; ocean, 255-256; *act.,* 254; *illus.,* 255, 256
Cutting, 29; *act.,* 31; *illus.,* 29

D

Deimos, 99; *illus.,* 99
Dental care, 331
Desalinization plant, *illus.,* 246

Diamond, 120, 136; *illus.,* 120
Diatoms, 257; *illus.,* 257
Diet, 337-352; food groups in, 346-350; nutrients in, 337-344; *act.,* 350; *tables,* 341, 343, 348-349
Discussing, 353
Dye, 14

E

Ear, 218-230; care of, 229-230; parts of, 220-222; *act.,* 224-225; *illus.,* 220, 221, 229
Earache, 230
Earth, 98; composition of, 118-136; plates of, 147; tides of, 251-253; *illus.,* 98, 238
Echo, 214
Eclipse: solar, 84-86; *act.,* 85; *illus.,* 84; *table,* 86
Edison, Thomas, 282
Egg cell, 24-25; *illus.,* 24
Electric charge, 286-291; *illus.,* 287, 289
Electricity, 282-298; current, 292-298; static, 285-291; *act.,* 288, 293, 295; *illus.,* 290, 291
Electromagnet, 308-312; *act.,* 309; *illus.,* 308, 310
Electron, 286-290; *illus.,* 290
Ellipse, 92; *illus.,* 92
Energy: from ocean, 253; solar, 80
Erosion, prevention of, 15; *illus.,* 15
Eustachian tube, 221-222

Exercise, 321-325; circulation and, 322; muscles and, 322; weight control and, 324; *act.,* 325; *illus.,* 321, 323

Exploration geologist, 137; *illus.,* 137

Extrusive igneous rock, 128; *illus.,* 128

Eye, 59-70; care of, 69-70; parts of, 60, 62; problems of, 64-69; reflex of, 181; *act.,* 60-61, 68; *illus.,* 60, 62, 63, 67, 69, 181; *table,* 70

Eye infection, 69

F

Farsightedness, 67
Fats, 340; *act.,* 342
Feathers, 163; *illus.,* 163
Feet, 165-166; *illus.,* 165-166
Fertilization, of plants, 25; *illus.,* 24
Fiber, 14, 339; *illus.,* 14
Fish, 263; behavior of, 184, 190; countershading of, 171; migration of, 184; protection of, 274-275; scales of, 161, 162; *act.,* 162; *illus.,* 160, 171, 184, 190, 262
Flower, 22-25, fertilization, 25; parts of, 22-23, 27; pollination, 24; *act.,* 27; *illus.,* 22, 23
Food, 336-352; age and, 351-352; nutrients in, 337-344; plants as, 12; *act.,* 350; *tables,* 324, 341, 343, 347, 348-349
Food groups, 346-350; *act.,* 350; *table,* 348-349
Fossil, 140-150; and artifacts, 145; kinds of, 142-144; mold and cast, 142; petrified, 144; using, 146-150; *act.,* 143, 149; *illus.,* 140, 141, 142, 144, 146, 148, 150
Frequency, 209
Fruit, 25-26
Fur, 164; *illus.,* 164
Fusion, 80

G

Galilei, Galileo, 76
Garden center, 17; *illus.,* 17
Gas, *act.,* 10
Generator, 310-311; *illus.,* 311
Geologist, 119
Geothermal energy, 307
Germination, 28-29; *illus.,* 28
Giotto **space probe,** 95, 109; *illus.,* 95, 109
Glacier, 147; *illus.,* 147
Globe, 241
Glossary, use of, 33
Gneiss, 131, 132; *illus.,* 131
Granite, 128; *illus.,* 128, 131
Graph, 111
Gravity, *act.,* 94
Grooming, 328-332

H

Hair care, 330; *illus.*, 330
Hammer, 220; *illus.*, 220
Hardness, 122
Health, 320-352; cleanliness, 328-331; exercise, 321-325; nutrition and, 336-352; sleep, 326-327; weight control, 324; *act.*, 325
Hearing, 218-230; limits of, 226-227; *act.*, 224-225, 228
Hematite, 120; *illus.*, 120
Horse head nebula, *illus.*, 44
Hypotheses about magnets, 313

I

Igneous rock, 127-128; extrusive, 128; intrusive, 128; *illus.*, 128
Image, 62-63
Inborn behavior, 180; *illus.*, 180
Inferring, 231
Insect: behavior of, 182, 184, 189; camouflage of, 171; mimicry in, 172-173; *act.*, 182; *illus.*, 170, 172, 173, 184, 189
Instinct, 183-185; *illus.*, 183, 184, 185
Insulator, 294; *illus.*, 294
Intrusive igneous rock, 128; *illus.*, 128
Io, *illus.*, 100
Iris, 60; *act.*, 60-61; *illus.*, 62

J

Jupiter, 93, 100-101; *illus.*, 101

K

Kelp, 266; *illus.*, 266

L

Latex, 14; *illus.*, 14
Lava, 128; *illus.*, 127
Learned behavior, 186-188; *act.*, 188; *illus.*, 186, 187
Lens, 62; concave, 66; convex, 66; corrective, 65-66; *act.*, 68; *illus.*, 66, 67
Light, 41-48; behavior of, 43-44; reflection of, 44; refraction of, 45-46; 48; white, 50; *act.*, 48; *illus.*, 43, 46, 50
Lightning, 291; *illus.*, 291
Limestone, 130; *illus.*, 130, 131
Lodestone, 303; *illus.*, 302
Lorenz, Konrad, 156
Luster, 124; *illus.*, 124

M

Magma, 127-128; 136, 270; *illus.*, 127
Magnet, 303-312; behavior of, 304-305; electromagnet, 308-312; *act.*, 309; *illus.*, 303, 304, 305, 308, 310

Magnetic field, 305-306; *illus.,* 306
Manganese, 248; *illus.,* 248
Marble, 131; *illus.,* 131, 132
Mariner spacecraft, *illus.,* 97
Mars, 98-99; *illus.,* 99
Mercury, 93, 96-97; *illus.,* 96
Metal, 294; *illus.,* 294
Metamorphic rock, 131-132; *illus.,* 131
Meteor, 109-110; *illus.,* 109
Meteorite, 110
Meteoroid, 109-110
Mica, 135
Mid-ocean ridge, 271
Migration, 183-184; *illus.,* 183, 184
Milky Way Galaxy, 90
Mimicry, 172-173; *illus.,* 172, 173
Mineral, 119-125; color of, 121; crystal shape in, 124-125; in diet, 340-341; hardness of, 122; luster of, 124; in ocean, 247-249; streak test of, 122; useful, 134-136; *act.,* 123; *illus.,* 119, 120, 121, 124, 125, 247, 248; *tables,* diet, 343; properties, 121
Mohs' scale, 122
Mold and cast fossil, 142
Moon: of Jupiter, 100; of Mars, 99; of Pluto, 105; of Saturn, 102; *illus.,* 99, 100
Mountains, under ocean, 270-271

Mouthparts, 166-167; *illus.,* 166, 167
Mummification, 142
Muscles, 322; *illus.,* 323

N

Nail care, 329-330; *illus.,* 329
Nearsightedness, 66
Nekton, 261
Neptune, 103; *illus.,* 77
Neutron, 286
Niépce, Joseph Nicéphore, 38
Nodule, 248; *illus.,* 248
Nucleus, 286
Nursery keeper, 175; *illus.,* 175
Nutrient, 256, 337-344; carbohydrates, 339; fats, 340, 342; minerals, 340-341, 343; protein, 338; vitamins, 340, 341; water, 343; *act.,* 342; *tables,* 341, 343
Nutrition, 346-352

O

Obsidian, 128; *illus.,* 128
Ocean, 236, 238-256; energy from, 253; mapping, 264-268; movements of, 250-256; pollution in, 275; properties of water, 242-246; protecting, 274-275; removing salt from, 246-247; resources of, 247-249;

temperature of, 244, 246; trenches in, 272; *act.*, 241, 245, 254; *illus.*, 239, 243, 244, 272

Ocean current, 255-256; *act.*, 254; *illus.*, 255, 256

Ocean floor, 264-273; *act.*, 273; *illus.*, 265, 266, 270, 271

Ocean floor plain, 268

Ocean life, 260-263, 271, 274-275; *illus.*, 260, 261, 262, 274

Ocean wave, 250-251; *illus.*, 250, 251

Oil, 248, 267

Opaque matter, 47

Ophthalmologist, 67

Optician, 67

Optic nerve, 62-63

Optometrist, 67

Orbit, 92-93; *illus.*, 92, 93

Ore, 134, 136

Outline, 71

Ovary, plant, 22-23

Oxygen, 249

P

Petal, 22; *illus.*, 22

Petrified fossil, 144; *illus.*, 144

Photography, 38-39

Photojournalist, 49; *illus.*, 49

Photosynthesis, 5-6; *illus.*, 6, 9

Physical property, 121; *act.*, 123, 133

Pinkeye, 69

Pistil, 22-23

Pitch, 206-207; 226-227; *act.*, 208

Plain, 268

Planet, 92-105; Earth, 98; Jupiter, 93, 100-101; Mars, 98-99; Mercury, 93, 96-97; Neptune, 103; orbit of, 92-93; Pluto, 105; Saturn, 101-102; Uranus, 103; Venus, 97; *act.*, 94, 104; *illus.*, 77, 92, 93, 96, 97, 98, 99, 101, 102, 105

Plankton, 261; *illus.*, 261

Plant, 5-16; in space, 11; photosynthesis by, 5-6; reproduction of, 20-32; respiration of, 8-9; uses of, 12-16; *act.*, 7, 10, 27, 31; *illus.*, 11, 12, 21, 22, 23, 25, 26, 28, 29, 30, 32

Plaque, 331

Plate, 147; *illus.*, 147

Pluto, 105; *illus.*, 105

Pole, 304-305; *illus.*, 305

Pollen grain, 23

Pollination, 24; *illus.*, 24

Pollution, of ocean, 275

Potato, 30; *illus.*, 30

Prism, 50; *illus.*, 50

Propeller planes, 223; *illus.*, 223

Property, physical, 121; *act.*, 123, 133

Protein, 338

Proton, 286

Pupil 60; *illus.*, 60, 62

Q

Quartz, *illus.*, 121
Quinine, 14

R

Rainbow, 52; *illus.*, 52
Raw material, from plants, 12-14
Reflection: of light, 44; of sound, 213, 214
Reflex, 181; *act.*, 182; *illus.*, 181
Refraction, 45-46; *act.*, 48; *illus.*, 46
Reproduction, of plants, 20-32; *act.*, 31; *illus.*, 24, 25, 26, 28, 29, 30
Resin, 14
Respiration, 8-9; *illus.*, 8, 9
Retina, 62, 63; *illus.*, 62, 63
Rhizome, 30; *illus.*, 30
Rift zone, 270-271; *illus.*, 270
Rock, 126-136; igneous, 127-128; metamorphic, 131-132; sedimentary, 129-130; useful, 134-136; *act.*, 133; *illus.*, 118, 126, 128, 129, 130, 131, 132
Rock record, 140-150
Rock salt, 135, 136
Roosevelt elk, 169; *illus.*, 169
Runner, 32

S

Safety goggles, 69; *illus.*, 69
Salt, 135, 136, 243, 246
Sandstone, 129, 135; *illus.*, 129
Saturn, 101-102; *illus.*, 102
Scales, 161; *act.*, 162; *illus.*, 161
Sediment, 129
Sedimentary rock, 129-130; *illus.*, 129, 130
Seed, 25-26; germination, 28-29; *illus.*, 25, 26
Senses: hearing, 218-230; sight, 58-70
Sepal, 22
Shale, 129; *illus.*, 129, 131
Sight, 58-70; problems with, 64-69; protection of, 69-70; *illus.*, 59
Silica, 247
Skin, 160-161; *illus.*, 160, 161
Skin care, 329; *illus.*, 329
Slate, 131, 132, 135; *illus.*, 131
Sleep, 326-327
Snake: skin of, 161; teeth of, 168; *illus.*, 161, 168
Social behavior, 189-190; *illus.*, 189, 190
Solar eclipse, 84-86; *act.*, 85; *illus.*, 84; *table*, 86
Solar flare, 82-83; *illus.*, 83
Solar system, 91; asteroids, 107; comets, 107-109; meteoroids, 109-110; planets, 92-105; sun, 78-86; *illus.*, 91

Sonar, 264-265; *illus.,* 264
Sound, 198-214; absorbed, 213, 214; behavior of, 210-211; frequency of, 209; hearing and, 218-230; making, 203-204; pitch of, 206-208; properties of, 201-202, 205-209; reflected, 213, 214; speed of, 211-212; volume of, 205-206; *act.,* 204, 208, 213, 224-225, 228; *table,* 212
Space satellite engineer, 87; *illus.,* 87
Spectrum, visible, 50-52; *illus.,* 50, 52
Speech therapist, 215; *illus.,* 215
Speed, of sound, 211-212
Sperm cell, 24-25; *illus.,* 24
Sphere, 80
Stamen, 23
Star, 79
Starch: in diet, 339; plant storage of, 6, 7; *act.,* 7
Static discharge, 290-291; *illus.,* 291
Static electricity, 285-291; *act.,* 288; *illus.,* 285, 291
Stimulus, 179
Stirrup, 220; *illus.,* 220
Strawberry plant, 32; *illus.,* 32
Streak, 122
Streak test, 122; *illus.,* 122; *table,* 122
Sugar: in diet, 339; plant storage of, 6

Sulfur, 135, 136; *illus.,* 136
Sun, 78-86; activity of, 81-83; corona of, 86; eclipse of, 84-86; energy from, 80; *act.,* 85; *illus.,* 78, 80, 81, 86
Sunspot, 81-82; *illus.,* 81, 82
Switch, 296-297

T

Talc, 120; *illus.,* 120
Tannic acid, 13
Tannin, 13
Teeth: adaptation and, 167-168; care of, 331; *illus.,* 165, 167, 168
Telescope, 76; *illus.,* 76
Territory, 191-192
Tidal power, 253
Tide, 251-253; *illus.,* 251, 252
Time travel television, 276-277; *illus.,* 276-277
Tomato, 26; *illus.,* 26
Tooth paint, 345; *illus.,* 345
Translucent matter, 47
Transparent matter, 46
Tree, fossil of, 146
Trench, 272; *illus.,* 272
Trough, 250; *illus.,* 250
Tsunami, 251; *illus.,* 251
Tuber, 30; *illus.,* 30
Turbine, 311-312; *illus.,* 311, 312

U

Understanding an outline, 71; *illus.,* 71
Understanding graphs, 111; *illus.,* 111
Underwater photography, 269; *illus.,* 269
Uranus, 103
Using a glossary, 33; *illus.,* 33

V

Vacuum, 211
Venus, 97; *illus.,* 97
Vesta, 107
Vibration, 203; *act.,* 204
Visible spectrum, 50-52; *illus.,* 50, 52
Vision. *See* Sight
Vitamins, 340; *table,* 341
Volcano, 116, 270; *illus.,* 116, 117
Volume, 205-206
Voyager, 76, 102, 103; *illus.,* 77, 101, 103

W

Warning coloration, 172
Watches: water powered, 299; *illus.,* 299
Water: desalinization of, 246-247; in diet, 343; ocean, 242-246
Water cycle, *illus.,* 243
Wave, 250-251; *illus.,* 250, 251
Weight control, 324; *tables,* 324
White light, 50
Wood pulp, 13; *illus.,* 13
Writing the results, 193

PHOTO CREDITS

COVER: Jet Propulsion Laboratory
viii, Commercial Image; **2, 3,** Milt and Joan Mann, inset Collections of the Passaic County Historical Society, Paterson, NJ; **4,** Elaine Shay; **5,** H. Reinhard/Bruce Coleman, Inc.; **6,** (t) Gerard Photography, (b) Breck P. Kent; **11,** NASA; **12,** (t) Jack Sekowski, (b) Gerard Photography; **13,** Roger K. Burnard; **14,** (t) Dr. Nigel Smith/Earth Scenes, (b) Grant Heilman Photography; **15,** Breck P. Kent; **16,** Zig Leszczynski/Earth Scenes; **17,** Commercial Image; **20,** D.R. Specker/Earth Scenes; **21,** (l) Gerard Photography, (c, r) Dwight R. Kuhn; **22,** (t) Grant Heilman Photography, (c, b) Steve Lissau; **24,** Dwight R. Kuhn; **25,** (l) Breck P. Kent, (r) Gerard Photography; **26,** Gerard Photography; **29,** (l) Victor Englebert/Photo Researchers, Inc., (r) Jack Sekowski; **30,** Gerard Photography; **32,** Dwight R. Kuhn; **38, 39,** Jack Sekowski, inset University of Texas at Austin/The Gernsheim Collection; **40,** Margaret C. Berg/Berg & Associates; **41,** (l) Norman L. Berg/Berg & Associates, (tr) Runk/Schoenberger from Grant Heilman, (br) Jack Sekowski; **43,** (l) Tom Pantages, (r) Jack Sekowski; **44,** Tersch; **46,** Pictures Unlimited; **47,** Jack Sekowski; **49,** Commercial Image; **50,** Courtesy of Eastman Kodak, 1978; **52,** (t) Grant Heilman Photography, (b) Jack Sekowski; **53,** (t) Bill Tronca/Tom Stack & Associates, (b) Jack Sekowski; **54,** Larry Hamill; **55,** Courtesy of Eye-Dentify, Inc.; **59, 60, 64,** Jack Sekowski; **65,** (t) Commercial Image, (b) Jack Sekowski; **66,** David Parker/Photo Researchers, Inc.; **69,** H.M. DeCruyenaere; **76,** Escorial/Arxiu Mas/Photograph Submitted and Authorized by Patrimonio Nacional; **78,** Tracy Borland; **79,** Jack Sekowski; **81,** Tersch; **83,** (t) NASA, (b) Don Benson/Tom Stack & Associates; **84,** Jack Sekowski; **86,** (t) Tersch, (b) NASA; **87,** Cobalt Productions; **90,** © 1980 Anglo-Australian Telescope Board; **95,** European Space Agency; **96, 97, 98, 99, 100, 101, 102, 103,** NASA; **107,** The Bettman Archive; **109,** (t) European Space Agency, (b) Tersch; **110,** Breck P. Kent; **116, 117,** Soames Summerhays/Photo Researchers, Inc., inset Breck P. Kent; **118,** Breck P. Kent; **119,** Jack Sekowski; **120,** (tl,tr) Pictures Unlimited, (bl) Breck P. Kent, (br) Doug Martin; **121, 122,** Doug Martin; **124,** (tl) Eric Hoffhines, (tr) Roger K. Burnard, (bl) Craig Kramer, (br) Doug Martin; **125,** (t) Breck P. Kent, (c) Eric V. Grave/Photo Researchers, Inc.; **126,** Doug Martin; **127,** (l) Doug Martin, (c,r) Breck P. Kent, (b) E. R. Degginger/Bruce Coleman, Inc.; **128,** (t,b) Breck P. Kent, (c) David Dennis; **129,** (t) Breck P. Kent, (b) Elaine Shay; **130,** (l) File Photos, (r) Rod Allin/Tom Stack & Associates, inset Breck P. Kent; **131,** (tl,tc) Elaine Shay, (tr) University of Houston, (b) Doug Martin; **132,** Gerard Photography; **134,** (t) Breck P. Kent, (b) Pictures Unlimited; **135,** Smithsonian Institution; **136,** C.C. Lockwood/Earth Scenes; **137,** Cobalt Productions; **140,** Courtesy of Takeo Susuki, UCLA; **141,** (l) Chip Clark, (r) Commercial Image; **142,** (t) Chip Clark, (b) William E. Ferguson; **144,** File Photo; **145,** Andrew Rakoczy; **146,** (l) Chip Clark, (r) Carl Roessler/Tom Stack & Associates; **147,** Breck P. Kent; **148,** (l)Chip Clark, (br) H.M. DeCruyenaere/Courtesy of The National History Museum of Los Angeles County, (tr) Tom Bean; **149,** Jack Sekowski; **150,** (l) Smithsonian Institution, (r) Library of Congress; **156, 157,** Courtesy of the Columbus Zoo, Columbus, OH, inset Harry Redl/Black Star; **158,** David Hiser/Aspen; **159,** (l) Stephen J. Krasemann, (r) Steve Lissau; **160,** (tl) Alan Carey, (cl) David R. Frazier, (bl) Mack Albin, (r) Stephen J. Krasemann; **161,** (tr) Lynn Stone, (cr) Stock Concepts, (l) Zig Leszczynski c/o Breck P. Kent; **163,** (t) G.I. Bernard/Animals Animals, (bl) Lynn Stone, (bc) Margot Conte/Animals Animals, (br) Sharon Kurgis; **164,** (l) Richard Kolar/Animals Animals, (r) Stephen J. Krasemann/DRK Photo; **165,** (t) William D. Popejoy, (bl) Mary Stouffer/Animals Animals, (br) Alan Carey; **166,** (tr) Lynn Stone, (cl) Roger K. Burnard, (bl) Stephen J. Krasemann; **167,** (tl) Gary R. Zahm/DRK Photo, (bl) Rex Schmidt, (c) Roger Altemus, (tr) Richard Brommer, (br) Gary Milburn/Tom Stack & Associates; **168,** Joe McDonald/Animals Animals; **169,** Tom and Pat Leeson; **170,** (l) James E. Stahl, (tr) Lynn Stone, (br) E.R. Degginger/Animals Animals; **171,** (t) Stephen J. Krasemann, (c) Breck P. Kent, (b) Fred Whitehead/Animals Animals; **172,** (t) Roger K. Burnard, (b) Dwight R. Kuhn; **173,** (tr) James E. Stahl, (c) Dwight R. Kuhn, (tr) Zig Leszczynski/Animals Animals, (br) Michael Fogden/Animals

Animals; **175,** Courtesy of the Columbus Zoo, Columbus, OH; **178,** Wendy Neefus/Animals Animals; **179,** (l) Ralph A. Reinhold/Animals Animals, (r) Jack Sekowski; **180,** (tl) G.I. Bernard/Animals Animals, (cl) Jack Sekowski, (bl) William J. Weber, (r) Dwight R. Kuhn; **181,** (l) Alan Carey, (r) Alvin Staffan; **183,** Alvin Staffan; **184,** (t) Leonard Lee Rue III/Animals Animals, (c) U.S. Fish and Wildlife Service, (b) Frank S. Balthis; **185,** File Photo; **186,** Jack Sekowski; **187,** (l) Commercial Image, (tr) David R. Frazier, (br) Tom McGuire; **189,** (t) Dwight R. Kuhn, (b) Lynn Stone; **190,** (t) J. Jacque, (b) Stephen J. Krasemann/DRK Photo; **191,** (t) DRK Photo, (b) Frank Roberts/Animals Animals; **192,** Perry D. Slocum/Animals Animals; **198, 199,** Dick Luria/Photo Researchers, Inc., inset The Metropolitan Museum of Art, gift of B.H. Homan 1929; **200,** Janet Adams; **201,** (l) Jack Sekowski, (tr) Pictures Unlimited, (br) H.M. DeCruyenaere; **202,** Scott Blackman/Tom Stack & Associates; **203,** (l) Pictures Unlimited, (r) Hickson-Bender Photography; **205,** (l) Matt Lindsay/Berg & Associates, (r) Jack Sekowski; **206,** Commercial Image; **207, 209,** Jack Sekowski; **210,** Cobalt Productions; **211,** FlexPhoto; **212,** Walter Grogan Jr./Spectra-Action, Inc.; **213,** Doug Martin; **214, 215,** Cobalt Productions; **218,** (tl) John Shaw/Tom Stack & Associates, (tr) Commercial Image, (bl) Milt and Joan Mann, (br) Alix Coleman from Grant Heilman; **219,** Royce Bair/The Stock Solution; **222,** Milt and Joan Mann; **223,** Courtesy of Beech Aircraft Corp.; **224,** Doug Martin; **226,** (tl) Commercial Image, (bl) Jack Fields/Photo Researchers, Inc., (r) First Image; **227,** Cobalt Productions; **229,** Jack Sekowski; **236, 237,** Herb Segars/Tom Stack & Associates, inset Randy Taylor/Black Star; **238,** NASA; **240,** Jeffrey W. Meyers/FPG; **242,** U.S. Geological Survey; **243,** FlexPhoto; **244,** (l) William Waterfall, (r) M.P. Kahl/Tom Stack & Associates; **246,** U.S. Dept. of the Interior; **247,** (l) William E. Townsend Jr./Photo Researchers, Inc., (r) Ed Robinson/Tom Stack & Associates; **248,** (t) Courtesy of Lawrence Sullivan, Lamont-Doherty Geological Observatory, (r) Jim McNee/Tom Stack & Associates; **249,** Ed Robinson/Tom Stack & Associates; **251,** Courtesy of National Geophysical Data Center; **252,** Terry Domico/Earth Images; **253,** Milt and Joan Mann; **255,** Steve Lissau; **257,** Rex Educational Resources Co.; **260,** Frank S. Balthis; **261,** (t) D.P. Wilson/Science Source, (c) David Denning/Earth Images, (b) David L. Shogren/Tom Stack & Associates; **264,** David R. Frazier; **265,** FPG; **266,** Tom Stack/Tom Stack & Associates; **268,** Wood's Hole Oceanographic Institution; **269,** Stock Concepts; **271,** Wood's Hole Oceanographic Institution; **274,** Jeff Foott/Tom Stack & Associates; **275,** (t) Martin Rogers/FPG, (b) Tom Stack/Tom Stack & Associates; **282, 283,** James N. Westwater; **284, 285, 289, 290,** Jack Sekowski; **291,** (l) Joe McDonald/Bruce Coleman Inc., (r) Tom Bean; **294,** (tl) Cliff Beaver, (tr) Don and Pat Valenti/DRK Photo, (bl) Commercial Image, (br) Pictures Unlimited; **296,** Doug Martin; **297,** (l) Gerard Photography, (tr) FlexPhoto, (cr,br) Pictures Unlimited; **298,** (tl,bl) Jack Sekowski, (r) FPG; **299,** Courtesy of VentuResearch, Inc.; **302, 303, 304, 305, 306,** Doug Martin; **307,** Cobalt Productions; **308,** Doug Martin; **310,** Frank Cezus; **311,** (t) First Image, (b) Earl Roberge/Photo Researchers, Inc.; **318, 319,** Lewis Portnoy/Spectra-Action, Inc., inset Culver Pictures; **320,** Jack Sekowski; **321,** (l) Jack Sekowski, (tr) Commercial Image, (br) Cobalt Productions; **326,** Elaine Shay; **327,** Doug Martin; **329,** (t) Jack Sekowski, (b) Hickson-Bender Photography; **330,** Doug Martin; **331,** Hickson-Bender Photography; **332, 333,** Commercial Image; **336, 337,** Hickson-Bender Photography; **338, 339, 340,** Jack Sekowski; **344,** Gerard Photography; **345,** Courtesy of Dr. Richard J. Simonsen; **347, 348,** Jack Sekowski; **349,** (l) Pictures Unlimited, (r) Jack Sekowski; **351,** Doug Martin; **352,** Frank Cezus.